THE SPOOKY ART

THE
SPOOKY
ART

Some Thoughts on Writing

NORMAN
MAILER

RANDOM HOUSE / NEW YORK

RANDOM HOUSE and colophon are registered trademarks of Random House, Inc.

Library of Congress Cataloging-in-Publication Data
Mailer, Norman.
The spooky art : some thoughts on writing / Norman Mailer.—1st ed.
p.   cm.
ISBN 0-394-53648-7 (acid-free paper)
1. Mailer, Norman.   2. Fiction—Authorship.   3. Authorship.   I. Title.
PS3525.A4152 S66   2003   808'.02—dc21   2002029170

Random House website address: www.atrandom.com
Printed in the United States of America on acid-free paper

2 4 6 8 9 7 5 3

First Edition

TO

J. MICHAEL LENNON

He lived at a little distance from his body, regarding his own acts with doubtful side-glances. He had an odd autobiographical habit which led him to compose in his mind from time to time a short sentence about himself . . .

James Joyce, "A Painful Case"

I was never so rapid in my virtue but my vice kept up with me. We are double-edged blades, and every time we whet our virtue the return stroke straps our vice.

Henry David Thoreau, *Journals*

A PREFACE
WITH THREE WARNINGS
AND ONE APOLOGY

During the seven years I worked on *Harlot's Ghost,* I perceived the CIA and its agents as people of high morals and thorough deceit, loyalty and duplicity, passion and ice-cold detachment. So many writers, including myself, have a bit of that in our makeup. It is part of what has made us novelists, even as intelligence agents are drawn to their profession by the striking opposites in their natures.

Let me assert from the outset, however, that *The Spooky Art* is not a book about intelligence agents. A work of that sort I might call *The Art of the Spooks.* This book, however, as the subtitle states, is about writing, its perils, joys, vicissitudes, its loneliness, its celebrity if you are lucky and not so very lucky in just that way. Needless to add, it speaks of problems of craft and plot, character, style, third person, first person, the special psychology of the writer. (I do not think novelists—good novelists, that is—are altogether like other people.) We novelists, good and bad, are also closet philosophers, and one is ready therefore—how not?—to offer one's own forays into the nature of such matters as being and nothingness, the near-to-unclassifiable presence of the unconscious and its demonic weapon—writer's block. En route, one looks into the need for stamina in doing a novel, and the relation of stamina to one's style. There are discussions of the differences and similarities between fiction and history, fiction and journalism, and, of course, I have often thought about the life of action and the life of meditation as it affects one's work. I have talked and written about the pitfalls of early success and how to cope with disastrous reviews and how we each do our best to live with the competitive spirit of the novelist rather than be eaten out by it. There is talk about identity and occasional crises of identity, as well as the presence of the unconscious in relation to the novelist, taken together with such strategems as when it is wise to enter a character's mind and when it is unwise to make characters out of real people in one's life.

All of that is Part I of this book. Part II concerns Genre and Colleagues. Since writers are often in search of how to work in other arts and crafts, Genre has to do with film and painting and journalism, with television and graffiti, as examples of some of the ways and by-ways down which writers search and/or flee from their more direct responsibility.

Finally, there is another section at the end called Giants and Colleagues, filled with a mix of thoughtful and/or shoot-from-the-hip candor about some of my contemporaries, rivals, and literary idols, as well as a few pieces of more formal criticism. Among the authors discussed, some in reasonable depth, others in no more than passing comment, are Hemingway, Faulkner, Dostoyevsky, Tolstoy, Updike, Cheever, Roth, Doctorow, Capote, Vidal, Bellow, Heller, Borges, James Jones, Styron, Chekhov, James T. Farrell, Henry Adams, Henry James, García Márquez, Melville, Proust, Beckett, Dreiser, Graham Greene, William Burroughs, Scott Fitzgerald, Nelson Algren, Kurt Vonnegut, Dwight Macdonald, Toni Morrison, Thomas Wolfe, Tom Wolfe, Jean Malaquais, Don DeLillo, Henry Miller, John Steinbeck, Christopher Isherwood, William Kennedy, Joan Didion, Kate Millett, Jonathan Franzen, Ralph Ellison, Joyce Carol Oates, John Dos Passos, D. H. Lawrence, Mark Twain, Freud, and Marx. Even Bill Buckley is mentioned (in relation to character versus plot). And Stephen King for style.

Taken all together, the result—one would hope—is a volume able to appeal to serious writers and to people who wish to write, to students, to critics, to men and women who love to read. But most of all, this may be a book for young novelists who wish to improve their skills and their commitment to the subtle difficulties and uncharted mysteries of serious novel-writing itself.

Now, for the warnings. A good deal of hesitation went along with the title. *Spooky* is virtually a child's word and seemed too casual. Besides, it does not always apply. Not all days at one's desk are odd or subtly frightening or, for that matter, full of scary fun. Novel-writing can be dogged. There are unproductive hours that feel like nothing so much as the act of trying to start an old car when the motor has gone dead on you.

Nor is this a geriatric analogy. It is usually young men who have old cars. Moreover, there is no sense of youth that a young man can feel on a truly bad day of writing. Young novelists do get to feel like old men on such unhappy occasions, as if whatever talent they once possessed is now gone. The first intimation of old age for many a young novelist is the day when the gift does not appear, or comes through hobbled. Scenes that one expected to be rich are without presence on the page. One's inner life—that exceptional sense of oneself as possessed of thoughts that are not like others'—is absent. The scene one is working on is as boring as one's breath on a dull day.

That is the worst, and there is nothing mysterious about such mornings, afternoons, or nights unless it is the new and intimate sense that destiny never guarantees a happy end. You are brought up close, on such occasions, to the future rigor of an unhappy denouement for yourself.

But there are also odd, offbeat, happy days when something does happen as you write and your characters take surprising turns, sometimes revealing themselves to you on the page in a manner other than you expected them to be. You discover that you know more about life and your characters than you thought you did. Such days are glorious. And they are certainly spooky in the most agreeable fashion. You feel close to all the outer stuff!

Of course, no two days of good work are necessarily the same. One may be practical and effective on certain mornings and the skill is actually in the sobriety of the effort. For another kind of hour, one takes risks. Yet if you have gotten good enough over the years (after decades of such varied mornings), there is also the sense of a governing hand (not necessarily and altogether your own) that keeps the highs and the lows from dashing away from one another so outrageously that your novel changes from chapter to chapter. (That is as bad as a car that pops out of gear at the damnedest times.)

All right. The point of this introduction has possibly been

made. In any event, I, as the author and assembler of this work, have succeeded in justifying the title to myself.

Let me add, however, a second warning. We have here a reasonably sized volume that will tell you a good deal of what I know about the problems of writing, and more than occasionally, they are advanced problems. So it is not a how-to-do-it for beginners who want basic approaches to plot, dialogue, suspense, and marketing of manuscripts all carefully laid out. This is, rather, a book for men and women who have already found some vocation to write in college or in graduate school, have perhaps taken courses on novel technique, are even advanced students who have begun to encounter the subtle perils and hazards of the writer's life.

I have also to offer a last warning, which concerns me most. *The Spooky Art,* by the nature of its sources (which derive from pieces I have written and extracts from interviews I have given), is without stylistic unity. The manner shifts at times from page to page. Given the separate components, there was no way to avoid this. Off-the-cuff remarks in an interview, even when polished to a modicum of good syntax, can hardly be the equal of an essay done at the top of one's form. Yet the scattered materials of a writer offer just such a spectrum of harsh perceptions roughly stated and insights good enough occasionally to startle even one's best perception of oneself. I have, however, tried to soften some of the transitions between reworked interviews and more formal essays, and in most places the reader should not suffer too many jolts.

Still, some of you may refuse to treat this as a consecutive work of printed pages so much as an unexpected and possibly dubious gift of chocolates into which they can dip and move on, pleasure alternating with displeasure. I cannot pretend to say this is wrong. I have tried to put some separate elements together with as much order as is possible under these curious circumstances—close to fifty years of reflecting, meditating, musing, and declaring my thoughts on a profession I practiced and could not always feel I understood—but to those readers for whom order in style is one of the cardinal literary virtues (and I am one of them), there may be no other way to treat this volume than as a gift of occasionally exceptional sweetmeats and disappointments. (Nor will every title and subtitle deliver its promise.)

Now, for the apology. By now, at least as many women as men

are novelists, but the old habit of speaking of a writer as *he* persists. So, I've employed the masculine pronoun most of the time when making general remarks about writers. I do not know if the women who read this book will be all that inclined to forgive me, but the alternative was to edit many old remarks over into a style I cannot bear—the rhetorically hygienic politically correct.

All this said, I still have a few hopes that the order imposed on these fifty years of opinions and conclusions will be read by some from the first page to the last, and that a few readers will find *The Spooky Art* to be an intimate handbook they can return to over the decades of their careers.

Here then is a collection of literary gleanings, aperçus, fulminations, *pensées,* gripes, insights, regrets and affirmations, a few excuses, several insults, and a number of essays more or less intact. May the critics feel bound to debate some of these notions in time to come.

It is interesting that my ceremonial sense intensifies as I grow older, and so I have looked to assemble this book in time for it to come out on January 31, 2003. I will be exactly eighty years old on that occasion. I would hope I am not looking for unwarranted easy treatment by this last remark. Can I possibly be speaking the truth?

CONTENTS

PART II

PART I

LIT BIZ

LIT BIZ

I am tempted to call this section Economics, for it concerns the loss and gain (economically, psychically, physically) of living as a writer. Let's settle, however, for a term that may be closer to the everyday reality: Lit Biz. Spend your working life as a writer and depend on it—your income, your spirit, and your liver are all on close terms with Lit Biz.

In 1963, Steve Marcus did an interview with me for *The Paris Review*, and I have taken the liberty of separating his careful and elegantly structured questions into several parts in order to give a quick shape to my first years as a writer. For those who are more interested in what I have to say about writing in general than about myself in particular, you are invited to skip over these autobiographical details and move on to a few comments on my first two books, *The Naked and the Dead* and *Barbary Shore*. Or, if you are in search of directly useful nitty-gritty, move even further, to "The Last Draft of *The Deer Park*."

STEVEN MARCUS: Do you need any particular environment in which to write?

NORMAN MAILER: I like a room with a view, preferably a long view. I like looking at the sea, or ships, or anything which has a vista to it. Oddly enough, I've never worked in the mountains.

SM: When did you first think of becoming a writer?

NM: That's hard to answer. I did a lot of writing when I was young.

SM: How young?

NM: Seven.

SM: A real novel?

NM: Well, it was a science fiction novel about people on Earth taking a rocket ship to Mars. The hero had a name which sounded like Buck Rogers. His assistant was called Dr. Hoor.

SM: Doctor . . . ?

NM: Dr. Hoor. *Whore,* pronounced H-O-O-R. That's the way we used to pronounce whore in Brooklyn. He was patterned directly after Dr. Huer in Buck Rogers, who was then appearing on radio. This novel filled two and a half paper notebooks. You know the type, about seven inches by ten. They had soft, shiny blue covers and they were, oh, only ten cents in those days, or a nickel. They ran to about a hundred pages each and I used to write on both sides. My writing was remarkable for the way I hyphenated words. I loved hyphenating, and so I would hyphenate "the" and make it "th-e" if it came at the end of the line. Or "they" would become "the-y." Then I didn't write again for a long time. I didn't even try out for the high school literary magazine. I had friends who wrote short stories, and their short stories were far better than the ones I would write for assignments in high school English and I felt no desire to write. When I got to college, I started again. The jump from Boys' High School in Brooklyn to Harvard came as a shock. I started reading some decent novels for the first time.

SM: You mentioned in *Advertisements for Myself* that reading *Studs Lonigan* made you want to be a writer.

NM: Yes. It was the first truly literary experience I had, because the background of Studs was similar to mine. I grew up in Brooklyn, not Chicago, but the atmosphere had the same flatness of affect. Until then I had never considered my life or the life of the people around me as even remotely worthy of— well, I didn't believe they could be treated as subjects for fiction. It never occurred to me. Suddenly I realized you could write about your own life.

SM: When did you feel that you were started as a writer?

NM: When I first began to write again at Harvard. I wasn't very good. I was doing short stories all the time, but I wasn't good. If there were fifty people in the class, let's say I was somewhere in the top ten. My teachers thought I was fair, but I don't believe they ever thought for a moment I was really talented. Then in the middle of my Sophomore year I started getting better. I got on *The Harvard Advocate* and that gave me confidence, and about this time I did a couple of fairly good short stories for English A-1, one of which won *Story* magazine's college contest for that year.

SM: Was that the story about Al Groot?

NM: Yes. And when I found out it had won—which was at the beginning of the summer after my Sophomore year [1941]— well, that fortified me, and I sat down and wrote a novel. It was a very bad novel. I wrote it in two months. It was called *No Percentage*. It was just terrible. But I never questioned any longer whether I was started as a writer.

SM: What do you think were some of the early influences in your life? What reading, as a boy, do you recall as important?

NM: *The Amateur Gentleman* and *The Broad Highway* were glorious works. So was *Captain Blood*. I think I read every one of Jeffrey Farnol's books, and there must have been twenty of them. And every one of Rafael Sabatini's.

SM: Did you ever read any of them again?

NM: No, now I have no real idea of their merit. But I never enjoyed a novel more than *Captain Blood*. Nor a movie. Do you remember Errol Flynn as Captain Blood? Some years ago I was asked by a magazine what were the ten most important books in my development. The book I listed first was *Captain Blood*. Then came *Das Kapital*. Then *The Amateur Gentleman*.

SM: You wouldn't say that *Das Kapital* was boyhood reading?

NM: Oh no, I read that many years later. But it had its mild influence.

SM: It's been said often that novelists are largely nostalgic for their boyhood, and in fact most novelists draw on their youthful experiences a great deal. In your novels, however, the evocation of scenes from boyhood is rare or almost absent.

NM: It's difficult to write about childhood. I never felt I understood it in any novel way. I never felt other authors did either. Not particularly. I think the portrait of childhood which is given by most writers is rarely true to anything more than the logic of their novel. Childhood is so protean.

SM: What about Twain, or Hemingway—who drew on their boy-hoods successfully?

NM: I must admit they created some of the psychological reality of my own childhood. I wanted, for instance, to be like Tom Sawyer.

SM: Not Huck Finn?

NM: The magic of Huck Finn seems to have passed me by, I don't know quite why. *Tom Sawyer* was the book of Twain's I always preferred. I remember when I got to college I was startled to find that *Huckleberry Finn* was the classic. Of course, I haven't looked at either novel in thirty years.

WRITING COURSES

———

I don't know if it still is true, but in the years I went to Harvard (so long ago as 1939 to 1943) they used to give a good writing course. In fact, it was not one good course but six. English A was compulsory for any Freshman who did not get a very good mark on the English College Entrance Boards, and five electives followed: English A-1, English A-2, up to English A-5, a vertiginous meeting place for a few select talents, whose guide was no less than Professor Robert Hillyer, the Pulitzer Prize–winning poet. By Senior year, I was taking English A-5. In fact, I must have been one of the few students in Harvard history who took all but one of the writing courses (A-4 was missed) and must even be one of the few living testimonials to the efficacy of a half-dozen classes in composition and the art of the short story. I entered college as a raw if somewhat generous-hearted adolescent from Brooklyn who did not know the first thing about a good English sentence and left four years later as a half-affected and much imperfect Harvard man who had nonetheless had the great good fortune to find the passion of his life before he was twenty. I wanted to be a writer. And had the further good luck to conceive this passion in Freshman year in a *compulsory* course in elementary composition. That much will be granted to the forces of oppression.

English A at Harvard in 1939 put its emphasis on teaching a student to write tolerably well—an ability we certainly had to call upon over the next three years. The first stricture of the course was a wise one: Writing is an extension of speech, we were told. So we were instructed to write with something of the ease with which we might speak, and that is a good rule for beginners. In time it can be absorbed, taken for granted, and finally disobeyed. The best writing comes, obviously, out of a precision we do not and dare not employ when we speak, yet such writing still has the ring of speech. It is a style, in short, that can take you a life to achieve.

At Harvard, however, they knew how to get us to begin, and there were fine men teaching English A, and they took me up the ladder of the electives. Over four years of such courses, one would have had to have a determined purchase on a lack of talent not to improve. I improved. In those four years, I learned a little about sentence construction and more about narrative pace; en route I was able to pick up some of the literary ego a young writer needs to keep going through the contradictory reactions of others to his work. If there is one reason above others for taking a writing course, it is to go through the agonizing but indispensable recognition that one's own short story, so clear, so beautiful, so powerful, and so *true,* so definite in its meaning or so well balanced in its ambiguity, has become a hundred different things for the other writers present. Even the teacher does not get your buried symbols, or, worse, does not like them. Being a young writer in such a course can bruise the psyche as much as being a novice in the Golden Gloves can hurt your head. There is punishment in recognizing how much more punishment will yet have to be taken. Yet the class has its unique and ineradicable value. For you get to see the faces of those who like your work, you hear their voices, and so you gain some comprehension of the perversities of an audience's taste (as when, for example, they like a story by a writer you despise). You can even come to recognize how a fine piece of prose can draw the attention of an audience together. If it happens to you, if you write a piece and everyone in the room listens as if there is nourishment for one ear—his own—then it will not matter afterward if you hear a dozen separate reactions, for you will have at last the certainty that you are a writer. Your work has effect: In some small way, you have begun to enter the life and intelligence of others.

Then you are not likely to stay away from writing. Indeed, if you get even a glimpse of that kind of reaction from one of your paragraphs, you will discover that you must have more such paragraphs. You will want the ineffable pleasure of such attention.

That is the best of it, but there are also perils. You can go through hell in a writing class, real, true hell. I remember in my second year at Harvard I was taking English A-1, with a very good man teaching it, Robert Gorham Davis. At a given moment, Davis said to the class, "I'd like to read to you an interesting story that's quite good but is totally destroyed at the end by the author."

The story, mine to be sure, was about a young bellhop working at a summer hotel. With other bellhops, he would talk about the wives of the businessmen who were having quick affairs with the hotel staff during the week. Their husbands, after all, only came out on weekends. One weekday night, however, one lonely businessman drove up unexpectedly from New York, came into the lobby, and headed right up to his room. The bellhops knew a disaster was coming before they even heard the shots. The narrator then went up to the room. Both the bellhop, who had been in bed with the wife, and the wife were dead. The wife had had her face blown off. The husband had committed suicide. The description given by the narrator went something like this: "I couldn't see her nose, or what was left of her mouth, and I didn't know whether all that was spread on the carpet by now and I was stepping on it, or whether I was still breathing it in."

At this point, the class started to laugh. My description had the misfortune to continue for another such paragraph. I was learning a frightful lesson in a terrible hurry: A story read aloud before an audience can have little in common with its mute presence on the page.

It became the worst single moment I ever had in a writing class. I didn't know whether to stand up and say, "I am the one who wrote that piece and you can all go to hell," or to remain totally silent. When you don't know what to do, you usually do nothing. I did nothing.

I hardly slept. Next day I had an appointment with Robert Gorham Davis. The first thing he said when I came into his office was, "Look, I owe you a serious apology. I had no idea the reaction would be so bad. I should have given you my criticisms privately. I hope you'll forgive me."

Of course I did. We even became friends.

But I can't tell you how my back was scalded by the laughter. In those years, scorn was a pure product of the superiority we felt about ourselves at being Harvard men. We used to be a force on Friday nights as we laughed at the filmic idiocies on display at the movie theatre in Harvard Square. During that stricken ten minutes in English A-1, I felt as if I had become one of those romantic dolts on the screen. In that year, 1940, we all looked upon films as being a sub-par art. Novelists were vastly more important.

In any event, on balance, I learned more than I lost from writing courses. For one thing, you certainly get used to how wide apart are reactions, even to pieces that present no striking disturbance. You also begin to pick up a lot about how power structures form. In the class, certain writers will make up a bloc, others an enclave. You soon learn a lot about manipulation and hypocrisy—"Oh, I absolutely love your story!" while lying through your teeth. You pick up a few random notes on human nature. Whether you glean enough for the time invested is another question. Indeed, there is a kind of signature today to many writers who come out of MFA programs. They tend to give you very good sentences and they move well on the page. Sometimes they have a tropism toward matters that are bizarre and/or intense. They also tend to be not terribly ambitious. Because in a writing course, nothing makes you crash with a louder sound than a bold attempt that doesn't come off. So, a built-in tendency develops to stay small. Nonetheless, a few very good writers do come out of the process.

What the course can't satisfy is the problem of experience. Young people who write well are not just reasonably sensitive; they are over-sensitive. Experience is usually painful and difficult for them. Moreover, to choose to go out and find a new subject to write about is always false to a degree. I would argue that your material becomes valuable only when it is existential, by which I mean an experience you do not control. Driving your car along a snowy road, you miscalculate a hairpin turn and are in a bad skid. For a fraction of a second, or for as much as a second and a half, you don't know if you're going to come out of it.

You may wreck your car. Or you may be dead in the next instant. A good deal goes through your mind at a good rate of speed—that's an existential moment. Another existential experience of wholly different character, ongoing, heavy, full of dread, common to many marriages, is where a woman is miserable with her husband but adores her child and hates the thought of divorce. Anna Karenina is one such lady.

In any event, there is no answer to the problem of how a young writer can pick up experience. If you search for it but are able to quit the experience if it gets too hot for you—then such a controlled adventure can be good conceivably for a magazine piece, but it's not necessarily there for bringing you to that deeper level of writing that young scriveners aspire to.

How I aspired! In those years at Harvard, if I had heard that Ernest Hemingway was going to speak in Worcester, Mass., I might have trudged the forty miles from Cambridge. That was how we felt then about writers. It is probably how I still feel. The shock, decades later, was to realize that this view of the writer is rare by now.

Full of the intensity of those feelings, I even wrote a long novel in the nine months between my graduation in 1943 and my induction into the Army in March 1944. What follows is the introduction to it, which I would write thirty-five years later, when the novel was brought out in an expensive limited edition.

Samuel Goldwyn once took a walk down the aisle of the writers' wing of his own studio and did not hear a sound. Supposedly, five writers were working behind five office doors, but Goldwyn did not pick up the clack of a single typewriter. Instead, there was a silence of the tombs. The writers were sleeping a sleep five thousand years old.

Goldwyn came to the end of the hall, turned around in a rage, his expressive face clenched like a fist, and he shouted down the corridor, "A writer should write!"

I never heard that story when I was young, but I had no need of it then. I wrote. It came as naturally to me as sexual excitement to an adolescent—I think from the time I was seventeen, I had no larger desire in life than to be a writer, and I wrote a great deal. Through my Sophomore, Junior, and Senior years at Harvard, and the summers between, I must have written thirty or forty short stories, a couple of plays, a novel, then a short novel, and then a long novel, which I called *A Transit to Narcissus*.

That was not the worst way to work up one's literary talent. There may be too much of a tendency among young intellectuals to think that if one can develop a consciousness, if one is able to brood sensitively and incisively on one's own life, and on the life of others for that matter, one will be able to write when the time comes. That assumption, however, may not recognize sufficiently that the ability to put words on a page also comes through years of experience and can become a skill nearly separate from consciousness and bear more resemblance to the sophisticated instinct of fingers that have been playing scales for a decade.

So I learned to write by writing. As I once calculated, I must have written more than half a million words before I came to *The Naked and the Dead*, and a large fraction of those words was in the several drafts of this novel. I no longer recall just when I began *A Transit to Narcissus*, although the spring of my Senior year at Harvard, March or April of 1943, seems a reasonable date, but indeed it was commenced earlier. In the summer before, between my Junior and Senior years, I had written a three-act play about a mental hospital and called it *The Naked and the Dead*. The play never interested anyone a great deal, most certainly not the Harvard Dramatic Society (although the title was to receive its full attention four years later, when it was transferred without a moment's shame to the war novel I started to write in the summer of 1946). By then, the play was long buried in a carton of papers, its best passages of dialogue—there were not many—cannibalized over to a few pages of *A Transit to Narcissus*.

Little enough, certainly, of those three acts are here. While I was writing the novel, a metamorphosis took place. The play, as I recollect, was stark, and its set was the screened-in porch of the violent ward of a mental hospital. In an area eight feet by forty feet, twenty or thirty actors were to mull insanely back and forth. It would have been a play of much shock, brutality, obscenity, and what they used to call untrammeled power, a crude but highly realistic work. I had, after all, spent the earlier part of the summer of 1942, one week, no more, working in the violent ward of a mental hospital for thirteen hours a day, five days a week (pay, nineteen dollars plus room and board). Then I quit. The experience was sufficient to write the play, digest a few of its faults, and embark less than a year later on that most peculiar novel we have here. Having just reread it after thirty-three years, I am all too unhappily aware that a seed of the psychotic, a whole field of the neurotic, and a crop of youthful energies obviously sprouted from a week of work in the insane asylum. If I was searching that summer for the experience to make me a better writer, most solemnly, of course, was I searching, I could hardly have recognized in advance that working in a mental hospital at the age of nineteen was equal to dropping myself precipitously into the lowest reaches of the proletariat—a charnel house of violence, a drudgery of labor, and a first coming to grips with a theme that would not so much haunt me as stalk me for the rest of my writing life: What is the relation between courage and brutality?

Being also a good son of the middle class, I could not stay rooted in such misery for too long. A week was enough to jolt my mind for a year. Since it was also the first social experience I came across that was cruel enough and crude enough to oblige me to write about it, I was bound to go back and try a novel. While graduating from a high school in Brooklyn into Freshman year at Harvard had offered a social transition that in its own way was virtually as abrupt, I would hardly have been able to write about it then; did I even know it was there to write about? On the other hand I was ready, in wholly inadequate fashion, of course, to take on the explosive and unmanageable themes of social corruption, insanity, and violence in a mental hospital; yes, I went right into the work and in less than a year was to write and rewrite a novel something like a hundred and eighty thousand words long.

I started on it in the last months of my Senior year, then plugged along from month to month, expecting any week to get drafted (it was the summer of '43), and unaccountably did not get drafted. The only explanation I can find for such delay is that my draft card must have fallen into the back of the file. I did not compose the novel, therefore, with any clear sense of how much time I had to work, nor even the confidence I could finish it. Rather, I worked on the book because I was out of college and my friends were at war and there was no sense in looking for a job if I would also be a soldier soon. So each month passed, and the novel proceeded. I was as lonely as I have ever been—which emotional tone is most certainly to be felt in the lugubrious weight of the style—and I was a little frightened of going to war and a great deal ashamed of not going to war and terrified of my audacity in writing so ambitious a novel—one part of me certainly knew how ignorant I was—and even more terrified I would not have time to finish, and therefore if I were soon killed in the war, nobody (except my family) would know that a young and potentially important author had lived among them: Such is the tone of the book. It is not a period I look back on with pleasure. Still, the novel got written, and I finished it in January of 1944.

It could not have seemed so bad a novel then as it does today. The politics of *A Transit to Narcissus*—during those war years when you went a long distance to the Right before you found a liberal who was not moving to the Left—were fashionable politics; its portrait of a mental hospital was without comparison, literally!—I cannot think of any other American novel, good or bad, written about an insane asylum before World War II. Moreover, the horror of the descriptions was accurate. In those years, before Thorazine and other tranquilizers changed the mood of our mental wards to the mood of our cancer wards, insane asylums, at least from the point of view of the inmates, had probably not improved significantly since the days of Hogarth. The beatings came every bit as frequently as they are portrayed in this novel, nor is the lack of medical care exaggerated. (That the real situation may not be better today—that Thorazine might do even less for a madman's soul than a brutal beating is a discussion belonging to R. D. Laing and will not be entered here.)

At any rate, this early novel, holding to its virtues and staggering under its faults, went out to publishers with the blessing of my agent, Berta Kaslow, who was beginning at William Morris then and loved the book; before she was done it went to twenty publishing houses. I was in the Army by then, of course, at last! I went into the Army the week *A Transit to Narcissus* went out to the first publisher, and all through basic training and replacement depots and on troop transports and in Leyte and Luzon and Japan, I would receive letters from Berta. Another publisher or two had just turned the book down, but she had not lost faith. Nor had I. Maybe we burned longer in our hopes for that book because the first editor to read it, Robert Linscott of Random House, then comparable in distinction to Maxwell Perkins, had liked *A Transit to Narcissus* enough to think of publishing it. The

other editors at Random House did not agree with him, however, and since I was in the Army and would not be able to work
with him on editing it (and, I'm certain, condensing it), Linscott
rejected the book reluctantly, and with a splendid letter to me
that I carried through the war.

Other readers were not to be as kind. Some editors thought
the book more depressing than anything, others were aghast at
the murkiness and/or depth of the sexual relations; the consensus suggested that the book had a power of a sort, and the author, considering his youth, might have yet a career, but the
work itself was too unpleasant to see print.

Oddly enough, there was, as I recollect, praise for the style.
Let us hope it was not a collective lack of taste so much as a collective hypocrisy of editors; if one can find nothing much good
to say about a manuscript, praise the style at least: It was obvious
I was proud of my style. But what awful stuff it is today! No little
word is ever used in *A Transit to Narcissus* when a polysyllabic
slab of jargon will do, and the meaning is not only fuzzy in the
pages but in the sentences. Maybe there has never been another
novel where as many characters take their psychic temperature
after every little event—where as many actually go out for walks
to think things through. One is even brought to remember that
the book takes place in the late Depression years of the thirties,
when the average American city and mill town was still interesting to walk around and nobody had money for more.

Yet if the style is monumentally bad, that is also a curiosity, for
all through college I had been writing better stuff. A short story
full of action and quick prose called "The Greatest Thing in the
World" had won a nationwide college short-story contest two
years before, and a short novel, *A Calculus at Heaven,* finished
at the beginning of my Senior year (indeed, right after the play
was written), had been far superior in style, if considerably less
ambitious in theme. But then, in a couple of years, I would be
writing simply again. The war squeezed more than a few pon-
derosities out of my fingers, and the lethargic dissonance of this
prose is soon replaced by the more digestible stylistic flaws of
The Naked and the Dead—the life of a soldier was good for one
writer! What may be interesting now is that *A Transit to Narcissus*
was done at a time when I was changing my literary gods, moving bag and borrowed baggage from Farrell, Hemingway, and
Dos Passos to Faulkner, Proust, Mann, Melville, Hawthorne,
Henry James, and an intense dose of F. O. Matthiessen's *Ameri-*

can Renaissance (which was the big book at Harvard my Junior and Senior years). So one's sure taste for low life in literature had been temporarily overwhelmed by the cultural reflexes of a half-educated Harvard man. One senses a literary prig working at these pages. As is usually true of young writers and long novels, the prose suffers from every intellectual sloth of the author's character. Indeed, without its operatic plot, the book would be close to unreadable.

Yet now I agree to publish it. True, it will appear in facsimile, and for a most limited audience. The general public will be protected (by the price of this work—$100!) from my youthful indulgences in prose.

But what is to be gained by showing it? My literary reputation is more likely to survive than be enhanced by this novel.

The answer is curious to myself. I do not recognize the young man who wrote this book, I do not even like him very much, and yet I know that he must be me because his themes are mine, his ambition is as large for his age as my ambition would ever become, and I am not even without an odd regard for him. If I understand what he is trying to say, then he is close to saying the unsayable. The most terrible themes of my own life—the nearness of violence to creation, and the whiff of murder just beyond every embrace of love—are his themes also. So I can recognize myself and realize that if I had not gone to war, I probably would have kept writing books like *A Transit to Narcissus,* although, in time, better, I hope, and with good fortune might have ended like Iris Murdoch, a writer I greatly admire.

Instead, my early talents, such as they were, went through the war, and the over-elaborated sinuosities and intercalations of that young man were hammered into shape by a crude anvil of American society—the American Army at war—and the social sense, lacking so conspicuously in *A Transit to Narcissus,* was now achieved. The writer would spend the rest of his working years in tension between two major themes rather than one, two mysteries to explore by literary means instead of a search for just one holy grail, and that, we may as well assume, was to his benefit. Maybe it is good to be aware early that society can be as much of a mystery as the individual, that Marx offers no more of a final answer than Freud, and that Satan is as profound an enigma as Jesus.

I stray, however. The point is that despite all its flaws, I am probably glad to see *A Transit to Narcissus* published. I cannot pretend to like it, but curiously, I respect the profundity of its impulse. Like a badly twisted arthritic who nevertheless engages in rock-climbing, I respect the effort, the confidence, and the peculiar bravery (since I do not feel I am speaking about myself) of a young man who was living in some private depth of the psyche and so comprehended early, as some people never do, that the unsayable was indeed all that would save him. That can be a lot for a young man to know—that even in our chaos we are individual works of art, maybe even of design—it is, indeed, a theme to live with for your life, and I have lived with it, or tried to, and now feel, I suppose, that we may as well reveal where it all began.

Soon after finishing *A Transit to Narcissus,* I entered another existence. It lasted for hardly more than two years but felt like a decade. I was a private in the Army. That gave real experience as opposed to the too-quick experience I was searching for in the week I spent working in the mental hospital. It's the life you can't escape that gives you the knowledge you need to grow as a writer.

STEVEN MARCUS: Can you say something about your methods of working?

NORMAN MAILER: They vary with each book. I wrote *The Naked and the Dead* on the typewriter. I used to write four days a week—Mondays, Tuesdays, Thursdays, and Fridays.

SM: Definite hours?

NM: Yes, very definite hours. I'd get up about 8:00 or 8:30 and I'd be at work by 10:00. And I'd work until 12:30; then I'd have lunch. I'd get back to work about 2:30 or 3:00 and work for another two hours. In the afternoon, I usually needed a can of beer to prime me. But I'd write for five hours a day. And I wrote a great deal. The average I tried to keep was seven typewritten pages a day, twenty-eight pages a week. The first draft took seven months; the second draft, which was really only half a draft, took four months. The part about the platoon went well from the beginning, but the Lieutenant and the General in the first draft were stock characters. If it had been published at that point, the book would have been considered an interesting war novel with some good scenes, no more. The second draft was the bonus. Cummings and Hearn were done in the second draft. If you look at the book, you

can see that the style shifts, that the parts about Cummings
and Hearn are written in a somewhat more developed vein.
Less forceful but more articulated. And you can see something of the turn my later writing would take in the scenes between Cummings and Hearn.

SM: Well, how did the idea of *The Naked and the Dead* come to
you?

NM: I wanted to write a short novel about a long patrol. All during the war I kept thinking about this patrol. I even had the
idea before I went overseas. Probably it was stimulated by a
few war books I had read: John Hersey's *Into the Valley,* Harry
Brown's *A Walk in the Sun,* and a couple of others I no longer
remember. Out of these books came the idea to do a novel
about a long patrol. And I began to create my characters. All
the while I was overseas a part of me was working on this long
patrol. I even ended up in a reconnaissance outfit which I had
asked to get into. A reconnaissance outfit, after all, tends to
take long patrols. Art kept traducing life. At any rate, when I
started writing *The Naked and the Dead* I thought it might be a
good idea to have a preliminary chapter or two to give the
readers a chance to meet my characters before they went on
patrol. But the next six months and the first 400 pages went
into that, and I remembered in the early days I was annoyed
at how long it was taking me to get to my patrol.

SM: Do you keep notes, or a journal? What's your preparatory
material?

NM: That varies. For *The Naked and the Dead* I had a file full of
notes and a long dossier on each man. Many of these details
never got into the novel, but the added knowledge made me
feel more comfortable with each character. Indeed, I even
had charts to show which characters had not yet had scenes
with other characters. For a book which seems spontaneous
on its surface, *The Naked and the Dead* was written mechanically. I studied engineering at Harvard, and I suppose it was
the book of a young engineer. The structure is sturdy, but
there's no fine filigree to the joints. And the working plan was
simple. I devised some preliminary actions for the platoon in
order to give the reader an opportunity to get to know the
men, but the beginning, as I said, took over two-thirds of the
book. The patrol itself is also simple, but I did give more
thought to working it out ahead of time.

SM: People have commented on the pleasure you seem to take in the military detail of *The Naked and the Dead*.

NM: Compared to someone like James Jones, I'm an amateur at military detail. But at that time I did like all those details, I even used to enjoy patrols, or at least did when I wasn't sick with jungle rot or Atabrine (which we took to avoid malaria). I was one of the few men in the platoon who could read a map and once I gave myself away. We used to have classes after a campaign was over. We'd come back to garrison—one of those tent cities out in a rice paddy—and they would teach us all over again how to read maps and compasses or they would drill us on the nomenclature of the machine gun for the eighth time. One day, very bored, I was daydreaming, and the instructor pointed to a part of the map and said, "Mailer, what are those coordinates?" If I had had a moment to think, I would never have answered. It was bad form to be bright in my outfit, but I didn't think: He caught me in a daze, and I looked up and said, "320.017 dash 146.814" and everyone's mouth dropped open. It was the first time anybody ever answered such a question thus briskly in the history of infantry map reading. At any rate, that was the fun for me, the part about the patrol.

I think I suffered more, however, from the reviews of *The Naked and the Dead* than any other of my books. I wanted to sit down and write a letter to each and every critic to tell how my work had been misinterpreted. I felt this way even when they enthused over the novel. It probably takes twenty years to appreciate book reviewing for what it is—a primitive rite. By then, you are able to ingest unkind reviews, provided they are well written. Sometimes, an off-the-wall review can be as nourishing as a wild game dinner. (And, by times, as indigestible.) I'd never dream, however, of not reading reviews. It would be like not looking at a naked woman if she happens to be standing in front of her open window. Whether ugly or lovely, she is undeniably interesting under such circumstances.

Fifty years after its publication in 1948, and thirty-two years after the interview with Steven Marcus, I wrote the following as a foreword to a new edition of the book.

—

I think it might be interesting to talk about *The Naked and the Dead* as a best-seller that was the work of an amateur. Of course, as best-sellers go, it was a good book, and the author who began it at the age of twenty-three and completed it in fifteen months had already written more than a half million words in college and so could be considered a hardworking amateur who loved writing and was prepared in the way of a twenty-four-year-old to fall on his sword in defense of literature.

He was naïve, he was passionate about writing, he knew very little about the subtle demands of a good style, he did not have a great deal of restraint, and he burned with excitement as he wrote. He hardly knew whether he should stand in the shadow of Tolstoy or was essentially without talent. He was an amateur.

He was also a writer of what soon became a big best-seller. Indeed, *The Naked and the Dead* was his only prodigious best-seller. It had a good story that got better and better, it had immediacy, it came out at exactly the right time, when, near to three years after the Second World War ended, everyone was ready for a big war novel that gave some idea of what it had been like—it thrived on its scenes of combat—and it had a best-seller style. The book was sloppily written (the words came too quickly and too easily), and there was hardly a noun in any sentence not holding hands with the nearest and most commonly available adjective—*scalding* coffee and *tremulous* fear are the sorts of things you will find throughout.

The book also had vigor. This is the felicity of good books by amateurs. They venture into scenes that a writer with more experience (and more professional concern) would bypass or eschew altogether. *The Naked and the Dead* took chances all over the place and more of them succeeded than not. It was rightly a best-seller; it fulfilled one of two profiles of such a category—for invariably these books are written by bold amateurs or by niche professionals, who know more about a given subject than they ought to.

All this said, one may now ask the professional what virtue he might ascribe to the work he did as an amateur. The answer is that he had the good luck to be influenced profoundly by Tolstoy in the fifteen months he was writing the opus back in 1946 and 1947—he read from *Anna Karenina* most mornings before he commenced his own work. Thereby, his pages, through the limited perceptions of a twenty-four-year-old, reflect what he learned about compassion from Tolstoy. For that is the genius of the old man—Tolstoy teaches us that compassion is of value and enriches our life only when compassion is severe, which is to say that we can perceive everything that is good and bad about a character but are still able to feel that the sum of us as human beings is probably a little more good than awful. In any case, good or bad, it reminds us that life is like a gladiators' arena for the soul and so we can feel strengthened by those who endure, and feel awe and pity for those who do not.

That fine edge in Tolstoy, the knowledge that compassion is valueless without severity (for otherwise it cannot defend itself against sentimentality), gave *The Naked and the Dead* whatever enduring virtue it may possess and catapulted the amateur who wrote it into the grim ranks of those successful literary men and women who are obliged to become professional in order to survive—no easy demand, for it would insist that one must be able to do a good day's work on a bad day, and indeed, that is a badge of honor decent professionals are entitled to wear.

STEVEN MARCUS: What methods did you pursue in your second novel?

NORMAN MAILER: Well, with *Barbary Shore,* I began to run into trouble. I started it in Paris about six months after I finished *The Naked and the Dead* and did about fifty pages. It was then called *Mrs. Guinevere* and was influenced by Sally Bowles in Isherwood's *Berlin Stories. Mrs. Guinevere* never went anywhere. It stopped, just ground down after those first fifty pages. I dropped it, thought I'd never pick it up again, and started to work on another novel. Did all the research, went to Indiana to do research.

SM: On what?

NM: On a labor novel. There was a union in Evansville with which I had connections. So I stayed for a few days in Indiana, and then went to Jamaica, Vermont, to write the novel. I spent four to five weeks getting ready to begin, made a great push on the beginning, worked for two weeks, and quit cold. I didn't have the book. I didn't know a damned thing about labor unions. In desperation (I was full of second-novel panic) I picked up *Mrs. Guinevere* and looked at it. And I found something there I could go on with. So I worked on it all through the spring of 1949, and then moved out to Hollywood for the summer. I finished the second half in Hollywood. *Barbary Shore* is really a Hollywood novel. I think it reflected the impact of Hollywood on me in some subterranean fashion. Certainly the first draft is the wildest draft of the three; it's almost insane, and the most indigestible portions were written in the first couple of months I was in Hollywood. I never knew where the book was going; I had no idea where it would be by tomorrow. I'd wake up and work the typewriter in great dread, in literal terror, wondering when this curious and doubtful inspiration was going to stop. It never quite did. It ground along at the rate of three pages, three difficult pages a day. I got a first draft done and was quite unhappy with it; it was a very bad book at that point. When I rewrote it later, in Provincetown, a summer later, again it went at the rate of three pages a day. The revision was different from the first draft, and I think much better. But working on *Barbary Shore*, I always felt as if I were not writing the book myself but rather as if I were serving as a subject for some intelligence which had decided to use me to write the book. It had nothing to do with whether the work was good or bad. I just had to make do with the fact that I had absolutely no conscious control of it. If I hadn't heard about the unconscious, I would have had to postulate one to explain this phenomenon. For the first time I became powerfully aware that I had an unconscious, which seemed to have little to do with me.

SM: How much of a plan did you have for *Barbary Shore*?

NM: None. As I indicated earlier, *Barbary Shore* just birthed itself slowly. The book came out sentence by sentence. I never knew where the next day's work was coming from.

SM: You don't mention [in your description of writing *Barbary Shore*] anything about politics. Wasn't your *engagement* at the time a considerable part of the plan?

NM: I think it was the unspoken drama in the working up of the book. I started *Barbary Shore* as some sort of fellow traveler and finished it with a political position that was a far-flung mutation of Trotskyism. And the drafts of the book reflected these ideological changes so drastically that the last draft of *Barbary Shore* is a different novel altogether and has almost nothing in common with the first draft but the names.

SM: Did Jean Malaquais [to whom the book is dedicated] have much to do with this?

NM: He had an enormous influence on me. He's the only man I know who can combine a powerfully dogmatic mind with the keenest sense of political nuance, and he has a formidable culture which seems to live in his veins and capillaries. Since he has also had a most detailed vision of the Russian Revolution—he was steeped in it the way certain American families are imbued with the records of their clan—I spent a year living more closely with the history of Russia from 1917 to 1937 than in the events of my own life. I doubt if I would even have gone back to rewrite *Barbary Shore* if I didn't know Malaquais. Certainly I would never have conceived McLeod. Malaquais, of course, bears no superficial resemblance whatsoever to McLeod—indeed, Malaquais was never even a Communist; he started as an anti-Stalinist, but he had a quality when I first met him which was pure Old Bolshevik. One knew that if he had been born in Russia, a contemporary of Lenin's, he would have been one of the leaders of the Revolution and would doubtless have been executed at the trials. So his personality—as it filtered through the contradictory themes of my unconscious—inhabits *Barbary Shore*.

SM: Would you care to discuss what you mean by the "contradictory themes" of your unconscious? It that related to what you said a little while ago about becoming aware of your unconscious while writing *Barbary Shore*?

NM: *Barbary Shore* was built on the division which existed then in my mind. My conscious intelligence, as I've indicated, became obsessed by the Russian Revolution. But my unconscious was much more interested in other matters: murder, suicide, orgy, psychosis, all the themes I discuss in *Advertisements*. Since the gulf between these conscious and unconscious themes was vast and quite resistant to any quick literary coupling, the tension to get a bridge across resulted in the peculiar feverish hothouse atmosphere of the book. My unconscious felt one kind of dread, my conscious mind another, and *Barbary Shore* lives somewhere in between. That's why its focus is so unearthly. And of course the difficulty kept haunting me from then on in all the work I did afterward. But it was a book written without any plan.

Barbary Shore, however, taught me one thing about myself: I could get up off the floor. The reviews were unbelievably bad. After all, I'd taken myself a little too seriously after *The Naked and the Dead*. Do that, and the book-review world will lie in wait for you. There are a lot of petty killers in our business. So there it was. My God, *Time* magazine's review of *Barbary Shore* ended by saying, "Paceless, tasteless, graceless, beached on a point of no fictional or intellectual return." When you realize that it didn't succeed in draining all your blood, you actually decide you're stronger than you thought you were. It's the way a young prize-fighter with a promising start can get knocked out early in his career and come back from that to have a good record. The time he was knocked out has become part of his strength. You start writing a novel and think, This could end up badly, but then you shrug: All right. I've been down before. It won't be the end of the world. That's important. I'm fond of *Barbary Shore* for this reason—not its in-and-out merits.

STEVEN MARCUS: What about *The Deer Park*?

NORMAN MAILER: For *The Deer Park* I didn't have much of a method. It was agony; it was far and away the most difficult of my three novels to write. The first and second drafts were written with the idea that they were only the first part of an eight-part novel. I think I used that enormous scheme as a pretext to get into the work. Apparently, I just couldn't sit down and write a nice modest Hollywood novel. I had to have something grandiose, in conception, anyway. I started *The Deer Park* with "The Man Who Studied Yoga." That was supposed to be a prologue to all eight novels. It went along nicely and was done in a few weeks. And then I got into *The Deer Park* and I forget what my methods were exactly; I think they varied. In the revisions of *Barbary Shore*, I had started working in longhand; as soon as I found myself blocked on the typewriter, I'd shift to longhand. By the time I got to *The Deer Park* I was writing in longhand all the time. I'd write in longhand in the morning and type up what I'd written in the afternoon. I was averaging about four–five pages a day, I think, three days a week; about fifteen pages a week. But I found it an unendurable book to write because I'd finish each day in the most profound black mood; as I found out later it was even physical. I was gutting my liver.

SM: It wasn't alcohol?

NM: No, I wasn't much of a drinker in those days. The liver, you see, is not unlike a car battery, and I was draining mine. I was writing with such anxiety and such fear and such distaste, and such gloom and such dissatisfaction that . . .

SM: Dissatisfaction with what?

NM: Oh, everything. My work, my life, myself. The early draft of *The Deer Park* was terrible. It had a few good things in it, but it was slow to emerge, it took years, and was stubborn.

For those who are interested, a long and detailed description of the anxiety, ambition, confusion, and fury that went into the *re-writing* of *The Deer Park* now follows.

THE LAST DRAFT OF
THE DEER PARK

———

In his review, Malcolm Cowley said it must have been a more difficult book to write than *The Naked and the Dead*. He was right. Most of the time, I worked in a low mood; my liver, which had gone bad in the Philippines, exacted a hard price for forcing the effort against the tide of a long depression, and matters were not improved when nobody at Rinehart & Co. liked the first draft of the novel. The second draft, which to me was the finished book, also gave little enthusiasm to the editors, and open woe to Stanley Rinehart, the publisher. I was impatient to leave for Mexico now that I was done, but before I could go, Rinehart asked for a week to decide whether he wanted to do the book. Since he had already given me a contract that allowed him no option not to accept the novel, any decision to reject the manuscript would cost him a sizable advance. (I later learned he had been hoping his lawyers would find the book obscene, but they did not, at least not then, in May 1954.) So he really had no choice but to agree to put the book out in February, and gloomily he consented. To cheer him a bit, I agreed to his request that he delay paying me my advance until publication, although the first half was due on delivery of the manuscript. I thought the favor might improve our relations.

Now, if a few of you are wondering why I did not take my book back and go to another publishing house, the answer is that I was tired, I was badly tired. Only a few weeks before, a doctor had given me tests for the liver, and it had shown itself to be sick and depleted. I was hoping that a few months in Mexico would give me a chance to fill up again.

But the next months were not cheerful. *The Deer Park* had been done as well as I could do it, yet I thought it was probably a minor work, and I did not know if I had any real interest in starting another book. I made efforts, of course; I collected notes, began to piece together a few ideas for a novel given to bullfighting, and another about a concentration camp; I read most of the work of the other writers of my generation (I think I was looking for a level against which to measure my third novel), went over the galleys when they came, changed a line or two, sent them back. Keeping half busy I mended a bit, but it was a time of dull drifting. When I came back to New York in October, *The Deer Park* was already in page proof. By November, the first advertisement was given to *Publishers Weekly*. Then, with less than ninety days to publication, Stanley Rinehart told me I would have to take out a small piece of the book—ten not very explicit lines about the sex of an old producer and a call girl. The moment one was ready to consider losing those lines, they moved into the moral center of the novel.* It would be no tonic for my liver to cut them out. But I also knew Rinehart was serious, and since I was still tired, it seemed a little unreal to try to keep the passage. Like a miser, I had been storing energy to start a new book; I wanted nothing to distract me now. I gave in on a word or two, agreed to rewrite a line, and went home from that particular conference not very impressed with myself. The next

---

*Here are the ten lines:

Tentatively, she reached out a hand to caress his hair, and at that moment Herman Teppis opened his legs and let Bobby slip to the floor. At the expression of surprise on her face, he began to laugh. "Just like this, sweetie," he said, and down he looked at that frightened female mouth, facsimile of all those smiling lips he had seen so ready to be nourished at the fount of power and with a shudder he started to talk. "That's a good girlie, that's a good girlie, that's a good girlie," he said in a mild lost little voice, "you're just an angel darling, and I like you, and you understand, you're my darling darling, oh that's the ticket," said Teppis.

morning I called up the editor in chief, Ted Amussen, to tell him I had decided the original words had to be put back.

"Well, fine," he said, "fine. I don't know why you agreed to anything in the first place."

A day later, Stanley Rinehart halted publication, stopped all promotion (he was too late to catch the first run of *Publishers Weekly,* which was already on its way to England with a full-page ad for *The Deer Park*), and broke his contract to do the book. I was started on a trip to find a new publisher, and before I was done, the book went to Random House, Knopf, Simon and Schuster, Harper's, Scribner's, and unofficially to Harcourt, Brace. Someday it would be fine to give the details, but for now little more than a few lines of dialogue and an editorial report:

BENNETT CERF: This novel will set publishing back twenty years.
ALFRED KNOPF TO AN EDITOR: Is this your idea of the kind of book which should bear a Borzoi imprint?

The lawyer for one publishing house complimented me on the ten lines, word for word, which had excited Rinehart to break his contract. This lawyer said, "It's admirable the way you get around the problem here." Then he brought out more than a hundred objections to other parts of the book. One was the line, "She was lovely. Her back was adorable in its contours." I was told that this ought to go because "the principals are not married, and so your description puts a favorable interpretation upon a meretricious relationship."

Hiram Hayden had lunch with me some time after Random House saw the book. He told me he was responsible for their decision not to do it, and if I did not agree with his taste, I had to admire his honesty—it is rare for an editor to tell a writer that kind of truth. Hayden went on to say that the book never came alive for him even though he had been ready to welcome it. "I can tell you that I picked the book up with anticipation. Of course I had heard from Bill, and Bill had told me that he didn't like it, but I never pay attention to what one writer says about the work of another. . . ." Bill was William Styron, and Hayden was his editor. I had asked Styron to call Hayden the night I found out Rinehart had broken his contract. One reason for asking the favor of Styron was that he sent me a long letter about the novel after I had shown it to him in manuscript. He had written, "I don't like *The Deer Park,* but I admire sheer hell out of it." So I thought to impose on him.

Other parts of the account are not less dreary. The only generosity I found was from Jack Goodman. He sent me a photostat of his editorial report to Simon and Schuster and, because it was sympathetic, his report became the objective estimate of the situation for me. I assumed that the book when it came out would meet the kind of trouble Goodman expected, and so when I went back later to work on the page proofs I was not free of a fear or two. But that can be talked about in its place. Here is the core of his report.

> Mailer refuses to make any changes. [He] *will* consider suggestions, but reserves the right to make final decisions, so we must make our decision on what the book now is.
>
> That's not easy. It is full of vitality and power, as readable a novel as I've ever encountered. Mailer emerges as a sort of post-Kinsey F. Scott Fitzgerald. His dialogue is uninhibited and the sexuality of the book is completely interwoven with its purpose, which is to describe a segment of society whose morality is nonexistent. Locale is evidently Palm Springs. Chief characters are Charles Eitel, movie director who first defies the House Un-American Committee, then becomes a friendly witness, his mistress, a great movie star who is his ex-wife, her lover who is the narrator, the head of a great movie company, his son-in-law, a strange, tortured panderer who is Eitel's conscience, and assorted demi-mondaines, homosexuals, actors.
>
> My layman's opinion is that the novel will be banned in certain quarters and that it may very well be up for an obscenity charge, but this should of course be checked by our lawyers. It it were possible to recognize this at the start, to have a united front here and treat the whole issue positively and head-on, I would be for our publishing. But I am afraid such unanimity may be impossible of attainment and if so, we should reject, in spite of the fact that I am certain it will be one of the best-selling novels of the next couple of years. It is the work of a serious artist. . . .

The eighth house was G. P. Putnam's. I didn't want to give it to them. I was planning to go next to Viking, but Walter Minton kept saying, "Give us three days. We'll give you a decision in three days." So we sent it over to Putnam, and in three days they took it without conditions, and without a request for a single change. I had a victory, I had made my point, but in fact I was not very happy. I had grown so wild on my diet of polite letters from publishing houses who didn't want me that I had been ready to collect rejections from twenty houses, publish *The Deer Park* at my own expense, and try to make a kind of publishing history. Instead I was thrown in with Walter Minton, who has since attracted some fame as the publisher of *Lolita*. He is the only publisher I ever met who would make a good general. Months after I came to Putnam, Minton told me, "I was ready to take *The Deer Park* without reading it. I knew your name would sell enough copies to pay your advance, and I figured one of these days you're going to write another book like *The Naked and the Dead*," which is the sort of sure hold of strategy you can have when you're not afraid of censorship.

Now I've tried to water this account with a minimum of tears, but taking *The Deer Park* into the nervous system of eight publishing houses was not so good for my own nervous system, nor was it good for getting to work on my new novel. In the ten weeks it took the book to travel the circuit from Rinehart to Putnam, I squandered the careful energy I had been hoarding for months; there was a hard comedy at how much of myself I would burn up in a few hours of hot telephone calls; I had never had any sense for practical affairs, but in those days, carrying *The Deer Park* from house to house, I stayed as close to it as a stage-struck mother pushing her child forward at every producer's office. I was amateur agent for it, messenger boy, editorial consultant, Machiavelli of the luncheon table, fool of the five o'clock drinks. I was learning the publishing business in a hurry, and I made a hundred mistakes and paid for each one by wasting a new bout of energy.

In a way there was sense to it. For the first time in years I was having the kind of experience which was likely to return someday as good work, and so I forced many little events past any practical return, even insulting a few publishers en route as if to discover the limits of each situation. I was trying to find a few new proportions to things, and I did learn a bit. But I'll never know what that novel about the concentration camp would have been like if I had gotten quietly to work when I came back to

New York and *The Deer Park* had been published on time. It is possible I was not serious about such a book, it is also possible I lost something good, but one way or the other, that novel disappeared in the excitement.

The real confession is that I was making a few of my mental connections those days on marijuana. Like more than one or two of my generation, I had smoked it from time to time over the years, but it never had meant anything. In Mexico, however, down in my depression with a bad liver, pot gave me a sense of something new about the time I was convinced I had seen it all, and I liked it enough to take it now and again in New York.

Then *The Deer Park* began to go like a beggar from house to house and en route Stanley Rinehart made it clear he was going to try not to pay the advance. Until then I had had sympathy for him. I thought it had taken a kind of displaced courage to be able to drop the book the way he did. An expensive moral stand, and wasteful for me; but a moral stand. When it turned out that he did not like to bear the expense of being that moral, the experience turned ugly for me. It took many months and the service of my lawyer to get the money, but long before that, the situation had become real enough to drive a spike into my cast-iron mind. I realized in some bottom of myself that for years I had been the sort of comic figure I would have cooked to a turn in one of my books, a radical who had the nineteenth-century naïveté to believe that the people with whom he did business were 1) gentlemen, 2) fond of him, and 3) respectful of his ideas even if in disagreement with them. Now I was in the act of learning that I was not adored so very much; that my ideas were seen as nasty; and that my fine America, which I had been at pains to criticize for so many years, was in fact a real country which did real things and ugly things to the characters of more people than just the characters of my books. If the years since the war had not been brave or noble in the history of the country, which I certainly thought and do think, why then did it come as surprise that people in publishing were not as good as they used to be, and that the day of Maxwell Perkins was a day which was gone, really gone, gone as Greta Garbo and Scott Fitzgerald? Not easy, one could argue, for an advertising man to admit that advertising is a dishonest occupation, and no easier was it for the working novelist to see that now were left only the cliques, fashions, vogues, snobs, snots, and fools, not to mention a dozen bureaucracies of criticism; that there was no room for the old literary idea of oneself as a major writer, a figure in the landscape. The day was gone when people held on to your novels no matter what others might say. Instead one's potential young readers waited now for the verdict of professionals.

I had begun to read my good American novels at the end of an era—I could remember people who would talk wistfully about the excitement with which they had gone to bookstores because it was publication day for the second novel of Thomas Wolfe, and in college, at a faculty tea, I had listened for an hour to a professor's wife who was so blessed as to have known John Dos Passos. My adolescent crush on the profession of the writer had been more lasting than I could have guessed. I had even been so simple as to think that the kind of people who went into publishing were still most concerned with the few writers who made the profession not empty of honor, and I had been taking myself seriously. I had been thinking I was one of those writers.

Instead I caught it in the face and deserved it for not looking at the evidence. I was out of fashion and that was the score; that was all the score; the publishing habits of the past were going to be of no help for my *Deer Park*. And so, as the language of sentiment would have it, something broke in me, but I do not know if it was so much a loving heart as a cyst of the weak, the unreal, and the needy, and I was finally open to my anger. I turned within my psyche, I can almost believe, for I felt something shift to murder in me. I finally had the simple sense to understand that if I wanted my work to travel further than others, the life of my talent depended on fighting a little more, and looking for help a little less. But I deny the sequence in putting it this way, for it took me years to come to this fine point. All I felt then was that I was an outlaw, a psychic outlaw, and I liked it, I liked it a good sight better than trying to be a gentleman, and with a set of emotions accelerating one on the other, I mined down deep into the murderous message of marijuana, the smoke of the assassins, and for the first time in my life I knew what it was to make your kicks.

I could write about that here, but it would be a mistake. Let the experience stay where it is, and on a given year it may be found again in a novel. For now it is enough to say that marijuana opens the senses and weakens the mind. In the end, you pay for what you get. If you get something big, the cost will equal it. There is a moral economy to one's vice, but you learn that last of all. I still had the thought it was possible to find something which cost nothing. Thus, *The Deer Park* resting at Putnam, and new friends found in Harlem, I was off on that happy ride where you discover a new duchy of jazz every night and the drought of the past is given a rain of new sound. What has been dull and dead in your years is now tart to the taste, and there is sweet in the illusion of how fast you can change. To keep up with it all, I began to log a journal, a wild set of thoughts and outlines for huge projects—I wrote one hundred thousand words in eight weeks, more than once twenty pages a day, in a style which came willy-nilly from the cramp of the past, a lockstep jargon of sociology and psychology that sours my teeth when I look at those pages today. Yet this journal has the start of more ideas than I will have again; ideas which came so fast and so rich that sometimes I think my brain was dulled by the heat of their passage.

The journal wore down by February, about the time *The Deer Park* had once been scheduled to appear. By then I had decided to change a few things in the novel, nothing in the way of lawyer's deletions, just a few touches for style. They were not happy about this at Putnam. Minton argued that some interest in the book would be lost if the text were not identical to Rinehart's page proofs, and Ted Purdy, my editor, told me more than once that they liked the book "just the way it is." Besides, there was thought of bringing it out in June as a summer book.

Well, I wanted to take a look. After all, I had been learning new lessons. I began to go over the page proofs, and the book read as if it had been written by someone else. I was changed from the writer who had labored on that novel, enough to be able to see it without anger or vanity or the itch to justify myself. Now, after three years of living with the book, I could at last admit the style was wrong, that it had been wrong from the time I started, that I had been strangling the life of my novel in a poetic prose which was too self-consciously attractive and formal, false to the life of my characters, especially false to the life of my narrator, who was the voice of my novel and so gave the story its air. He had been a lieutenant in the Air Force, he had been cool enough and hard enough to work his way up from an orphan asylum, and to allow him to write in a style which at its best sounded like Nick Carraway in *The Great Gatsby* must of course blur his character and leave the book unreal. Nick was legitimate, out of fair family, the Midwest and Yale—he would write as he did, his style was himself. But the style of Sergius O'Shaugnessy, no matter how good it became (and the Rinehart *Deer Park* had its moments), was a style which came out of nothing so much as my determination to prove I could muster a fine style.

If I wanted to improve my novel yet keep the style, I would have to make my narrator fit the prose, change his past, make him an onlooker, a rich pretty boy brought up let us say by two old-maid aunts, able to have an affair with a movie star only by luck and/or the needs of the plot, which would give me a book less distracting, well written but minor. If, however, I wanted to keep that first narrator, my orphan, flier, adventurer, *germ*—for three years he had been the frozen germ of some new theme—well, to keep him I would need to change the style from the inside of each sentence. I could keep the structure of my book, I thought—it had been put together for such a narrator—but the style could not escape. Probably I did not see it all so clearly as I now suggest. I believe I started with the conscious thought that I would tinker just a little, try to patch a compromise, but the navigator of my unconscious must already have made the choice, because it came as no real surprise that after a few days of changing a few words I moved more and more quickly toward the eye of the problem, and in two or three weeks I was tied to the work of doing a new *Deer Park*. The book was edited in a way no editor could ever have time or love to find; it was searched sentence by sentence, word for word, the style of the work lost its polish, became rough, and I can say real, because there was an abrupt and muscular body back of the voice now. It had been there all the time, trapped in the porcelain of a false style, but now as I chipped away, the work for a time became exhilarating in its clarity—I never enjoyed work so much—I felt as if finally I was learning how to write, learning the joints of language and the touch of a word, felt as if I came close to the meanings of sound. I even had a glimpse of what Flaubert might have felt, for as I went on tuning the book, often five or six words would pile above one another in the margin at some small crisis of choice. As I worked in this fine mood, I kept sending pages to the typist, yet so soon as I had exhausted the old galley pages, I could not keep away from the new typewritten copy—it would be close to say the book had come alive, and was invading my brain.

Soon the early pleasure of the work turned restless; the consequences of what I was doing were beginning to seep into my stamina. It was as if I were the captive of an illness whose first symptoms had been excitement, prodigies of quick work, and a confidence that one could go on forever, but that I was by now close to a second stage where what had been quick would be more like fever, a first wind of fatigue upon me, a knowledge that at the end of the drunken night a junkie cold was waiting. I was going to move at a pace deadly to myself, loading and overloading whatever little centers of the mind are forced to make the hard decisions. In ripping up the silk of the original syntax, I was tearing into any number of careful habits as well as whatever subtle fleshing of the nerves and the chemicals had gone to support them.

For six years I had been writing novels in the first person; it was the only way I could begin a book, even though the third person was more to my taste. Worse, I seemed unable to create a narrator in the first person who was not over-delicate, over-sensitive, and painfully tender, which was an odd portrait to give, because I was not delicate, not physically; when it was a matter of strength I had as much as the next man. In those days I would spend time reminding myself that I had been a bit of an athlete (house football at Harvard, years of skiing), that I had not quit in combat, and once when a gang broke up a party in my loft, I had taken two cracks on the head with a hammer and had still been able to fight. Yet the first person seemed to paralyze me, as if I had a horror of creating a voice which could be in any way bigger than myself. So I had become mired in a false style for every narrator I tried. If now I had been in a fight, had found out that no matter how weak I could be in certain ways, I was also steady enough to hang on to ten important lines, that may have given me new respect for myself, I don't know, but for the first time I was able to use the first person in a way where I could suggest some of the stubbornness and belligerence I also might have, I was able to color the empty reality of that first person with some real feeling of how I had always felt, which was to be outside, for Brooklyn, where I grew up, is not the center of anything. I was able, then, to create an adventurer whom I believed in, and as he came alive for me, the other parts of the book which had been stagnant for a year and more also came to life, and new things began to happen to Eitel, my director, and to Elena, his mistress, and their characters changed. It was a phenomenon. I learned how real a novel is. Before, the story of Eitel had been told by O'Shaugnessy of the weak voice; now by a confident young man: When the new narrator would remark that Eitel was his best friend and so he tried not to find Elena too attractive, the man and woman he was talking about were larger than they had once been. I was no longer telling of two nice people who fail at love because the world is too large and too cruel for them; the new O'Shaugnessy had moved me by degrees to the more painful story of two people who are strong as well as weak, corrupt as much as pure, and fail to grow despite their bravery in a poor world, because they are finally not brave enough, and so do more damage to one another than to the unjust world outside them. Which for me was exciting, for here and there *The Deer Park* now had the rare tenderness of tragedy. The most powerful leverage in fiction comes from point of view, and giving O'Shaugnessy courage gave passion to the others.

But the punishment was commencing for me. I was now creating a man who was braver and stronger than me, and the more my new style succeeded, the more was I writing an implicit portrait of myself as well. There is a shame about advertising yourself that way, a shame which became so strong that it was a psychological violation to go on. Yet I could not afford the time to digest the self-criticisms backing up in me. I was forced to drive myself, and so more and more I worked by tricks, taking marijuana the night before and then drugging myself into sleep with an overload of Seconal. In the morning I would be lithe with new perception, could read new words into the words I had already, and so could go on in the pace of my work, the most scrupulous part of my brain too sluggish to interfere. My powers of logic became weaker each day, but the book had its own logic, and so I did not need close reason. What I wanted and what the drugs gave me was the quick flesh of associations, and there I was often over-sensitive, could discover new experience in the lines of my text like a hermit savoring the revelation of Scripture; I saw so much in some sentences that more than once I dropped into the pit of the amateur: Since I was receiving such emotion from my words, I assumed everyone else would be stimulated as well, and on many a line I twisted the phrase in such a way that it could read well only when read slowly, about as slowly as it would take for an actor to read it aloud. Once you write that way, the quick reader (who is nearly all your audience) will stumble and fall against the vocal shifts of your prose. Then you had best have the cachet of a Hemingway, because in such a case it is critical whether the reader thinks it is your fault or is so in awe of your reputation that he returns on the words, throttles his pace, and tries to discover why he is so stupid as not to swing on your style.

An example: In the Rinehart *Deer Park* I had this:

"They make Sugar sound so good in the newspapers," she declared one night to some people in a bar, "that I'll really try him. I really will, Sugar." And she gave me a sisterly kiss.

I happened to change that very little. I put in "said" instead of "declared" and later added "older sister," so that it now read:

And she gave me a sisterly kiss. Older sister.

Just two words, but I felt as if I had revealed some divine law of nature, had laid down an invaluable clue—the kiss of an older sister was a worldly universe away from the kiss of a younger sister—and I thought to give myself the Nobel Prize for having brought such illumination and *division* to the cliché of the sisterly kiss.

Well, as an addition it wasn't bad fun, and for two words it did a bit to give a sense of what was working back and forth between Sergius and Lulu, it was another small example of Sergius's hard eye for the world, and his cool sense of his place in it, and all this was to the good, or would have been for a reader who went slowly, and stopped, and thought.

There was a real question, however, whether I could slow the reader down, and so as I worked on further, at some point beginning to write paragraphs and pages to add to the new Putnam galleys, the attrition of the drugs and the possibility of failure began to depress me, and Benzedrine entered the balance, and I was on the way to wearing badly. Because, determined or no that they would read me slowly, praying my readers would read me slowly, there was no likelihood they would do anything of the sort if the reviews were bad. As I started to worry this it grew worse, because I knew in advance that three or four of my major reviews had to be bad—*Time* magazine for one, because Max Gissen was the book review editor, and I had insulted him in public once by suggesting that the kind of man who worked for a mind so exquisitely and subtly totalitarian as Henry Luce was not likely to have any ideas of his own. I could spin this out, but what is more to the point is that I had begun to think of the reviews before finishing the book, and this doubtful occupation came out of the kind of inner knowledge I had of myself in those days. I knew what was good for my energy and what was poor, and so I knew that for the vitality of my work in the future, and yes, even the quantity of my work, I needed a success and I needed it badly if I was to shed the fatigue I had been carrying since *Barbary Shore*. Some writers receive not enough attention for years, and so learn early to accommodate the habits of their work to little recognition. I think I could have done that when I was twenty-five. With *The Naked and the Dead* a new life had begun, however. I had gone through the psychic labor of changing a good many modest habits in order to let me live a little more happily as a man with a name which could arouse quick reactions in strangers. If that started as an over-large work, because I started as a decent but scared boy, well, I had come to live with the new life, I had learned to like success—in fact I had probably come to depend on it, or at least my new habits did.

When *Barbary Shore* was ambushed in the alley, the damage to my nervous system was slow but thorough. My status dropped immediately—America is a quick country—but my ego did not permit me to understand that, and I went through tiring years of subtle social defeats because I did not know that I was no longer as large to others as I had been. I was always over-matching myself. To put it crudely, I would think I was dropping people when they were dropping me. And of course my unconscious knew better. There was all the waste of ferocious if unheard discussion between the armies of ego and id; I would get up in the morning with less snap in me than I had taken to sleep. Six or seven years of breathing that literary air taught me a writer stayed alive in the circuits of such hatred only if he was unappreciated enough to be adored by a clique, or was so overbought by the public that he excited some defenseless nerve in the snob. I knew if *The Deer Park* was a powerful best-seller (the magical figure had become one hundred thousand copies for me) that I would then have won. I would be the first serious writer of my generation to have a best-seller twice, and so it would not matter what was said about the book. Half of publishing might call it cheap, dirty, sensational, second-rate, and so forth, but it would be weak rage and could not hurt, for the literary world suffers a spot of the national taint—a serious writer is certain to be considered major if he is also a best-seller; in fact, most readers are never convinced of his value until his books do well. Steinbeck is better known than Dos Passos; John O'Hara is taken seriously by people who dismiss Farrell, and indeed it took three decades and a Nobel Prize before Faulkner was placed on a level with Hemingway. For that reason, it would have done no good if someone had told me at the time that the financial success of a writer with major talent was probably due more to what was meretricious in his work than what was central. The argument would have meant nothing to me—all I knew was that seven publishing houses had been willing to dismiss my future, and so if the book did poorly, a good many people were going to congratulate themselves on their foresight and be concerned with me even less. I could see that if I wanted to keep on writing the kind of book I liked to write, I needed the energy of new success, I needed blood. Through every bit of me, I knew *The Deer Park* had damn well better make it or I was close to a real apathy of the will.

Every now and again I would have the nightmare of wondering what would happen if all the reviews were bad, as bad as for *Barbary Shore*. I would try to tell myself that could not happen, but I was not certain, and I knew that if the book received a unanimously bad press and still showed signs of selling well, it was likely to be brought up for prosecution as obscene. As a delayed convulsion from the McCarthy years, the fear of censorship was strong in publishing, in England it was critically bad, and so I also knew that the book could lose such a suit—there might be no one of reputation to say it was serious. If it were banned, it could sink from sight. With the reserves I was throwing into the work, I no longer knew if I was ready to take another beating—for the first time in my life I had worn down to the edge, I could see through to the other side of my fear, I knew a time could come when I would be no longer my own man, that I might lose what I had liked to think was the incorruptible center of my strength (which of course I had had money and freedom to cultivate). Already the signs were there—I was beginning to avoid new lines in the Putnam *Deer Park* which were legally doubtful, and once in a while, like a gambler hedging a bet, I toned down individual sentences from the Rinehart *Deer Park*, nothing much, always a matter of the new O'Shaugnessy character, a change from "at last I was able to penetrate into the mysterious and magical belly of a movie star" to what was more in character for him: "I was led to discover the mysterious brain of a movie star." Which "brain" in context was fun, for it was accurate, and "discover" was a word of more life than the legality of "penetrate," but I could not be sure if I was chasing my new aesthetic or afraid of the cops. The problem was that *The Deer Park* had become more sexual in the new version, the characters had more force, the air had more heat, and I had gone through the kind of galloping self-analysis which makes one very sensitive to the sexual nuance of every gesture, word, and object— the book now seemed over-charged to me, even a terror of a novel, a cold chisel into all the dull mortar of our guilty society. In my mind it became a more dangerous book than it really was, and my drug-hipped paranoia saw long consequences in every easy line of dialogue. I kept the panic in its place, but by an effort of course, and once in a while I would weaken enough to take out a line because I could not see myself able to defend it happily in a court of law. But it was a mistake to nibble at the edges of censoring myself, for it gave no life to my old pride that I was the boldest writer to have come out of my flabby time, and I think it helped to kill the small chance of finding my way into what could have been a novel as important as *The Sun Also Rises*.

But let me spell it out a bit: Originally, *The Deer Park* had been about a movie director and a girl with whom he had a bad affair, and it was told by a sensitive but faceless young man. In changing the young man, I saved the book from being minor, but put a disproportion upon it because my narrator became too interesting, and not enough happened to him in the second half of the book, and so it was to be expected that readers would be disappointed by this part of the novel.

Before I was finished, I saw a way to write another book altogether. In what I had so far done, Sergius O'Shaugnessy was given an opportunity by a movie studio to sell the rights to his life and get a contract as an actor. After more than one complication, he finally refused the offer, lost the love of his movie star, Lulu, and went wandering by himself, off to become a writer. This episode had never been an important part of the book, but

I could see that the new Sergius was capable of accepting the offer, and if he went to Hollywood and became a movie star himself, the possibilities were good, for in O'Shaugnessy I had a character who was ambitious yet, in his own way, moral, and with such a character one could travel deep into the paradoxes of the time.

Well, I was not in shape to consider that book. With each week of work, bombed and sapped and charged and stoned with lush, with pot, with benny, saggy, coffee, and two packs a day, I was working live, and over-alert, and tiring into what felt like death, afraid all the way because I had achieved the worst of vicious circles in myself; I had gotten too tired, I was more tired than I had ever been in combat, and so as the weeks went on, and publication was delayed from June to August and then to October, there was only a worn-out part of me to keep protesting into the pillows of one drug and the pinch of the other that I ought to have the guts to stop the machine, to call back the galleys, to cease—to rest, to give myself another two years and write a book which would go a little further to the end of my particular night.

But I had passed the point where I could stop. My anxiety had become too great. I did not know anything anymore. I did not have that clear sense of the way things work, which is what you need for the natural proportions of a long novel, and it is likely I would not have been writing a new book so much as arguing with the law. Of course another man might have had the stamina to write the new book and manage to be indifferent to everything else, but it was too much to ask of me. By then I was like a lover in a bad but uncontrollable affair; my woman was publication, and it would have cost too much to give her up before we were done. My imagination had been committed—to stop would leave half the psyche in limbo.

Knowing, however, what I had failed to do, shame added momentum to the punishment of the drugs. By the last week or two, I had worn down so badly that with a dozen pieces still to be fixed, I was reduced to working hardly more than an hour a day. Like an old man, I would come up out of a Seconal stupor with four or five times the normal dose in my veins and drop into a chair to sit for hours. It was July, the heat was grim in New York, the last of the book had to be in by August 1. Putnam had been more than accommodating, but the vehicle of publication was on its way, and the book could not be postponed beyond the middle of October or it would miss all chance for a large fall sale. I would sit in a chair and watch a baseball game on television, or get up and go out in the heat to a drugstore for a sandwich and malted—it was my outing for the day: The walk would feel like a patrol in a tropical sun, and it was two blocks, no more. When I came back, I would lie down, my head would lose the outer wrappings of sedation, and with a crumb of Benzedrine, the first snake or two of thought would wind through my brain. I would go for some coffee—it was a trip to the kitchen, but when I came back I would have a scratch-board and pencil in hand. Watching some afternoon horror on television, the boredom of the performers coming through their tense hilarities with a bleakness to match my own, I would pick up the board, wait for the first sentence—like all working addicts I had come to an old man's fine sense of inner timing—and then slowly, but picking up speed, the actions of the drugs hovering into collaboration like two ships passing in view of one another, I would work for an hour, not well but not badly either. (Pages 195 to 200 of the Putnam edition were written this way.) Then my mind would wear out, and new work was done for the day. I would sit around, watch more television, and try to rest my dulled mind, but by evening a riot of bad nerves was on me again, and at two in the morning I'd be having the manly debate of whether to try sleep with two double capsules or settle again for my need of three.

Somehow I got the book done for the last deadline. Not perfectly—doing just the kind of editing and small rewriting I was doing, I could have used another two or three days, but I got it almost the way I wanted, and then I took my car up to the Cape and lay around in Provincetown with my wife, trying to mend, and indeed doing a fair job, because I came off sleeping pills and the marijuana and came part of the way back into that world which has the proportions of the ego. I picked up on *The Magic Mountain,* took it slowly, and lowered *The Deer Park* down to modest size in my brain. Which, events proved, was just as well.

A few weeks later we came back to the city, and I took some mescaline. Maybe one dies a little with the poison of mescaline in the blood. At the end of a long and private trip which no quick remark should try to describe, the book of *The Deer Park* floated into mind, and I sat up, reached through a pleasure garden of velveted light to find the tree of a pencil and the bed of a notebook, and brought them to union together. Then, out of some flesh in myself I had not yet known, with the words coming one by one, in separate steeps and falls, hip in their turnings, all cool with their flights, like the touch of being coming into other being, so the last six lines of my bloody book came to me, and I was done. And it was the only good writing I ever did directly from a drug, even if I paid for it with a hangover beyond measure.

That way the novel received its last sentence, and if I had waited one more day it would have been too late, for in the next twenty-four hours, the printers began their cutting and binding. The book was out of my hands.

Six weeks later, when *The Deer Park* came out, I was no longer feeling eighty years old but something like a vigorous, hysterical sixty-three—I was actually thirty-three—and I laughed like an old pirate at the indignation I had breezed into being. The important reviews broke about seven good and eleven bad, and the out-of-town reports were almost three-to-one bad to good, but I was not unhappy, because the good reviews were lively and the bad reviews were full of factual error.

More interesting is the way reviews divided in the New York magazines and newspapers. *Time,* for example, was bad, *Newsweek* was good; *Harper's* was terrible, but the *Atlantic* was adequate; the daily *Times* was very bad, the Sunday *Times* was good; the daily *Herald Tribune* gave a mark of zero, the Sunday *Herald Tribune* was better than good; *Commentary* was careful but complimentary, the *Reporter* was frantic; the *Saturday Review* was a scold, and Brendan Gill, writing for *The New Yorker,* put together a series of slaps and superlatives, which went partially like this:

> . . . a big, vigorous, rowdy, ill-shaped, and repellent book, so strong and so weak, so adroit and so fumbling, that only a writer of the greatest and most reckless talent could have flung it between covers.

It's one of the three or four lines I've thought perceptive in all the reviews of my books. That Malcolm Cowley used one of the same words in saying *The Deer Park* was "serious and reckless" is also, I think, interesting, for reckless the book was—and two critics, anyway, had the instinct to feel it.

One note appeared in many reviews. The strongest statement of it was by John Hutchens in the daily New York *Herald Tribune:*

. . . the original version reputedly was more or less re-
written and certain materials eliminated that were deemed
too erotic for public consumption. And, with that, a book
that might at least have made a certain reputation as a large
shocker wound up as a cipher. . . .

I was bothered to the point of writing a letter to the twenty-
odd newspapers which reflected this idea. What bothered me
was that I could never really prove I had not "eliminated" the
book. Over the years all too many readers would have some
hazy impression that I had disemboweled large pieces of the best
meat, perspiring in a coward's sweat, a publisher's directive in
my ear. (For that matter, I still get an occasional letter which asks
if it is possible to see the unbowdlerized *Deer Park*.) Part of the
cost of touching the Rinehart galleys was to start those rumors,
and in fact I was not altogether free of the accusation, as I have
tried to show. Even the ten lines which so displeased Rinehart
had been altered a bit; I had shown them once to a friend whose
opinion I respected, and he remarked that while it was impossible to accept the sort of order Rinehart had laid down, still a
phrase like the "fount of power" had a Victorian heaviness about
it. Well, that was true, it was out of character for O'Shaugnessy's
new style, and so I altered it to the "thumb of power" and then
other changes became desirable, and the curious are invited
to compare the two versions of this particular passage,* but the
mistake I made was to take a small aesthetic gain on those lines
and lose a larger clarity about a principle.

What more is there to say? The book moved fairly well. It
climbed to seven and then to six on the *New York Times* best-seller
list, stayed there for a week or two, and then slipped down. By
Christmas, the tone of the *Park* and the Christmas spirit being
not all that congenial, it was just about off the lists forever. It did

---

*Here are the ten lines as changed:

Tentatively, she reached out a hand to finger his hair, and at that moment
Herman Teppis opened his legs and let Bobby fall to the floor. At the expression of surprise on her face, he began to laugh. "Don't you worry, sweetie," he
said, and down he looked at that frightened female mouth, facsimile of all
those smiling lips he had seen so ready to serve at the thumb of power, and
with a cough, he started to talk. "That's a good girlie, that's a good girlie, that's
a good girlie," he said in a mild little voice, "you're an angel darling, and I like
you, you're my darling darling, oh that's the ticket," said Teppis.

well, however; it would have reached as high as three or two or even to number one if it had come out in June and then been measured against the low sales of summer, for it sold over fifty thousand copies after returns, which surprised a good many in publishing, as well as disappointing a few, including myself. I discovered that I had been poised for an enormous sale or a failure—a middling success was cruel to take. Week after week I kept waiting for the book to erupt into some dramatic change of pace which would send it up in sales instead of down, but that never happened. I was left with a draw, not busted, not made, and since I was empty at the time, worn-out with work, waiting for the quick transfusions of a generous success, the steady sales of the book left me deeply depressed. Having reshaped my words with an intensity of feeling I had not known before, I could not understand why others were not overcome with my sense of life, of sex, and of sadness. Like a starved revolutionary in a garret, I had compounded out of need and fever and vision and fear nothing less than a madman's confidence in the identity of my being and the wants of all others, and it was a new dull load to lift and to bear, this knowledge that I had no magic so great as to hasten the time of the apocalypse but that instead I would be open like all others to the attritions of half-success and small failure. Something God-like in my confidence began to leave, and I was reduced in dimension if now less a boy. I knew I had failed to bid on the biggest hand I ever held.

The proper end to this account is the advertisement I took in *The Village Voice*. It was bought in November 1955, a month after publication, it was put together by me and paid for by me, and it was my way I now suppose of saying good-bye to the pleasure of a quick triumph, of making my apologies for the bad flaws in the bravest effort I had yet pulled out of myself, and certainly for declaring to the world (in a small way, mean pity) that I no longer gave a sick dog's drop for the wisdom, the reliability, and the authority of the public's literary mind, those creeps and old ladies of vested reviewing.

Besides, I had the tender notion—believe it if you will—that the ad might after all do its work and excite some people to buy the book.

But here it is:

BEST-SELLERS

———

Now that this once-outsized lust in me for large sales has settled into more reasonable expectations, I may as well offer some later thoughts on the subject.

Writing a best-seller with conscious intent to do so is, after all, a state of mind that is not without comparison to the act of marrying for money only to discover that the absence of love is more onerous than anticipated. When a putative and modest writer of best-sellers finally becomes professional enough to write a winner, he or she thinks that a great feat has been brought off, even as a man void of love (and money) will see a wealthy marriage as a splendid union.

The ideal, and as you get older you do try to get closer to the ideal, is to write only what interests you. It will prove of interest to others or it won't, but if you try to steer your way into success, you shouldn't be a serious writer. Rather, you will do well to study the tricks of consistent best-seller authors while being certain to stay away from anything that's *well written*. Reading good books could poison your satisfaction at having pulled off a best-seller. I don't think Jackie Susann went to bed with Rainer Maria Rilke on her night table.

—

Today, large literary canvases are usually left to best-selling novelists. They will have a cast of forty or fifty characters, and stories
that traverse fifty to a hundred years. They'll have several world
wars, plus startling changes in the lives of several families. They
do all that to keep their book moving. What usually characterizes these novels is that nothing is in them that you haven't come
across before. Most good writers tend these days to work on
smaller canvases. Then, at least, you have the confidence that
what you're doing has some fictional truth. That's reasonable. At
least you're contributing to knowledge rather than adding to
the sludge of the culture. Of course, that can make it more difficult to take on a large topic. At the moment the only great writer
who can handle forty or fifty characters and three or four decades is García Márquez. *One Hundred Years of Solitude* is an amazing work. He succeeds in doing it, but how, I don't know. In my
Egyptian novel, it took me ten pages to go around a bend in the
Nile.

It's counterproductive to think, I'm going to put this in because
it will sell copies. Usually, that doesn't work. There is an integrity
to best-sellerdom—it is the best book that the author is capable
of writing at that time. He or she believes in the book. That's one
reason it's a best-seller. Stephen King was a desperately clumsy
and repetitive writer when he started, but best-seller book readers responded to his sincerity. That was present on every badly
written page. The popularity of bad writing is analogous to the
enjoyment of fast food.
  I must say King has improved in style since he started. Hopefully, his readers also have, but that is not as certain.

A best-seller strategy is to keep cooking up new ingredients for
the story. But beware! Plot is equal to a drug. It can stimulate
a novelist into hordes of narrative energy, and will certainly keep
a reader on the page, but sooner or later, plot presents its bill,
and dire exigencies come down upon the writer. The author
who is over-burdened with plot is sometimes obliged to enter
the character's mind in order to keep things clear.
  Right here is where it all bogs down. A reader's confidence
in what he is reading will be subtly betrayed or even squandered
should a novelist choose to enter the mind of a character but
fail to bequeath the indispensable gift that the reader can now

know more about the character than before. The internal mono-logues are usually routine and insist on telling us what we know already. There is almost no signature quality of mind.

Of course, the damage is limited, since the internal rumina-tions of the characters in most mega-best-sellers are about what you would expect. Mega-best-seller readers want to be able to read and read and read—they do not want to ponder any truly unexpected revelations. Reality might lie out there, but that is not why they are reading.

Editing tends to make best-sellers read more like each other. As one instance, few best-sellers don't suffer from a spate of adjec-tives. For when a writer can't find the nuance of an experience, he usually loads up with adjectives. That tells the reader what to think. This goes along with a tendency in publishing houses to get the emphasis on entertainment at all costs. Of course, a per-vasive weariness could come into us because of the rate at which we are being entertained.

My literary generation was under the umbrella of Maxwell Perkins—anyone who became an editor wanted to be like him. Young editors felt a loyalty toward their writers. There were spiritual marriages, if you will. It's still true to a degree, but the odds against sustaining such loyalty are now much higher. Today's publishing dictates that an editor has to bring in books which make money. This near-absolute has to enter the inter-stices of a young editor's thinking. (And his or her intestines.) I imagine it would be hard for most young editors not to start pushing their authors just a bit in the direction of trying to be more popular. That, of course, strains the bond.

Right now the smart money would bet against the serious novel. The publishing houses are getting depressed about the future of good fiction, and the publishers are obviously the ones who most determine that future. Survival probably comes down to the young editors. When a serious novel by an unknown gets published these days, it's usually because some young editor has made an issue of it. The publisher generally goes along. In ef-fect, it's the charitable side of publishing, and it will continue so long as publishers keep a little faith in their young editors, who, in turn, manage to hold on to their nerve.

—

Bookstore managers may ask, "Why don't you write a short book?" They don't have to state their motive. We both know. Short books are thin books, and so take up less space on shelves. Ergo, the shelves can bring in more income per foot. But short novels? Unfortunately, I was co-opted at an early age by Thomas Mann, who said that only the exhaustive is truly interesting. Trust Mann to make one a closet elitist.

REVIEWS, PUBLICITY, AND SUCCESS

I treat bad reviews in the manner that a politician running for office treats a loss of support. A couple of friends called up after a very bad review of *Ancient Evenings* appeared in *The New York Times Book Review* and asked, "Are you all right?" I'd seen it a week before, so my unhappiness was now digested. I told them that it was like realizing the county chairman in Schenectady had decided against your candidacy. But to lose a primary in Schenectady doesn't mean you stop running for governor. It isn't my ego that's hurt, it's my damn pocketbook. Getting a bad review these days in the Sunday *Times* affects my wallet. My ego, however, remains relatively intact. Whereas, when I was younger, I used to consider a bad review a personal insult. The guy who wrote it was evil. In fact, however, I have never actually punched out a reviewer, which I say with a certain wistfulness. I did sit next to Philip Rahv after he had written an atrocious review of *An American Dream*. Rahv had his virtues, bless him, but physical courage was not one of them. So I made a point of installing myself beside him on a couch at a party, and while I smiled at him, I kept my body firmly pressed into his, leaning into him all the while that we had a long thirty-minute conversation about something else altogether. I was perfectly pleasant the entire time and everything seemed all right, except we were both tilted alarmingly from my leaning into him. He was in an absolute panic, waiting for me to strike. It must have seemed an odd sight from across the room: He was a heavy man, and the two of us probably looked like two doughnuts crushed together at one end of the box.

MICHAEL SCHUMACHER: Should a writer be concerned about looking foolish when taking risks?

NORMAN MAILER: You want to stay above that fear, but once in a great while, I'll still think, "This is going to get the world's worst reviews. I'm diving into something that's going to make no one happy and will leave certain people very unhappy." On the other hand, the good side of such risk is that it is exciting. You feel like a free man.

Sometimes, you can tell in advance you're headed for trouble. Obviously, with a book about ancient Egypt, everyone would have been happier if some unknown author had written it. There might have been then a lively curiosity about the author. Who is this unknown and most curious talent? One hurdle I had to overcome with *Ancient Evenings* was knowing in advance that a lot of people would pick it up and spend the first fifty pages saying, "What is Norman Mailer up to?" It makes them uncomfortable, because these days we all pride ourselves on our acumen. We want to think we're in control of the scene. When someone refutes our expectations, it does irritate the hell out of us.

MS: How do you deal with it?

NM: Professional confidence. Not arrogance—professional confidence. If I'm not, in the literary sense, smarter than the reviewer, I'm in a lot of trouble. After all, I should know more about my book than he or she does. So, I can read a very bad review and shrug it off. That works until it *doesn't* work. If all the reviews are bad, it could feel like a catastrophe.

It usually doesn't matter if your book is good or bad. Across the country, you're going to get more or less the same number of good and bad reviews. A dreadful book will probably get three good reviews in ten, and a very good book may get six. Occasionally, a work will receive all good or all bad reviews across the board and this happens because something in its pages outrages or soothes some part of the national temper to which the media is sensitive.

Crude example: a work that is insensitive to 9/11.

Large literary success is so often a matter of fortuitous publication. *The Naked and the Dead* had the luckiest timing of my career. By 1946, people were no longer that interested in novels about the Second World War. But *The Naked and the Dead* didn't come out until 1948, and by then readers were ready. If it had appeared earlier, I don't know that it would have had equal impact.

On the other hand, when I wrote *Ancient Evenings* (and that novel took eleven years), I ended up wishing I had been a bit more productive on a few of those working days and so could have come out twelve months earlier. That might have offered me a following breeze. There was large interest in the Egyptian dynasties just the year before. New York had had a massive museum exhibit at the Metropolitan that then proceeded to travel all over the country. By the time *Ancient Evenings* appeared, I was in the wake. The curious had, for the most part, lost interest.

Something of the same happened with *Harlot's Ghost*. When it was published in 1992, the Cold War was over. Much direct attention was gone. When I'd begun seven years earlier, people were still fascinated (as I certainly was) by the CIA. My point is, don't write a book with the idea people are going to be attracted by the subject and therefore you have a good chance to do well with your sales. The situation is bound to be different by the time the work is ready to show itself. No need to calculate. It's a crapshoot.

Ah, publicity! One has written a book and the publisher intends to do a bit with it—the faint hope arises that it will become a bestseller—and so the author is ready to do a tour and excite some attention.

I think for any novelist who's had a great deal of early success, as Capote did and Vidal did and Styron and I did, it was not automatic or easy to look upon other people with simple interest, because, generally speaking, they were more interested in us. One is never more aware of this vanity than when on a publicity tour. You are the center of attention. But there is a price. You are also an object to be manipulated as effectively as possible. The career of media interviewers conceivably rises or falls a little by how well they handle you.

Moreover, count on it: Three out of four interviewers will not have read your book. That tends to make them ask questions which cost them 2 percent and you 98 percent. For example: "Tell me all about your book." After you've answered that a few times, you begin to feel as if the limousine in which you are traveling is out of gas and you have to push it up the hill.

For literary people who are on a tight budget, buying a good hardcover book does bear some slight relation to a sacramental act, so it's best if they feel a certain respect, even a touch of awe, for you as the author. If you're unsavory in public life, it doesn't matter that everyone knows your name—you are not going to sell as many hardcover books as you should. The good authors who do well are usually careful not to be in the public eye—Saul Bellow and John Updike for two. Very few can flout that law. Capote has. So has Vidal. I certainly haven't.

Every time a story about me appears in a newspaper, I am injured professionally. I don't think there's anything to do about it. One of the reasons I'm in all the time is that the columns keep using the same people. It's a game, and there may not be many more than a few hundred players on the board. If I were in a Tarot deck, I'd be the Fool. I used to try to keep a stern separation between the public legend and myself, but you know, you get older, and after a while, you can feel at times like an old gink in Miami with slits in his sneakers. At that juncture, it's pointless to fight the legend. The legend has become a lotion for your toes.

If you are ever in a situation where you've had enough commercial success to be dealing with a movie company—don't worry about the number-one man or woman. Do your best to have Number Two approve of what you're doing. Because if Number One likes what you offer him and Number Two doesn't, Number One will almost never give the go-ahead. It's to his or her advantage to go along with Number Two's declared opinion.

We can approach it as a logical proposition. If One insists on doing your book and the movie that comes out doesn't do well, then Two now has a real edge. Conceivably—if the stakes have been high—he or she might someday be in a position to take over One's job. On the other hand, if One was right in going ahead with you and your property does well for the company, then Two may never forgive One for exhibiting superior acumen.

On the other hand, if One turns to Two and says, "Okay, we won't take it on," and the film that is made by others from your book or script does not do well, then Two can feel genial enough to say, "I'm working for a pretty good guy. He pays attention to me; he respects me. That is because he knows I'm usually right." Of course, if the company who picks it up makes real money, Two is left at a whole disadvantage.

Ergo, the rule suggests: Get to the number-two man and hope he likes your work.

On the other hand, if you've written your best, forget about these matters. It's taken me fifty years to learn this sort of thing. In that sense, it's not worth learning. After all, I still have to find out how to get to Number Two.

On this practical note, let me add another tip: *An American Dream* was originally published in *Esquire* in 1964 and had a scene where a black man said *shit* about twenty times. Now, I didn't really need all twenty. Twelve would have been better, but I also knew that if I put in twelve, the editors would take out five, so I put in twenty. And the editors screamed, but I ended up with my twelve. They were happy and I was happy.

THE BITCH

I remember, years ago, talking about the novel with Gore Vidal. We were reminiscing in mutually sour fashion over the various pirates, cutthroats, racketeers, assassins, pimps, rape artists, and general finks we had encountered on our separate travels through the literary world, and we went on at length, commenting—Gore with a certain bitter joy, I with some uneasiness— upon the decline of our métier in recent years. We were speaking as trade unionists. It was not that the American novel was necessarily less good than it had been immediately after the war so much as that the people we knew seemed to care much less about novels. The working conditions were not as good. One rarely heard one's friends talking about a good new novel anymore; it was always an essay in some magazine or a new play which seemed to occupy the five minutes in a dinner party when writers are discussed rather than actors, politicians, friends, society, or, elevate us, foreign affairs. One could not make one's living writing good novels anymore. With an exception here and there, it had always been impossible, but not altogether—there used to be the long chance of having a best-seller. Now with paperback books, even a serious novel with extraordinarily good reviews was lucky to sell thirty or forty thousand copies—most people preferred to wait a year and read the book later in its cheap edition.

So we went on about that, and the professional mediocrity of book reviewers and the indifference of publishers, the lack of community among novelists themselves, the backbiting, the glee with which most of us listened to unhappy news about other novelists, the general distaste of the occupation—its lonely hours, its jealous practitioners, its demands on one's character, its assaults on one's ego, its faithlessness as inspiration, its ambushes as fashion. Since we had both begun again to work on a novel after some years of taking on other kinds of writing, there was a pleasant irony to all we said. We were not really as bitter as we pretended.

Finally, I laughed. "Gore, admit it. The novel is like the Great Bitch in one's life. We think we're rid of her, we go on to other women, we take our pulse and decide that finally we're enjoying ourselves, we're free of her power, we'll never suffer her depredations again, and then we turn a corner on a street, and there's the Bitch smiling at us, and we're trapped. We know the Bitch has still got us."

Vidal gave that twisted grin of admiration which is extracted from him when someone else has coined an image that could fit his style. "Indeed," he said, "the novel *is* the Great Bitch."

Every novelist who has slept with the Bitch (only poets and writers of short stories have a *Muse*) comes away bragging afterward like a G.I. tumbling out of a whorehouse spree—"Man, I made her moan" goes the cry of the young writer. But the Bitch laughs afterward in her empty bed. "He was so sweet in the beginning," she declares, "but by the end he just went, 'Peep, peep, peep.'"

A man lays his character on the line when he writes a novel. Anything in him which is lazy, or meretricious, or unthought-out, complacent, fearful, overambitious, or terrified by the ultimate logic of his exploration will be revealed in his book. Some writers are skillful at concealing their weaknesses; some have a genius for converting a weakness into an acceptable mannerism of style. Nonetheless, no novelist can escape his or her own character altogether. That is, perhaps, the worst news any young writer can hear.

One more note on the Bitch. A friend, after reading the above paragraphs, said, "There's the title for your book—*I Made Her Moan.*" I assured him that I never had a day so brave as to be ready to use that title.

SOCIAL LIFE,
LITERARY DESIRES,
LITERARY CORRUPTION

One of the cruelest remarks in the language is: Those who can, do; those who can't, teach. The parallel must be: Those who meet experience, learn to live; those who don't, write.

The second remark has as much truth as the first—which is to say, some truth. Of course, many a young man has put himself in danger in order to pick up material for his writing, but as a matter to make one wistful, not one major American athlete, CEO, politician, engineer, trade-union official, surgeon, airline pilot, chess master, call girl, sea captain, teacher, bureaucrat, Mafioso, pimp, recidivist, physicist, rabbi, movie star, clergyman, or priest or nun has also emerged as a major novelist since the Second World War.

What with ghostwriters, collaborators, and editors hand-cranking the tongues of the famous long enough to get their memoirs into tape recorders, it could be said that some dim reflection can be found in literature of the long aisles and huge machines of that social mill which is the world of endeavor—yes, just about as much as comes back to us from a photograph insufficiently exposed in the picture-taking, a ghost image substituted for the original lights and deep shadows of the object. So, for every good novel about a trade union that has been written from the inside, we have ten thousand better novels to read about authors and the social activities of their friends. Writers tend to live with writers just as automotive engineers congregate in the same country clubs of the same suburbs around Detroit.

But even as we pay for the social insularity of Detroit engineers by having to look at the repetitive hump of their design until finally what is most amazing about the automobile is how little it has been improved in the last fifty years, so literature suffers from its own endemic hollow: We are overfamiliar with the sensitivity of the sensitive and relatively ignorant of the cunning of the strong and the stupid, one—it may be fatal—step removed from good and intimate perception of the inside procedures of the corporate, financial, governmental, Mafia, and working-class establishments. Investigative journalism has taken us into the guts of the machine, only not really, not enough. We still do not have much idea of the soul of any inside operator; we do not, for instance, yet have a clue to what makes a quarterback ready for a good day or a bad one. In addition, the best investigative reporting of new journalism tends to rest on too narrow an ideological base—the rational, ironic, fact-oriented world of the media liberal. So we have a situation, call it a cultural malady, of the most basic sort: a failure of sufficient information (that is, good *literary* information) to put into those centers of our mind we use for assessment. No matter how much we read, we tend to know too little of how the world works. The men who do the real work offer us no real writing, and the writers who explore the minds of such men approach from an intellectual stance that distorts their vision. You would not necessarily want a saint to try to write about a computer engineer, but you certainly would not search for the reverse. All too many saints, monsters, maniacs, mystics, and rock performers are being written about these days, however, by practitioners of journalism whose inner vision is usually graphed by routine parameters. Our continuing inability to comprehend the world is likely to continue.

Being a novelist, I want to know every world. I would never close myself off to a subject unless it's truly repulsive to me. While one can never take one's imperviousness to corruption for granted, it is still important to have some idea of how the world works. What ruins most writers of talent is that they don't get enough experience, so their novels tend to develop a certain paranoid perfection. That is almost never as good as the rough edge of reality. (Franz Kafka immaculately excepted!)

For example, how much of the history that's made around us is conspiracy, how much is simple fuckups? You have to know the world to get some idea of that.

It's not advisable for a novelist, once he is successful!, to live in an upper-class social milieu for too long. Since it is a world of rigid rules, you cannot be yourself. There's a marvelous built-in reflex in such society. It goes: If you are completely one of us, then you are not very interesting. (Unless you have prodigious amounts of money or impeccable family.) If you have any entrée, it's because that world is always fascinated with mavericks, at least until the point where they become bored with you. Then you are out. On the other hand, while in, even as a maverick, there are certain rules you have to obey, and the first is to be amusing. (Capote and Jerzy Kosinski come to mind.) If you start accepting those rules past the point where you enjoy going along as part of the game, then you are injuring yourself. Capote played con-sigliere to New York society until he could bear it no longer and then he commenced his self-destruction with *Answered Prayers*. Kosinski, who may have been the most amusing guest of them all in New York, committed suicide during an ongoing illness.

I remember saying in 1958, "I am imprisoned with a perception that will settle for nothing less than making a revolution in the consciousness of our time." And I certainly failed, didn't I? At the time, I thought I had books in me that no one else did, and so soon as I was able to write them, society would be altered. Kind of grandiose.

Now, the things I've stood for have been roundly defeated. Literature, after all, has been ground down in the second half of the twentieth century. It's a gloomy remark, but consider that literature was one of the forces that helped to shape the latter part of the nineteenth century—naturalism, for example. One can fear that in another hundred years the serious novel will bear the same relation to serious people that the five-act verse play does today. The profound novel will be a curiosity, a long cry away from what great writing once offered. Where indeed would England be now without Shakespeare? Or Ireland without James Joyce or Yeats? If you ask who has had that kind of influence today in America, I'd say Madonna. Some years ago, the average young girl was completely influenced by her. She affected the way girls dressed, acted, behaved. So far, she's had more to do with women's liberation than Women's Liberation. I mean, for every girl who was affected by feminist ideology, there must have been five who tried to live and dress the way they thought Madonna did. They had their own private revolution without ever hearing about *Ms.* magazine.

Sometimes you write a novel because it comes out of elements in yourself that—no better word—are deep. The subject appeals to some root in your psyche, and you set out on a vertiginous venture. But there are other times when you may get into an altogether different situation. You just damn well have to write a book for no better reason than that your economic problems are pressing.

Tough Guys Don't Dance comes under that rubric. After I finished *Ancient Evenings,* I was exhausted. I also felt spoiled. So I did no writing for ten months. Unfortunately, my then-publisher Little, Brown and I were parting company. (They weren't mad about authors who took eleven years on a massive tome like *Ancient Evenings.*) However, there was one more book owed to them. And my feeling was, Well, they won't want the book right away even if they have been paying me good money every month to write it and I haven't been doing the job. Reality had not tapped on any of my windows for all those months. If it sounds silly that a grown man could be that naïve, well, we are all, you know, somewhat less than our sophistication.

So, on month ten, they said to me in effect, "Are you going to give us a novel or will you repay us the money?" Now, I had to recognize that if I ended up owing them a year of sizable monthly stipends, I would never catch up with the IRS.

The only thing was to come up with a book in sixty days! I couldn't possibly give them non-fiction. The research would take too long—no, I had to do a novel that would be quick and comfortable. First thing, therefore, was to make a decision on whether to do it in first person or third. First person is always more hospitable in the beginning. You can give a sense of the immediate almost at once. It would be first person, then.

But where would it take place? New York is too complicated to write about quickly. Besides, given the constrictions of time, I had to know the place well. All right, it would have to be a book about Provincetown. At that time, in the early Eighties, I had been going there off and on for forty years. For practical purposes, it was all the small town I would ever have.

What should it be about? Well, I could take my cue from *An American Dream,* make it a story of murder and suspense. But who would the narrator be? An easy decision: Let him be a writer. In first person, a writer is the single most cooperative character to deal with. Let him be between thirty-five and forty, frustrated, never published, bitter, quite bright, but not as bright as myself. After all, I had to be able to write this book in a hurry. Then, having subscribed to these quick guidelines, I thought if I had one pious bone in my body, just one, I would now get down and pray. Because I was still in trouble. Sixty days to produce a novel!

I set out. It's one of the few times I've felt blessed as a writer. I knew there was a limit to how good the book could be, but the style came through, and that is always half of a novel. You can write a very bad book, but if the style is first-rate, then you've got something that will live—not forever, but for a decent time. The shining example might be G. K. Chesterton's *The Man Who Was Thursday.* It has an undeniably silly plot unless you invest a great deal into it. A worshipful right-wing critic can do a blitheringly wonderful thesis on the symbolic leaps and acrobatics of *The Man Who Was Thursday,* but actually, it's about as silly as a Jules Verne novel. Yet the writing itself is fabulous. The style is extraordinary. The aperçus are marvelous. *The Man Who Was Thursday* proves the point: Style is half of a novel.

And for some good reason, unknown to me, the style came through in *Tough Guys Don't Dance.* The writing was probably, for the most part, as good as I can muster. The plot, however, was just as close to silly. That was the price to pay for the speed of composition. The irony is that the book did not end up at Little, Brown. I was able to pay off my debt because Random House wanted me, and I have been with them ever since.

I expect we are now ready to talk about the writer's daily work.

CRAFT

HAZARDS

———

Before we can talk about lore, skill, or practice, it may prove of use to discuss the most common occupational hazard of the writer—a bad mood. The indispensable element in craft is learning to live with the problems and perils of the profession. They do weigh on one in a special fashion.

The piece that follows may be a touch too hortatory, but then, it was delivered as a speech at the University of Michigan Hopwood Awards in 1984. Originally called "The Hazards and Sources of Writing," I have broken it into several sections. Stories about Kurt Vonnegut, Robert Rauschenberg, and Willem de Kooning appear in other portions of this book, and the last few pages (Sources) have been moved over to "The Occult," where I try to talk about the mysterious origin of some novelistic choices.

This portion, however, is complete in itself, and does deal with the difficulties of writing a novel when the winds of one's creative spirit threaten oncoming squalls or, worse, long periods of no wind—becalmed by writer's block.

I am going to speak of the working state of the novelist once he has passed his apprenticeship—and to avoid saying *his or her* on every occasion, let me repeat that I will often use the possessive pronoun *his* to indicate all of humankind. The apprenticeship of a writer is, of course, subject to all the later hazards of the profession, those perils of writer's block and failing energy, alcoholism, drugs, and desertion. For many a writer deserts writing to go into a collateral profession in advertising or academia, trade journals, publishing—the list is long. What is not routine is to become a young writer with a firmly established name. Luck as well as talent can take one across the first border. Some do surpass the trials of acquiring technique and commence to make a living at our bizarre profession. It is then, however, that less-charted perils begin. I would like to speak at length of the hazards of writing, the cruelties it extorts out of mind and flesh. I know something of these hazards and I ought to. My first story was published, after all, more than forty years ago and the first novel I wrote that saw print is going to be thirty-six years old in a month. Obviously, for a long time I have been accustomed to thinking of myself as a writer, even as others see me that way. So I hear one lament over and over from strangers: "Oh, I too would have liked to be an author." You can almost hear them musing aloud about the freedom of the life. How felicitous to have no boss and to face no morning rush to work, to know all the intoxications of celebrity—how they long to satisfy the voice within that keeps saying, "What a pity no one will know how unusual my life has been! There are all those secrets I cannot tell!" Years ago, I wrote, "Experience, when it cannot be communicated to another, must wither within and be worse than lost." I often ponder the remark. Once in a while your hand will write out a sentence that seems true and yet you do not know where it came from. Ten or twenty words seem able to live in balance with your experience. It may be one's nicest reward as a writer. You feel you have come near the truth. When that happens, you can look at the page years later and meditate again on the meaning, for it goes deep. So how can I not understand why people want to write? All the same, I am also a professional and so there is another part of me that is ready to laugh when strangers tell me of their aspirations. I am not free of the scorn of a veteran prize-fighter who hears someone say, "I'd like to flatten that bully." The speaker does not know how many years of discipline and dull punishment must be given over to the ability to throw a good punch at will. I say to myself, "They can write an interesting letter so they assume they are ready to tell the story of their lives. They do not understand how much it will take to pick up even the rudiments of narrative." If I believe that the person who has spoken to me in that fashion is serious, I warn them as gently as I can. I say, "Well, it's probably as hard to learn to write as to play the piano." Then if their only reason for wanting to be a writer is to pull in some quick success, they feel deflated and that's okay with me. One shouldn't encourage people to write for too little. It's a splendid life when you think of its emoluments, but it can be death to the soul if you are not good at it.

Let me keep my promise, then, and go on a little about the negative part of being a writer. To skip at one bound over all those fascinating and relatively happy years when one is an apprentice writer and learning every day, at least on good days, there is in contrast the more or less constant pressure on the life of the professional novelist. For soon after you finish each hard-earned book, the reviews come in and the reviews are murderous. Contrast an author's reception to an actor's. With the notable exception of John Simon, theater critics do not often try to kill performers. I believe there is an unspoken agreement that thespians deserve to be protected against the perils of first nights. After all, the actor is daring a rejection that can prove as fearful as a major wound. For sensitive human beings like actors, a hole in the ego can be worse than a hole in the heart. Such moderation does not carry over, however, into literary criticism. *Meretricious, dishonest, labored, loathsome, pedestrian, hopeless, disgusting, disappointing, raunchy, ill-wrought, boring*—these are not uncommon words for a bad review. You would be hard put to find another professional field where criticism is equally savage. Accountants, lawyers, engineers, and doctors do not often speak publicly in this manner.

Yet the unhappiest thing to say is that our critical practice may even be fair, harsh but fair. After all, one prepares a book in the safety of the study and nothing short of your self-esteem, your bills, or your editor is forcing you to show your stuff. You put your book out, if you can afford to take the time, only when it is ready. If economic necessity forces you to write somewhat faster than is good for you—well, everybody has his sad story. As a practical matter, not that much has to be written into the teeth of a gale and few notes need be taken on the face of a cliff. An author usually does his stint at the desk, feeling not too hungry and suffering no pains greater than the view of his empty pad of paper. Now, granted, that white sheet can look as blank as a television screen when the program is off the air, but that is not a danger, merely a deadening presence. The writer, unlike more active creative artists, works in no immediate peril. Why should not the open season begin so soon as the work comes out? If talented authors were to have it better than actors in all ways, there would be a tendency for actors to disappear and talented authors to multiply, so the critics keep our numbers down.

In fact, not too many good writers remain productive through the decades. There are too many other hazards as well. We are jerked by the media in and out of fashion, and each drop from popularity can feel like a termination to your career. Such insecurity is no help to morale, for even in the best periods every writer always knows one little terror: *Does it stop tomorrow? Does it all stop tomorrow?* Writing is spooky. There is no routine of an office to keep you going, only the blank page each morning, and you never know where your words are coming from, those divine words. So your professionalism at best is fragile. You cannot always tell yourself that fashions pass and history will smile at you again. In the literary world, it is not easy to acquire the stoicism to endure, especially if you've begun as a vulnerable adolescent. It is not even automatic to pray for luck if it has been pessimism itself which gave force to your early themes. Maybe it is no more than blind will, but some authors stay at it. Over and over they keep writing a new book and do it in the knowledge that upon its publication they will probably be savaged and will not be able to fight back. An occasional critic can be singled out for counterattack, or one can always write a letter to the editor of the book section, but such efforts at self-defense are like rifle fire against fighter planes. All-powerful is the writer when he sits at his desk, but on the public stage he may feel as if his rights are puny. His courage, if he has any, must learn to live with the bruises left by comments on his work. The spiritual skin may go slack or harden to leather, but the honor of the effort to live down bad reviews and write again has to be analogous to the unspoken, unremarked courage of people who dwell under the pressure of a long illness and somehow resolve enough of their inmost contradictions to be able to get better. I suppose this is equal to saying that you cannot become a professional writer and keep active for three or four decades unless you learn to live with the most difficult condition of your existence, which is that superficial book reviewing is irresponsible and serious literary criticism can be close to merciless. The conviction that such a condition is fair has to take root deep enough to bear analogy to the psychology of a peasant who farms a mountain slope and takes it for granted that he or she was meant to toil through the years with one foot standing higher than the other.

Every good author who manages to forge a long career must be able, therefore, to build a character that will not be unhinged by a bad reception. That takes art. Few writers have rugged personalities when they are young. In general, the girls seldom look like potential beauty contest winners and the boys show small promise of becoming future All-Americans. They are most likely to be found on the sidelines, commencing to cook up that warped, passionate, bitter, transcendent view of life which will bring them later to the attention of the American public. But only later! The young writer usually starts as a loser and so is obliged to live with the conviction that the world he knows had better be wrong or he or she is wrong. On the answer depends one's evaluation of one's right to survive. Thanks to greed, plastics, mass media, and various abominations of technology—lo, the world is wrong. The paranoid aim of a cockeyed young writer has as much opportunity to hit the target as the beauty queen's wide-eyed lack of paranoia. So occasionally this loser of a young writer ends up a winner, for a while. His vision has projected him forward; he is just enough ahead of his time. But dependably, that wretched, lonely act of writing will force him back. Writing arouses too much commotion in one's psyche to allow the author to rest happily.

It is not easy to explain such disturbances to people unless they do write. Someone who has never tried fiction will hardly be quick to understand that in the study, a writer often does feel God-like. There one sits, ensconced in judgment on other people's lives. Yet contemplate the person in the chair: He or she could be hungover and full of the small shames of what was done yesterday or ten years ago. Those flashes of old fiascoes wait like ghosts in the huge house of the empty middle-aged self. Sometimes the ghosts even appear and ask to be laid to rest. Consciously or unconsciously, writers must fashion a new peace with the past every day they attempt to write. They must rise above despising themselves. If they cannot, they will probably lose the sanction to render judgment on others.

Yet the writer at work does not tolerate too much good news

either. At your desk, it is best if you do not come to like yourself too much. Wonderfully agreeable memories may appear on certain mornings, but if they have nothing to do with the work, they must be banished or they will leave the writer too cheerful, too energetic, too forgiving, too horny. It is in the calm depression of a good judge that one's scribblings move best over the page. Indeed, just as a decent judge will feel that he has injured society by giving an unjust verdict, so does an author have to ask himself constantly if he is being fair to his characters. For if the writer does violate the life of someone who is being written about—that is, proceeds in the ongoing panic of trying to keep a book amusing to distort one's characters to more comic, more corrupt, or more evil forms than one secretly believes they deserve—then one may be subtly injuring the reader. That is a moral crime. Few authors are innocent of such a practice; on the other hand, not so many artists can be found who are not also guilty of softening their portraits. Some writers don't want to destroy the sympathy their readers may feel for an appealing heroine by the admission that she shrieks at her children. Sales fly out the window. It takes as much literary integrity to be tough, therefore, as to be fair. The trail is narrow. It is difficult to keep up one's literary standards through the long, slogging reaches of the middle of a book. The early pleasures of conception no longer sustain you; the writer plods along with the lead feet of habit, the dry breath of discipline, and the knowledge that on the other side of the hill, the critics—who also have their talent to express—are waiting. Sooner or later you come to the conclusion that if you are going to survive, you had better, where it concerns your own work, become the best critic of them all. There is a saying among boxers that the punch you see coming hurts less than the one you never saw at all. An author who would find the resources to keep writing from one generation to the next does well to climb above his own ego high enough to see every flaw in the work. Otherwise he will never be able to decide what are its true merits.

Let yourself live, however, with an awareness of your book's lacks and shortcuts, its gloss where courage might have produced a little real shine, and you can bear the bad reviews. You can even tell when the critic is not exposing your psyche so much as taking off his own dirty socks. It proves amazing how many evil reviews one can digest if there is a confidence one has done one's best on a book, written to the limit of one's honesty, even scraped off a little of one's dishonesty. Get to that point of purity and your royalties may be injured by a small welcome but not your working morale. There is even hope that if the book is better than its reception, one's favorite readers will come eventually to care for it more. (It is, after all, a lovely but hitherto unloved child!) The prescription, therefore, is simple: One must not put out a job that has any serious taint of the meretricious. At least the prescription ought to be simple, but then how few of us ever do work of which we are not in fact a bit ashamed. It comes down to a matter of degree. There is that remark of Engels to Marx, "Quantity changes quality." A single potato is there for us to eat, but ten thousand potatoes are a commodity and have to be put in bins or boxes. A profit must be made from them or a loss will certainly be taken. By analogy, a little corruption in a book is as forgivable as the author's style, but a sizable literary delinquency is a diseased organ, or so it will feel if the critics begin to bang on it and happen to be right for once. That will be the hour when one's creditors do not go away. I wonder if we have not touched the fear that is back of the writing in many a good novelist's heart, the hazard beneath all others.

To the risks I just cited, let me add what may be the subtlest one of all. Some talented people feel they still haven't read enough to sit down and write. That is paralyzing. My great friend Malaquais had a terrible time. He had read more than anyone I knew. Like many another self-educated man, he had a powerful mind. But he couldn't write quickly, because he could see everything that was wrong in what he did. He'd realize that so-and-so—whoever: Stendhal, Racine, Molière—had done it better. This even extended into the narrowest corners. Some unheralded Polish novelist who was known for one small ability— Malaquais had read him, too. What an agony that he couldn't write a book as large as his vision of society. He was forever living in the harshest judgment on his talents. He could sit for twelve or fourteen hours at his desk and end with a page of work, no more, for the day. He had a good style but not good enough for him. "You must be ready," he would say, "to piss blood in order to find the right tone."

STYLE

———

S tyle, of course, is what every good young author looks to acquire. In lovemaking, its equivalent is grace. Everybody wants it, but who can find it by working directly toward the goal?

In my case, *Advertisements* was the first work I wrote with a style that I could call my own, but I didn't begin it until 1958, ten years after *The Naked and the Dead* was published. In between had come *Barbary Shore* and *The Deer Park* and I never want to have again two novels as hard to write.

I did not know what I was doing. Apart from the psychological vertigo that will attack any athlete, performer, or young entrepreneur who has huge early success, I had my own particular problem, a beauty—I did not know my métier. *The Naked and the Dead* had been written out of what I could learn from reading James T. Farrell and John Dos Passos, with good doses of Thomas Wolfe and Tolstoy, plus homeopathic tinctures from Hemingway, Fitzgerald, Faulkner, Melville, and Dostoyevsky. With such help, it was a book that wrote itself.

I knew, however, it was no literary achievement. I had done a book in a general style borrowed from many people and did not know what I had of my own to say. I had not had enough of my own life yet. The idea could even be advanced that style comes to young authors about the time they recognize that life is also ready to injure them. Something out there is not necessarily fooling. It would explain why authors who were ill in their childhood almost always arrive early in their career as developed stylists: Proust, Capote, and Alberto Moravia give three examples; Gide offers another. This notion would certainly account for the early and complete development of Hemingway's style. He had, before he was twenty, the unmistakable sensation of being wounded so near to death that he felt his soul slide out of him, then slip back.

The average young author is not that ill in childhood or that harshly used by early life. His little social deaths are sometimes balanced by his small social conquests. So he writes in the style of others while searching for his own, and tends to look for words more than rhythms. In his haste to dominate the world (rare is the young writer who is not a consummate prick), he also tends to choose his words for their precision, their ability to define, their acrobatic action. His style often changes from scene to scene, from paragraph to paragraph. He may know a little about creating mood, but the essence of good writing is that it sets a mood as intense as a theatrical piece and then alters that mood, enlarges it, conducts it over to another mood. Every sentence, precise or imprecise, vaulting or modest, is careful not to poke a hyperactive finger through the tissue of the mood. Nor do the sentences ever become so empty of personal quality that the prose sinks to the ground of the page. It is an achievement that comes from having thought about one's life right to the point where one is living it. Everything that happens seems capable of offering its own addition to one's knowledge. One has arrived at a personal philosophy or has even reached that rare plateau where one is attached to one's philosophy. At that juncture, everything one writes comes out of one's own fundamental mood.

Some such development may have gone on in me over the ten years from the publication of *The Naked and the Dead* to the commencement of work on *Advertisements for Myself.* In any event, it became the book in which I tried to separate my legitimate spiritual bile from my self-pity, and maybe it was the hardest continuing task I had yet set myself. What aggravated every problem was that I was also trying to give up smoking, and as a corollary of kicking nicotine, I was thrust into the problem of style itself.

In those days, my psyche felt as different without cigarettes as my body felt in moving from air to water. It was as if I perceived with different senses, and clear reactions were blunted. Writing without cigarettes, the word I looked for almost never came, not in quick time. In compensation, I was granted a sensitivity to the rhythm of what I wrote and that helped to turn my hand in the direction of better prose. I began to learn how difficult it is to move from the hegemony of the word to the resonance of the rhythm. This can be a jump greater than a leap into poetry. So, *Advertisements for Myself* was a book whose writing changed my life.

In *The Deer Park* I had been trying to find a style through three drafts. The first had been Proustian—not first-rate Proust, of course. Attempted Proust. Failed Proust. The second draft was located somewhere between the English novel of manners and Scott Fitzgerald—not good, but in that general direction. Then I found a tone that was not like the others. It fit the essential material. So I learned how style literally repels certain kinds of experience and can be equal to a dominating wife who is ever ready to select your suits. If a writer insists on a specific tone, despite all inner warnings, it can even limit the varieties of experience that will enter the book.

Finding one's own manner is elusive. While it certainly helps to develop a unique style, first you have to learn how to write. Back in the Fifties, Nelson Algren was giving a writing class in Chicago and invited me to sit in. He read a story by one of the kids. Third-rate Papa. Afterward, I said to Nelson, "Why did you pay that much attention? He was just copying Hemingway." And Algren, who was about ten years older than me and knew that much more, said, "You know, these kids are better off if they attach themselves to a writer and start imitating him, because they learn a lot doing that. If they're any good at all, sooner or later they'll get rid of the influence. But first, they have to get attached to somebody." That was useful.

On the other hand, it takes so long to find your own manner. It comes down to a set of decisions on which word is valuable and what is not, in every sentence you write. That's one element. Another is the overall consistency. You have writers who are exceptionally talented but are still what I would call great amateurs. The most notable example would be a writer as significantly gifted as Toni Morrison. Her style can shift from chapter to chapter—her strength is not in protecting the tone. She can write beautifully for pages, and then in a following chapter dawdle along in pedestrian mode. It violates what she is at her best, her distinctive voice, those distinctive insights.

Style is character. A good one will not come from a bad, undisciplined character. Now, a man may be evil, but I believe that people can be evil in their essential nature and still have good character. Good in the sense of being well tuned, flexible, supple, adaptable, principled. Even an evil man can have principles; he can be true to his own evil, which is not so easy either. And then I think one has to develop one's physical grace. Writers who are possessed of some may tend to write better than writers who are physically clumsy. It's my impression this is so. I certainly couldn't prove it.

Style is also a reflection of identity. Given a firm sense of yourself, you can write in a consistent vein. But should your identity shift, so will your presence change in your prose. Needless to say, illness, tragedy, huge frustration, age itself are bound to alter every firm notion of yourself.

And, of course, one's subject matter will also affect one's words. A journalistic voice can get into the workings of a good many topical novels. But then you wouldn't want Henry James to describe the life of Gary Gilmore. There is such a vice as too much splendid writing. For what Henry James wanted to do, however, his language was ideal. He recognized before anyone else that polite social life, despite its ridiculous or affected aspects, also presents a spectrum of small options present at every moment. In social life, a person often chooses among three or four equally agreeable alternatives, even to making the choice of being a little warmer or a little cooler than he or she originally expected to be toward a given person. James had an extraordinary sense of that unforeseen vibration in the almost wholly expected, and he created a fictional world out of such insight, a world that depended altogether on his unique voice.

It is comforting to argue that some major writers develop a style out of the very avoidance of their major weakness. Hemingway was not capable of writing a long, complex sentence with good architecture in the syntax. But he turned that inability into his personal skill at writing short declarative sentences or long run-on sentences connected by conjunctions. Faulkner, to the contrary, was not capable of writing simply, but his over-rich, congested sentences produced an extraordinary mood. In turn, Henry Miller could rarely tell a full story well. He preferred his excursions away from the story, and those asides are what make him exceptional.

You know, a good skier rarely worries about a route. He just goes, confident that he'll react to changes in the trail as they come upon him. It's the same thing in writing: You have to have confidence in your technique. That is the beauty of mustering the right tone at the right time—it enables you to feel like a good skier, nice and relaxed for the next unexpected turn.

There are two kinds of writers. Faulkner, Fitzgerald, and Hemingway, Melville and James, write with an air that is inimitable. There are other writers, usually less famous, who go along in a variety of modes. I'm in the latter camp. The same can be said of painters. Matisse painted in one recognizable vein, while Picasso entered a hundred before he was done. Style was the cutting tool by which he could delineate a reality. He saw it as a tool rather than as an extension of his identity. I've found his attitude to be useful for myself. It's better if one's writing is close to the material one is working with—a fairly formal prose for one occasion, casual for another.

Metaphors? You ask about metaphors. I had a dear friend, Charlie Devlin, who helped me greatly with *The Naked and the Dead,* and in fact was the model, considerably removed, for the character named McLeod in *Barbary Shore.* Charlie was a quiet, saturnine forty-year-old Irishman who was living full-time in the small rooming house where I took a cubicle (four dollars a week) to finish *The Naked and the Dead.* We used to have long literary conversations. At a certain point I showed him the manuscript. He tore it apart. He could be a severe critic. He said, "It's a better book than I thought it would be, but you have no gift for metaphor." Then he said, "Metaphor reveals a writer's true grasp of life. To the degree that you have no metaphor, you have not yet lived much of a life." I never forgot this lecture, and

began to work with might and main on my life and my metaphors. I would claim they have improved with age.

On the other hand, good dialogue depends on your ear. There
has to be something in each speech that relies on the previous
one. But I don't even want to talk about dialogue. Some people
have marvelous stuff, some don't, but that's only one aspect of
writing, it is not *the* aspect, and besides, I don't think you can
teach it. Most kids who have talent start off with good dialogue.
They're happy it's there, and they have fun—that can start you
as a writer. Those who are not gifted at dialogue will, hopefully,
be endowed with philosophy or good language.

If one wants an example of superb dialogue where the bar is
set about as high as it can go, then read William Kennedy or
Joan Didion. But make no attempt to imitate either. Superb dialogue is inimitable. It is the indispensable aid, however, to most
short stories.

A short fictional piece has a tendency to look for climates of
permanence—an event occurs, a man is hurt by it in some small
way forever. The novel moves as naturally toward flux. An event
occurs, a man is injured, and a month later is working on something else. The short story likes to be classic. It is most acceptable
when one fatal point is made. Whereas the novel is dialectical. It
is most alive when one can trace the disasters which follow victory or the subtle turns that sometimes come from a defeat. A
novel can be created out of short stories only if the point in each
story is consecutively more interesting and incisive than the
point before it, when the author in effect is drilling for oil.

LARRY SHAINBERG: You used a phrase I want you to elaborate on:
    "the tensile strength of a sentence."
NORMAN MAILER: Yes. That you can learn from a writing course.
LS: Tell me what you mean by the tensile strength.
NM: You can't change a single word. What is tensile strength? It
    is that all the components are working together. I repeat: You
    can't change a single word. The best short stories are built on
    this premise.

While Dwight Macdonald gave us no great body of books, he did
spend his talents in writing some of the better political and literary criticism of our time. More important than his oeuvre, how-

ever, was his influence. He was one of the best teachers of writing in the world. He gave no classes, but if one had learned a little about writing already, there were so many avenues to follow in the felicities of his style. Dwight had something fabulous to offer. It was to search for the *feel* of the intellectual phenomenon. Describe what you see as it impinges on the sum of your passions and your intellectual attainments. Bring to the act of writing all of your craft, care, devotion, lack of humbug, and honesty of sentiment. And then write without looking over your shoulder for the literary police. Write as if your life depended on saying what you felt as clearly as you could, while never losing sight of the phenomenon to be described. If something feels bad to you, it is bad. Others received the same message from Hemingway, but it took Dwight Macdonald to give the hint to many a young intellectual that the clue to new discovery rests not so much on the idea with which you begin a sentence as in the closeness of your attack on the continuation, and your readiness to depart from preconceived intentions by the insight provided in an unexpected and happy turn of phrase.

As a corollary to the above: To know what you want to say is not the best condition for writing a novel. Novels go happiest when you discover something you did not know you knew: an insight into one of your more opaque characters, a metaphor that startles you even as you are setting it down, a truth—it certainly feels like a truth—that used to elude you.

Reading the work of good writers is, of course, an indispensable nutrient for developing your style when you are young. After you have arrived, however, there comes a point where perversely, or from necessity, you don't want to read too much. It becomes impossible to look at each good novel as it comes out. If you're trying to do your own writing, it's distracting. Generally, you stay away from the work of contemporaries for a year or two at a time: It saves a good deal of reading. It is amazing how many much-touted novels disappear in eighteen months. The underlying force in book reviewing is journalism. The editor of a book review has a section which he hopes to make interesting. If, for two or three days, a newspaper is filled with news about a murder, one can be certain it is treated implicitly as the most exciting murder in the last twenty years. So it is with war novels, first novels, novels about homosexuality or politics, novels by authors of the Establishment, and historical novels. If I had a chapter of a novel for each review I've read of a new war novel which was said to be as good as *The Naked and the Dead* or *From Here to Eternity,* I would have fifty chapters. One never knows, of course. Maybe a few of these books are as good as they're said to be, and even if they've since disappeared, they will emerge again in ten or twenty years or in a century, but it is sensible to ignore what is said about a book when it first appears. There is too much direct and personal interest in the initial opinions, and much too much log-rolling. The editor of a large book review is of course not owned by the Book-of-the-Month Club or the Literary Guild, but on the other hand, the editor would just as soon not give more than two or three bad reviews in a year to book-club choices. Nor is his attitude dissimilar when it comes to choosing a reviewer for the novel that a big publishing house has chosen for its big book of the season. Considering how bad these books can be, it's impressive what attention they get. The slack (since a book review, depending on local tradition, can have just a certain proportion of good reviews or it will be seen as no more than a puff sheet) is taken up by misassigning small, determined literary types onto most of the medium good novels, which then receive snide treatment and/or dismissal.

The point is that any serious novelist knows enough to stay out of the flurry which hits a new book. Every year, whether the books deserve it or not, four or five first novelists will be provided a brilliant debut and four or five respectable young novelists will receive the kind of review that "enhances their reputation as one of the most serious and dedicated voices in the vineyard of literature."

So you stay away. If your friends and young writers and girls at cocktail parties keep talking about certain books, if the talk is intriguing because you begin to have less and less of a clear impression of the books as the months go by, then they come to install themselves on your reading list. And every year, or two years, or three, you go off on a binge for a month and gorge on the novels of your contemporaries and see how they made out on their night with the Bitch.   ,

Nor is it always natural for magazine writers to be at home in the novel. Even in the upper reaches of feature work, you still move on quickly to a new subject, another set of people. So you do not form those novelistic habits that are learned best when you are young, exactly the need never to be satisfied with any of your characters just because they have come alive for you. Indeed, the intoxication of creating a person on a page can prove blinding to an untried novelist's vision of what the character is going to need in his or her development through the narrative. What the young novelist learns, and it can take half a life, is that it is much easier to create a character than to develop him, or, even harder, *her*. So an inner caution develops. Unless your literary figures keep growing through the events of the book, your novel can go nowhere that will surprise you. Because if the character comes alive on one particular note and stays alive on that note, then there is nowhere to proceed but into the plot.

Part of the problem for feature writers is that they have to bring to life the figures they write about, and must not only do it in a few days or a few weeks but be sharp in every sentence and entertaining (if possible), and then on the next assignment they move on to another person in another occupation. Tom Wolfe became the best of them when it came to capturing the off-edge of each person's dialogue and all the details of their shoes, asses, hairdos, and stomach rumblings. He saw a room in the way a shark sees prey. Details were ectoplasm to him, and luminescence.

He worked for years doing bigger and better articles, then books, high-octane books, but he had formed bad habits. The basic pattern was to go right into new material, bring it off, and move on to the next job. Your characters had to come alive, but since you didn't stay with them, you hardly needed a second note. You could always hold the reader for the length of a magazine piece.

Of course, a great many of Dickens's characters were also Johnny One-Note. Yet, what notes! Besides, one did not read at that time to explore into character in the way we feel is necessary today. The stakes are higher now. Given the Twentieth Century, so full of vast achievements and horrors, it is viscerally important that our understanding of men and women keep pace with the mechanisms of society. If Wolfe is as good as or better than any other American writer in his power to capture the surface of wholly diverse elements in America, he comes in last of all major American writers when it's a matter of comprehending a little more about men and women. Indeed, this may be the most important purpose of the novelist today. Surely we are not going to leave it to the jargon-ridden expertise of the oral guns-for-hire in the TV human relations media business, or the fundamentalists' search for the all-purpose power-grip over other humans. We need only contemplate one more time how we are steeped in a nausea-broth of TV pundit-heads, coming to an intellectual climax every night.

FIRST PERSON VERSUS
THIRD PERSON

Third person and first person are at least as different as major and minor keys in music.

In the first person, you gain immediacy but lose insight, because you can hardly move into other people's heads without using a few devices, usually dubious.

The Deer Park underlined the difficulty. At one point, the young man who was telling the story stated that he was shifting from first person to third. He was now old enough, went his claim, to understand people he had not understood before. Because he now had more of an idea of how they think, he would write about them in third person. I believe it worked, but I would not swear to it.

In first person, the style has to be altogether tuned to the man who's telling the story. (Only once did I have a woman as the narrator. And that was Marilyn Monroe in *Of Women and Their Elegance.*)

When your prime character is a man, the key choice is not how bright he is, because however smart, he can't be more intelligent than you are. That's easy. You dumb him down to taste or bring him up to your level. The real question is, How tough is he? Do you have the inner sanction to create a man who's braver and tougher than yourself? The answer is yes. Contra Heming-way—yes! You can do that by exercising your *critical* imagination. It must not be wish fulfillment! You are entitled to guess how you might act if you were that much more of a hero.

I don't know how to pose the question for an author who's female. Can she, for example, write about a woman who is more sensitive than herself? Probably not. She could write about a woman who uses her sensitivity and sensibility more than herself, because she can then key on all the frustrated times in her existence when the sensitivity and sensibility she possessed were not appropriate to a harsh occasion. Following question: Can a woman write about another woman more passionate than herself? Probably. Or a woman who's colder than herself? Without doubt.

In the third person, there's a different set of difficulties.

With a full use of the third person, you are God—well, of course, not quite, but, one way or another, you are ready to see into everyone's mind. That is never routine. There is, of course, an easier approach—point-of-view third person, where you remain in one character's mind but are still viewing your protagonist from outside, and usually from above. In the classic vein of third person, however, where you enter each and every one's consciousness, it is not routine to get over the embarrassment that you are able to accommodate certain characters' minds with considerably more skill than you can with others'. This Olympian third person, this Tolstoyan presence, needs experience, confidence, irony, insight, and lordly detachment. When it can be done, hurrah. Most of the great nineteenth-century novels achieve just that tone. Today, it's usually up to the novelists who write best-sellers. In their case, God is always ready to offer an adjective adequate to their means. Teeming excitement, unendurable suspense, delightful joy, grim misery, dogged courage. But let me not froth at the mouth. There was a time when I used to do that myself.

First person point of view, however, remains a fine tool. You can get to places you don't arrive at any other way. Of course, you can also injure your writing hand. As an instrument, it's double-edged. Hemingway had a marvelous sense of its limitations and used it to create his style. He dramatized its first edict: Do not talk about things that could prove embarrassing. They don't feel right in the telling, not when the "I" stands at the head of the sentence. So there's a tendency, most marked in Hemingway, to keep most of his revelations at arm's length. As, for example, the famous last sentences of *A Farewell to Arms*.

We live in a time that is astonishingly more open, but the edict, adjusted, still remains. First person cannot be as free as the separation between author and protagonist offered by the third person.

It was not until I struggled with *Advertisements for Myself* that I began to recognize how curious it was to be working in the first person. Now, many writers good and bad have been employing that mode for centuries, but I had to come to this remarkable conclusion on my own. The first person was not all that available a way to write. It proved to be a very interesting and exciting mode of literary presence, with large limitations, and you really do have to understand it as such—especially if you're dealing with your own presence. Nothing is more difficult than to become comfortable writing about yourself in the first person. It's highly unnatural, because "I" makes up only about a third of the consciousness of any human being. "I" may be the prow of the ego, but you do get into all sorts of other places where you want "one" to talk about different aspects of yourself. And then there is even second person, *you*, employed as if it is first person: "You get up, you brush your teeth, you feel lousy this morning." (In the first period of awakening, you can indeed feel like a vague entity slightly outside yourself.) And there is also the third person when used as a substitute for "I"—for one, the character named Norman Mailer in *The Armies of the Night*. Using the third person in this manner may be a special condition of first person, but it is legitimate. There is a part of the ego that is superior to ourselves—that person who observes us carefully even as we're doing bizarre things, that special persona, possessed of immaculate detachment, who is always saying, "Oh, are we really doing well right now?" A wonderful voice. Because it enables you to treat yourself as one more character in a field of characters.

Nonetheless, I have considerable regard for the first person. Once I even dared to cross the line with it. That began on a given night, in a small Paris hotel room, when I couldn't sleep.

The room was tiny, the double bed took up almost all the floor, and you could break your toe trying to walk around. I didn't want to go rummaging in my suitcase for a book, so I picked up a Gideon Bible (in English!) on my bedside table and started reading. I hadn't looked at the New Testament for thirty or forty years, but I recalled that a man named Fulton Oursler once sold over a million copies of a book called *The Greatest Story Ever Told*. Now, with the bona fide Gospels in my hand, I thought, Well, this may be the greatest story, but it is certainly being told abominably. Sayings popped out of the New Testament that were worthy of Shakespeare, but much in the double columns was poorly described. An ungainly prose pronged with golden nuggets. I thought, There have got to be a hundred novelists in the world who can do a better job. I'm one of them.

The notion was intriguing. When I thought of all the hypocrites and corruptibles and power seekers who had been living with the Gospel for centuries, standing foursquare on any gnomic chunk of text they could use to abet their aims, I decided, Why not just tell the *story*? It is, in fact, a fascinating one. The narrative keel is mind-boggling. We are dealing with a man who is obliged to recognize through the evidence itself that he is the Son of God. The difficulty of such a book would be to write about a man considerably nicer than myself. That is never easy. To fashion a character who is meaner than yourself—a piece of cake. But to do someone who is better? Jean Malaquais once remarked that you can write about any character but one. "Who is that?" "A novelist more talented than yourself."

I thought, This is analogous. A finer sense of morality is also a higher talent. Yes, the problems were interesting.

I decided my character had to be more of a man than a god, an existential man, dominated by the huge cloud that he is the Son of God. Jesus, as the protagonist, doesn't feel worthy, but he is ready nonetheless to do his best every step of the way. Not in command of every situation, but will do his best. And he does have his startling successes.

Moreover, I had to decide whether to travel in first person or third. First person would have everyone saying: "That egomaniac. Does Mailer now think he's Jesus Christ? What an overinflamed vanity!" That's the bad side, I thought, but at least I can avoid the larger mistake of doing it in the third person. Because that would soon get mixed up with the actual text of the

Gospels, and the reader would wonder, Is this sentence from the New Testament or was it added? That can only make for a squirrelly experience as one reads. All right, then. First person. Damn the torpedoes, first person. Play the Ace.

It became interesting. If it was too biblical in the beginning, I did have an editor who is totally irreligious, Jason Epstein. He was appalled that I was writing this book. We're friends, but he's one tough editor. And he's most often all too right or altogether wrong. So, you have to make a quick decision. Yes, the style was too biblical.

After which, it was relatively easy. The book was short enough for me to work up seven variations on the style. I had to find the balance between a biblical rhythm and a contemporary one—something that would not inflict a biblical grip on one's mind yet would keep the echo. Before I was done, it all took a year from that night in that much-too-small hotel room on the Ile St.-Louis.

REAL LIFE VERSUS
PLOT LIFE

———

The CIA, in its actual workings, is the antithesis of the average spy novel, which, best-seller-oriented, tends to present a perfect clock that ticks to its conclusion. In *Harlot's Ghost,* one of my characters remarks that she came into the CIA because she loved spy novels. Now, her complaint was that she could never—precisely because she was inside—experience the full run of a scenario. On occasion, her work put her into the equivalent of a spy novel, but only, let us say, for Chapters Five and Six. She hadn't been there at the beginning, and was soon shifted to another assignment. Often, one did not learn how it all turned out. That struck me as being about what life is like: The gun over the mantelpiece does not often get fired. We live in and out of ongoing plots every day of our lives, but they are discontinuous. Nothing can be more difficult to encounter than a life story that accompanies us through a beginning, middle, and end. There is only our own that is not missing most of the pages, yet how discontinuous it seems all the same! One could make the case that our love of plot—until it gets very cheap indeed—comes out of our need to find the chain of cause and effect that so often is missing in our own existence.

—

The decisions you make while writing fiction can leave you uneasy. If your characters come alive, that's fine; they will carry you a part of the way. But finally, your people have to make what might be termed career decisions. Does your protagonist want to go abroad in the foreign service, or does he decide to stay in New York with the amazing young model he has just met? Needless to say, such choices are non-operative for writers who have the story complete in their mind before they begin. So I repeat: I look to find my book as I go along. Plot comes last. I want a conception of my characters that's deep enough so that they will get me to places where I, as the author, have to live by my wits. That means my characters must keep developing. So long as they stay alive, the plot will take care of itself. Working on a book where the plot is already fully developed is like spending the rest of your life filling holes in rotten teeth when you have no skill as a dentist.

Working on *The Executioner's Song,* I came to the realization that God is a better novelist than the novelists. The story was not only incredible, but it most certainly had happened. If I had conceived it, the work would have been more dramatic but less true. I learned all over again that the way things come about in life is not the way they work in novels. (Unless you are Theodore Dreiser!) It would have seemed wasteful to me to have a novel with two really fascinating characters who didn't get together for a scene. Whereas, what I discovered in *The Executioner's Song* was that the characters I was most interested in didn't always meet, and when they did, the results were often disappointing.

It took some time to learn that this did not necessarily diminish the drama. It could increase it. Most of our lives are spent getting ready for dramatic moments that don't take place. Or if they do, are less than we expected. About the time we say, "Well, nothing really big ever happens to me," you can get knocked down with something larger by far than you expected. All the frustrations of all the little narratives in your life that never had a real climax can be present in the rare denouement that life also offers once in a great while.

I no longer work up a master plan before I begin a novel. When I was younger I used to sit down and write out such plans, but I never finished such projects. Even with *The Executioner's Song,* where, after all, I knew the end of the story, I was careful not to be too versed in too many details ahead. I preferred to do my research up to no more than a hundred pages ahead of where I was. I wanted to keep the feeling that I didn't know how it was all going to turn out. I needed something like the illusion that I was inventing each detail. Obviously, I prefer doing a book that is not too carefully prepared. Some of my best ideas come because I haven't fixed my novel's future in concrete. Once you know your end, it's disastrous to get a new idea. That can only take you away from your prearranged conclusion. Yet the new idea that you didn't follow may be worth more than the denouement you planned in advance.

For that matter, the moment I think of a good plot, I find that the book becomes almost impossible to write, because I know I won't believe it. Life may consist of people plotting all the time, but the plots rarely develop. We decide: I'll make this move in my life, and that should result in the following—then life confounds us. So I prefer a story that develops out of the writing. I don't like one that moves ahead of my characters, because then my people won't live. Tie your characters to a prearranged plot, and you are doing to them what we would do to our children if we carefully selected their colleges, their spouses, and their jobs without ever consulting them. The same unspoken despondency weighs on characters who are treated that way in a novel: They never get to fulfill their own perverse (that is, surprising to the novelist) capabilities; they never come alive. Bill Buckley is wonderful at plots—his mind may work that way—but nobody lives and breathes in his novels with any more three dimensionality than some passing movie star who can't act.

Many young novelists tend to draw for their material on family or the near world of friends. How, goes the question, do you manage that without making these near and dear people too recognizable? Can you treat the familiar in such a way as not to incur the rage and tears of those who are close to you?

It is next to impossible. You cannot write about people you care about and not hurt them or, to the contrary, even worse, allow too little to be wrong with them. They then come through as boring. That is the first mark of bottom-level amateur writing.

I've always stayed away from such close material, have never written directly about my parents or my sister. Those experiences are so basic that I encircle them with a favorite word: I characterize these fundamental and primary experiences as *crystals*. The crystals can be simple or extraordinarily developed. But provided you don't use them directly, you can sometimes send a ray of your imagination through the latticework in one direction or another and find altogether different scenarios. If you've got a relative in mind who's, let's say, a pretty tough kid, you can, if you don't write about him head-on, make the boy a bullfighter or put him in Special Forces, even turn him into a bank robber or an honest cop. So long as you don't use the core of your experience, you will be in command of many possibilities. But if you are determined to get it all accurately on paper, then at a given moment you will have to face the fact that you are going to hurt people who are close to you.

When a surgeon operates on a young girl, he isn't saying, "I'm going to make an incision on this young lady's stomach that is not only going to scar her but will affect her future sex life to some degree for the next thirty years." He just says, "Scalpel, nurse," and does it. The surgeon is focused on the act, not its reverberations.

Novelists are engaged in something analogous. If they start thinking of all the damage they are going to do, they can't write the book—not if they're reasonably decent.

The point is that one is facing a true problem. Either you produce a work that doesn't approach what really interests you or, if you go to the root with all you've got, there is no way you won't injure your family, friends, and innocent bystanders.

Some of my characters do come from real people. One might emerge out of five individuals, another from one person, greatly altered. Still another is imagined. No matter by which route, there's pleasure when a character becomes, in a sense, independent of yourself.

Graham Greene once said that there were certain characters who took care of themselves. He never had to bother about them in the writing. Others, he had to go to great pains with. He would work very hard on them. Later, when he'd read a review and it would mention one of his resistant characters as "well drawn," he used to think, Well dragged.

—

Up to now, I've not liked writing about people who are close to me, because their actual presence interferes with the reality one is trying to create. They become alive not as creatures in your imagination but as actors in your life. And so they seem real while you write, but you're not developing their novelistic reality into more and more. For example, it's not a good idea to try to put your wife into your novel. Not your latest wife, anyway. In practice, I prefer to draw a character from someone I hardly know, who excites my novelist's instinct. I sense that I will be able to add a great deal to the portrait by what I've learned from other people.

The question remains: How do you turn a real person into a fictional one? If I have an answer, it is that I try to put the model in situations which have very little to do with his or her real situations in life. Very quickly, the original disappears. The private reality can't hold up. For instance, I might take somebody who is a professional football player, a man whom I know slightly, let's say, and turn him into a movie star. In a transposition of this sort, everything that relates particularly to the professional football player quickly disappears, and what is left, curiously, is what is *exportable* in his character. But this process, while interesting in the early stages, is not as exciting as the more creative act of allowing your characters to grow once you've separated them from the model. It's when they become as complex as real people that the fine excitement begins. Because now they're not really characters any longer—they're *beings,* which is a distinction I like to make. A character is someone you can grasp as a whole—you can have a clear idea of him—but a being is someone whose nature keeps shifting. In *The Deer Park,* Lulu Meyers is a being rather than a character. If you study her closely, you will see that she is a different person in every scene. Just a little different. I don't know whether initially I did this by accident or purposefully, but at a certain point I made the conscious decision not to try to straighten her out; she seemed right in her changeableness.

I've spoken of characters *emerging.* Quite often they don't emerge; they fail to. And one is left with the dull compromise that derives from two kinds of experience warring with each other within oneself. A character who should have been brilliant is dull. Or even if a character does prove to be first-rate, it's possible you could have done twice as much. A novel has its own laws. After a while, it becomes a creature. One can feel a bit like a rider who's got a fine horse. Very often, I'll suffer shame for what I've done with a novel. I won't say it's the novel that's bad; I'll say it's I who was bad, as if the novel were a child raised by me, but improperly. I know what's potentially beautiful in my novel, you see. Very often after I'm done, I realize that the beauty I recognize in it is not going to be perceived by the reader. I didn't succeed in bringing it out. It's very odd—it's as though I had let the novel down, owed it a duty which I didn't fulfill.

Hearn's death in *The Naked and the Dead* was supposed to be shocking. I haven't thought of Hearn's death in years. I stole the way of doing it directly from E. M. Forster. In *The Longest Journey,* he created a character who was most alive for the reader, then destroyed him on the next page. As I recall the line, it went: "Gerald died next day. He was kicked to death in a football game." You get an idea what a rifle shot is like at that point. In my book, it may have been too big a price to pay, because the denouement of the novel was sacrificed. I don't think I was aware of the size of the problem. Today I'd be much more alert to that. If I were to do the book now, I might keep Hearn alive until the very end, and it would probably be a phonier book as a result. One of the things you always have trouble with when you talk about "true" or "not true" is, of course, the relative truth of the novel. In a way, if you get a fairly good novel going, then you have a small universe functioning, and this universe lives or does not live in relation to its own scheme of cause and effect.

Looking back on it, I can give you a good and bad motive that I had for killing Hearn where I did. The good motive is that it was a powerful way to show what death is like in war. The shoddy motive was that I wasn't altogether sure in my heart that I knew what to do with him or how to bring him off.

I think that I truly work on impulse in all of my writing. That's why I don't like to plan too far ahead. I've gotten into this before, but it's worth repeating. Planning too carefully makes it almost impossible for one of your characters to go through a dramatic shift of heart, because it's going to violate your larger scheme. It's better if this larger scheme unfolds at a rate that is compatible with your characters.

When it comes to entering a man or woman's mind, a writer has to be good, even brilliant. So long as you stay outside that head, your character can retain a certain mystery. We walk around such figures with the same respect we offer strangers who come into a room with force. Part of the meaning of charisma is that we don't know the intimate nature of the human presence we're facing. Characters in novels sometimes radiate more energy, therefore, when we don't enter their mind. It is one of the techniques a novelist acquires instinctively—don't go into your protagonist's thoughts until you have something to say about his or her inner life that is more interesting than the reader's suppositions. To jump in only to offer banal material is a fatal error. It is the worst of best-sellerdom. Second-rate readers enjoying the insights of second-rate writers.

I'd say try not to think of your characters as victims. That sort of classification narrows them. In reality, very few victims ever see themselves exclusively as victims, and when they do, their spirit turns stale. There is a certain sort of self-pitying victim one wishes to walk away from, and they can be even worse in a book. Unless one is Dickens. (Scrooge, Scrooge, Scrooge.)

Hemingway suffered from the honorable need to be the equal of his male characters, particularly since he used the first person so much. It is not easy to write in the first person about a man who's stronger or braver than yourself. It's too close to self-serving. All the same, you have to be able to do it. Because if every one of your characters is kept down to your own level, you do not take on large subjects. You need people more heroic than yourself, more enterprising, less timid, sexier, more romantic, more tragic. You've got to be able to create people greater than yourself and not be ashamed of the damnable fact that the "I" who is being promoted is offering a false picture of himself to all those readers, who will predictably assume that the author is the man they are now encountering in the first person.

I've been asked when the idea of using a hornet's nest to thwart the climbers in *The Naked and the Dead* came to me. In truth, the idea was there before I wrote the first sentence of the book. The incident happened to my reconnaissance platoon on the most ambitious patrol we ever took. They sent out thirty of us to locate and destroy one hundred Japanese marines, but we did get stuck climbing one hell of an enormous hill with a mean, slimy trail, and when we were almost up to the ridge, somebody kicked over a hornet's nest. Half of us went tearing up the hill, but the machine-gun squad was behind us and went flying down to the valley. We never did find each other again that day. We just slunk back to our bivouac.

There are some who feel it was not a satisfactory device, but I think I'd do it the same way again. War is disproportions, and the hornet's nest seemed a perfect one to me. We were ready to lose our lives that day, but we weren't up to getting stung by a hornet.

If a novelist can take people who are legendary figures and invent episodes for them that seem believable, then he has done something fine. There's that meeting between J. P. Morgan and Henry Ford in E. L. Doctorow's *Ragtime*—I think it's one of the best short chapters in American literature. It told me an awful lot about Morgan and an awful lot about Henry Ford, and the fact that it obviously never took place made it more delicious.

The characters you create in a novel become as real in your mind as movie stars. That is no small equation. To a lot of people, Humphrey Bogart might, for example, be the psychic equivalent of an influential uncle, given the presence he exerts on those who love his work.

INSTINCT AND
INFLUENCE

———

I am not sure it is possible to describe how it feels to write a
novel. It may be that it is not an experience. It may be more
like a continuing relation between a man and his wife. You can't
necessarily speak of that as an experience, since it may consist of
several experiences braided together; or of many experiences
all more or less similar; or indeed it may consist of two kinds of
experiences that are antagonistic to one another.

In large part, writing may be an instinctive process, but it's not
always clear what the instinct is saying. Sometimes you feel no
more than a dull pressure to go in a certain direction for the oncoming chapter. You have to be able to hear the faint voice which
prods you toward an honest continuation of the work. That can
be hard to hear. A writer is also open to the temptation to take
the immediate advantage, even if it doesn't feel quite right. And
we all do that in various ways. And pay for it with falsities that
burrow directly into our intent.

One example I always give to a writing class: A very young
writer sits on a park bench with his girl. He kisses her. He's seventeen. He's never had such a kiss before. Later that night, he
tries to capture the event. He writes:

I love you, he said.
I love you, she said.
He stops, throws down his pen, and says, "I'm a great writer!"
Sometimes you have to wait.

I think Capote's book and mine are formally similar, but vastly different. Obviously, I'll be the first to state that if he hadn't done *In Cold Blood,* it's conceivable that I wouldn't have thought of taking on *The Executioner's Song.* Nonetheless, it's also possible that something about *The Executioner's Song* called for doing it in the way I chose. In any event, its flavor is different from *In Cold Blood.* Truman retained his style. Not the pure style—he simplified it—but it was still very much a book written by Truman Capote. You felt it every step of the way. The difference is that he tweaked it more, where I was determined to keep the factual narrative. I wanted my book to read like a novel, and it does, but I didn't want to sacrifice what literally happened in a scene for what I would like to see happen. Of course, I could afford to feel that way. I had advantages Truman didn't. His killers were not the most interesting guys in the world, so it took Truman's exquisite skills to make his work a classic. I was in the more promising position of dealing with a man who was quintessentially American yet worthy of Dostoyevsky. If this were not enough, he was also in love with a girl who—I'll go so far as to say—is a bona fide American heroine. I didn't want, therefore, to improve anything. Dedicated accuracy is not usually the first claim a novelist wishes to make, but here it became a matter of literary value. What I had was gold, if I had enough sense not to gild it.

If you find some theme that keeps you working, don't question it. Let that theme be sufficient to fuel your work. If you start using the value judgments of others, you're never going to get much done. If I find something is stimulating to me and arousing my energy, that's fine; I'll trust it. If you're a serious young writer and find that you're writing a lot, then don't listen to what anyone else says—do your book. There is probably a deeper truth than you'll ever know in the fact that you're able to work so well. Of course, you could be writing in absolutely the wrong direction. You could be doing a dreadful book.

No matter what you find yourself writing about, if it's giving you enough energy to continue, then the work bears a profound relationship to you at that point and you don't question it.

—

Let me take this further. You can write a book with a powerful sense of inner conviction and a year or two later say, "How could I have so deluded myself? This is awful." Your instinct can betray you, but you still have to go with it. Very often the instinct sees some light at the end of the tunnel, but that's because you've been trapped in a situation where your creative energies can't get together. Now, at last, you've found a way to work. You may be writing out some very bad tendencies in yourself, but this can be good, too. You might be feeling happy because soon you're going to be done with that malfunctioning side of yourself. That's what your enthusiasm can be about.

Only rarely is one's instinct analogous to a fast highway, but that's exactly when things get hairy. The slow twists and turns of one's creative impulse can be a form of protecting oneself from the driving force, which sometimes is manic.

The influence of Henry Adams on *The Armies of the Night* is peculiar. I had never read much Adams. In my Freshman year at Harvard, we were assigned one long chapter of *The Education of Henry Adams,* and I remember thinking at the time what an odd thing to write about yourself in the third person. Who is this fellow, Henry Adams, talking about himself as Henry Adams? I remember being annoyed in that mildly irritable way Freshmen have of passing over extraordinary works of literature. To my conscious recollection, I hardly ever thought about him again. Yet, start reading *The Armies of the Night,* and immediately you say—even I said—"My God, this is pure Henry Adams." It's as if I were the great-grandson. Contemplate, therefore, how peculiar is influence: Adams must have remained in my mind as a possibility, the way a painter might look at a particular Picasso or Cézanne and say to himself, "That's the way to do it." Yet the influence might not pop forth for twenty or thirty years. When it does, the painter could say, "Oh yes, that was a Picasso I saw at MoMA twenty-five years ago, and I've always wanted to try such a palette, and now I have." In effect, that's what happened with Henry Adams.

Literary influence remains endlessly curious. I happened to pick up *Moby-Dick.* I hadn't thought about Melville ten times in the last thirty years, but as soon as I read the first page, I realized my later style was formed by Melville, shaped by his love of

long, rolling sentences full of inversions and reverses and paradoxes and ironies and exclamation points and dashes. Of
course, to be as good as Melville—that's another matter.

It's disturbing to read a novelist with a good style when you're in
the middle of putting your work together. It's much like taking
your car apart and having all the pieces on the floor just as
somebody rides by in a Ferrari. Now, you may hear a note in the
Ferrari that isn't good and say, "His motor needs a little tuning."
But nonetheless the car and its roar are still there in your ear
while your parts remain on the floor. So while I'm working on a
book I rarely read more than *The New York Times*—which could
have the long-term effect of flattening my style. I'd rather blame
the *Times* than old age.

STAMINA

I'm now eighty, but some people still regard me as a wild man. Even at my peak, that was only five to ten percent of my nature. The rest was work. I like work. I remember Elia Kazan saying one day at Actors Studio, "Here, we're always talking about the work. We talk about it piously. We say *the work. The work.* Well, we do work here, and get it straight: Work is a *blessing.*" He said this, glaring at every one of us. And I thought, He's right. That's what it is. A blessing.

Of course, if you ask what work is dependent upon, the key word, an unhappy one, is *stamina.* It's as difficult to become a professional writer as a professional athlete. It often depends on the ability to keep faith in yourself. One must be willing to take risks and try again. And it does need an enormous amount of ongoing working practice to be good at it. Since you are affected by what you read as a child and adolescent, it also takes a while to unlearn all sorts of reading reflexes that have led you into bad prose.

I remember in the summer before my Junior year, working on my very first novel, *No Percentage* (which will remain forever unpublished), I ran into a phrase by Henry James. He spoke of "the keeping up." That can be the first horror to face when you're young. Your novel tends to change all too quickly. It may even be the cardinal reason why people in college tend to stay away from longer fiction. Young short-story writers, no matter how good, often blow up when they attempt a longer work. They'll have a good beginning, but the second chapter goes off and they never get it back. The sad truth is that a would-be novelist possibly has to start a few books that do give out, or even crash, before a sense of the difficulties is acquired. If the same likelihood of early failure applied to young race-car drivers, there would not be speedways.

A large part of writing a novel is to keep your tone. I love starting a book; I usually like finishing one. It's the long middle stretches that call on your character—all that in-between!—those months or years when you have to report to work almost every day. You don't write novels by putting in two brilliant hours a week. You don't write novels if you lose too many mornings and afternoons to a hangover.

Sometimes, when you're in a bad period, you must in effect contract yourself for weeks running. "I'm going in to write tomorrow," you have to declare, and, indeed, show up at your desk, even though there's nothing in you, and sit there for hours, whatever number of hours you told yourself you were going to put in. Then, if nothing happens, you still show up the next day and the next and the next, until that recalcitrant presence, the unconscious, comes to decide you can finally be trusted. Such acceptance is crucial. The unconscious expects that what it has prepared for you in your sleep should be expressed, ideally, the next day. We live, you see, in an arm's-length relationship to our unconscious. It has to be convinced over and over again to believe in you. Sometimes when you're writing a novel, you have to live as responsibly as a good monk. That does get easier as you grow older.

Writing is wonderful when you talk about it. It's fun to contemplate. But writing as a daily physical activity is not agreeable. You put on weight, you strain your gut, you get gout and chilblains. You're alone, and every day you have to face a blank piece of paper.

There's nothing glorious about being a professional. You become more dogged. You probably relinquish the upper reaches of the mind in order to be able to do your stint of work each day: That means you are ready to endure a certain amount of drudgery. But your mind is, obviously, not enthralled by such dull conditions. Professionalism probably comes down to being able to work on a bad day.

I used to have a little studio in Brooklyn, a couple of blocks from my house—no telephone, not much else. The only thing I ever did there was work. It was perfect. I was like a draft horse with a conditioned reflex. I came in ready to sit at my desk. No television, no way to call out. Didn't want to be tempted. There's an old Talmudic belief that you build a fence around an impulse. If that's not good enough, you build a fence around the fence. So, no amenities. (But for a refrigerator!) I wrote longhand with a pencil and I gave it to my assistant, Judith McNally. She would type it for me and next day I would go over it. Since at my age you begin to forget all too much, I would hardly remember what I had written the day before. It read, therefore, as if someone else had done it. The critic in me was delighted. I could now proceed to fix the prose. The sole virtue of losing your short-term memory is that it does free you to be your own editor.

When I read something good, I want to do a critical piece. I want to expand on where I think the author is terrific and where he or she is lacking—especially if reviewers are blowing it up too high. I may feel, It's good but not that good—let's get into it. So it can be immensely distracting. Your mind settles on the work you are reading rather than the one you're supposed to be laboring on. A tendency grows to protect yourself by not reading anything that's too good. Stendhal, for instance, used to peruse the Code Napoléon every day in the loo before he'd start to write.

Now, I didn't always follow that rule. When I was doing *The Naked and the Dead,* I used to pick up Thomas Wolfe and Tolstoy. I didn't read them every day, but they were on my writing desk and they were perfect for what I needed, Tolstoy particularly. The tone of *Anna Karenina* was wonderful for *The Naked and the Dead*. And then there was Thomas Wolfe to steam up the descriptions. If I needed a tropical sunset or the smell of the jungle, I had Wolfe. For the characters, Tolstoy.

I never know what the style of a book will be until I get into it. Sometimes you aim high and don't get it—you have to settle for a more functional tone. After all, style is very much like the pace a serious jogger sets for himself. You have to be able to maintain it. In that sense, style is an offshoot of character. With all else, character is the wise or foolish estimate of your resources.

I think it's important for a writer to keep in shape. But it's hard to talk about. Harry Greb, for example, was a fighter who used to keep in shape. He was completely a fighter, the way one might wish to be completely a writer. He always did the things that were necessary to him as a fighter. Now, some of these things were extremely irrational from a prize-fight manager's point of view. That is, before he had a fight he would go to a brothel and he would have two prostitutes, not one, taking the two of them into the same bed. And this apparently left him feeling like a wild animal. Don't ask me why. Perhaps he picked the two meanest whores in the joint and so absorbed into his system all the small, nasty, concentrated evils that had accumulated from carloads of men. Greb was known as the dirtiest fighter of his time. He didn't have much of a punch, but he could spoil other fighters and punish them; he knew more dirty tricks than anyone around, and the two whores were an essential part of his training methods. He did it over and over again until he died at a relatively early age of a heart attack on an operating table. I think he died before he was thirty-eight. They operated on him, and bang, he went.

The point I want to make is that he stayed in training by the way he lived his life. The paramount element was to keep in shape. If he was drinking, you see, the point was to keep in shape *while* drinking. I'm being a touch imprecise. . . . Put it this way: He would not drink just to release his tension. Rather, what went on was that there was tension in him which was insupportable, so he had to booze. But reasoning as a professional, he felt that if he was going to drink, he might as well use that too. In the sense that the actor uses everything which happens to him, so Greb as a fighter used everything. As he drank, he would notice the way his body moved. One of the best reasons one drinks is to become aware of the way your mind and body move. Now, let me try to apply this.

Craft is a grab bag of procedures, tricks, lore, formal gymnastics, symbolic superstructures—methodology, in short. It's the compendium of what you've acquired from others. And since great writers communicate a vision of experience, one can't usually borrow their methods. Their method is married to the vision. Therefore, one acquires craft more from good writers and mediocre writers with a flair. Craft, after all, is what you can take out whole from their work. But keeping in shape is something else. For example, you can do journalism and it can be terrible for your style. Or it can temper your style. In other words, you can become a better writer by doing a lot of different kinds of writing. Or you can deteriorate. There's a book that came out a few years ago which was a sociological study of some Princeton men—I forget the name of it. One of them said something which I thought was extraordinary. He wanted to perform the sexual act under every variety of condition, emotion, and mood available to him. I was struck with this not because I ever wanted necessarily to have that kind of sexual life but because it seemed to me that was what I was trying to do with my writing. I edit on a spectrum which runs from the high, clear manic impressions of a drunk that has made one electrically alert all the way down to the soberest reaches of a low mood where I can hardly bear my words. By the time I'm done with writing I care about, I usually have worked on it through the full spectrum of my consciousness. If you keep yourself in this peculiar kind of shape, the craft will take care of itself. Craft is very little, finally. But if you're continually worrying about whether you're growing or deteriorating as a man, whether your integrity is turning soft or firming itself, why, then, it is in that slow war, that slow rearguard battle you fight against diminishing talent, that you stay in shape as a writer and have a consciousness. You develop a consciousness as you grow older which enables you to write about anything, in effect, and write about it well. That is, provided you keep your consciousness in shape and don't relax into flabby styles of thought. They, after all, surround one everywhere. The moment you borrow other writers' styles of thought, you need craft to shore up the walls. But if what you write is a reflection of your own consciousness, then even journalism can become interesting. One wouldn't want to spend one's life at it, and I wouldn't ever want to be caught justifying journalism as a major activity (it's obviously less interesting than to write a novel), but it's legitimate to see it as a venture of one's ability to keep in shape rather than as an essential betrayal of the chalice of your art.

Indeed, many good writers get smashed en route. In that

sense, they are like race-car drivers, and the punishment they take stops them eventually. They write less well, or they take a tremendously long time to write, or they lose the desire to write.

Of course, it's virtually as if writers are there to be ruined. Look at the list: booze, pot, too much sex, too little, too much failure in one's private life, too much attrition, too much recognition, too little recognition, frustration. Nearly everything in the scheme of things works to dull a first-rate talent. But the worst probably is cowardice—as one gets older, one becomes aware of one's cowardice. The desire to be bold, which once was a joy, gets heavy with caution and duty. And finally there's apathy. About the time it doesn't seem too important anymore to be a major writer, you know you've slipped far enough to be doing your work on the comeback trail.

The hardest thing for an older writer to decide is whether he's burned-out or merely lying fallow. I was ready to think I was burned-out before I even started *The Naked and the Dead*. I had written a few good things in college and now had to wonder whether my time in the Army had blunted that talent. That is exactly how little sense a young writer can have of his or her own literary future.

If you can, I think it's a good idea to rotate your crops. Once you've written a novel that's factual and realistic and big, awfully close to what happened, then it's probably a good idea that your next novel be as fanciful as possible. Yes—if you can, rotate those crops.

Once you are committed to earning your living from your pen, you discover that you can push yourself. It's analogous to what athletes do when they take steroids to gain more strength. Ultimately damaging, but they set records. We do the same thing. You can force yourself to write much more than you want to. And the writing will not necessarily deteriorate. Not necessarily. But you can end up with a bad nervous system or a shortened life. Of course, one can always hope for transcendence. Sometimes working much harder than one wants to work can liberate energy. Sometimes.

I've often felt that those times when you can work or make love with great energy occur when your best and worst motives are working in cooperation for once.

The literary life is not all about envy. There is a corollary. Good writers are as competitive as good athletes. When I come across an interesting novel, I don't go at it as other people do. I read critically, the way one athlete will watch another's performance. Not watch it with venom—quite the contrary. You might say to yourself, "His spiral is tighter than mine and he's got five more yards on me at least, but I scramble better." The ideal is to give a good novel its credit and never overlook its power by deciding too quickly that the work is overrated, which is exactly the dreadful tendency underwritten by the envy chronic to the writer's occupation. Is this because we are obliged to work alone so much of the time?

A few words on rewriting and research.

Rewriting is where your working experience over the years has its day. There comes a time when you know how to get the maximum out of what you've done. The only way to accelerate this skill when you are young is to have the courage to look at it when you're about ready to destroy it. If something still comes through, then it may well have the merit to be worked upon further. It is also not bad to read things at the top of your feelings in order to get a sense of what the maximum might be. If nothing else, all this will give you a tolerance for the extraordinary range of reaction you can receive in the classroom. You realize that the people who don't like your work aren't necessarily evil and the people who love your stuff don't have to be altogether illustrious.

Research is another matter. The trick in doing a historical novel, for example, is to digest the research. You have to avoid that awful stance where you say, in effect, "Hello, I'm Saint-Simon and I'm at the court of Louis XIV. Madame de Maintenon is very angry this morning." Better to remind yourself that Madame de Maintenon does not necessarily feel that she is the Madame de Maintenon we know through Saint-Simon.

In addition, one must always be on guard against anachronisms. You learn how hard it is to separate what belongs only to your time from the era you are trying to re-create.

A CODA TO "CRAFT"

————

By now, I'm a bit cynical about craft. I think there's a natural mystique in the novel that is more important. One is trying, after all, to capture reality, and that is extraordinarily and exceptionally difficult. Craft is merely a series of way stations. I think of it as being like a Saint Bernard with that little bottle of brandy under his neck. Whenever you get into trouble, craft can keep you warm long enough to be rescued. Of course, this is exactly what keeps good novelists from becoming great novelists. Robert Penn Warren might have written a major novel if he hadn't had just that extra little bit of craft to get him out of all the trouble in *All the King's Men*. If Penn Warren hadn't known anything about Elizabethan literature, the would-be Elizabethan in him might have brought off a fantastic novel. As it was, he knew enough about craft to use it as an escape hatch. And his plot degenerated into a slam-bang of exits and entrances, confrontations, tragedies, quick wails, and woe. But he was really forcing an escape from his literary problem, which was the terror of confronting a political reality that might open into more and more anxiety. Craft protects one from facing endless expanding realities—the terror, let us say, of losing your novel in the depths of philosophical insights you are not ready to live with. I think this sort of terror so depresses us that we throw up evasions—such as craft. Indeed, I think this adoration of craft makes a church of literature for that vast number of writers who are somewhere on the bell-shaped curve between mediocrity and talent.

PSYCHOLOGY

LEGEND AND IDENTITY

If I place a large emphasis on the word, it is because our identity on a given day or year is the seat from which we speak to
the world. Any shifts of identity, any sense that the seat is not fast
on its foundations but is sliding away, will play hell with the
modicum of stability that one needs to write at a given moment.

So this discussion of psychology as it refers to writing can
begin with some thoughts about identity and its huge overgrown
sibling—legend.

Having, at the age of twenty-five, broken away from the pack,
I lived with a swollen sense of importance. At the same time, I
wasn't ready. Much too much well-founded modesty. One part
of you shoots up, another lags behind. It's like having a prima
donna of a hard-on. You just can't depend on it. The stamina
you look to develop comes later, as does your new identity.

Some artists have, however, a powerful, consistent sense of
themselves. I think the best American examples might be Henry
Miller, Hemingway, Faulkner, Thomas Wolfe, Henry James, Sinclair Lewis. In contrast, a writer like Steinbeck kept changing his
persona with every book he did. As other examples, one could
add Ed Doctorow or myself. Picasso, however, comes more to

mind than any of us. His many changes of style are generally seen as a reaction to the different women in his life. I might have to say the same about myself. Up to a point. You can become a different man in each marriage. On the other hand, Henry Miller married a number of times and that did not change his personality. I expect that Miller had to fight to establish his identity very early in life. This is probably the case for people who grow up in unsympathetic families—they must arrive at an inner presence sooner, a hard, often hostile identity that the family cannot mess with too easily.

My case was different. My family was sympathetic; it was the world outside that proved hard. For seven or eight years after the success of *The Naked and the Dead,* I kept saying nobody treats me as if I'm real; nobody wants me for my five feet eight inches and my medium good looks. I am only wanted for my celebrity. Therefore my experience is not real to me. The sense of how to perceive life and new material that I had formed up to that point was as an observer on the sidelines. Now, willy-nilly, I was the center of many a room, and so, regardless of how I carried myself, everything I did was noted. To myself, I complained about the unfairness of it, until the day I realized that it was fair, that that was now going to be my experience. It's the simplest remark to make, but it took years to get to that point. Then I began to realize that the kind of writing I was now going to do would be on new and unfamiliar themes. After *The Naked and the Dead,* I had assumed I would work on large, collective novels about American life, books that required venturing out to get experience, but my celebrity took away much of the necessary anonymity I needed personally for that. There was, however, something else I might express. I was, after all, having a form of twentieth-century experience that might become more and more prevalent—I was separated from my roots. People who suffer such an identity crisis generally have to take all sorts of curious steps to locate who they are. They succeed here, they fail there, and the process gives them points of reference. So I began to have a public life even though I was eccentrically shy in those years—that is, half-shy and half-arrogant. Like most young writers. I discovered, however, that I had gregarious gifts and started to employ them. Before long, I began to enjoy them. I also wasted a lot. You gain, you lose, and it makes for a new kind of life. Eventually, you have a new identity. I was successful and alienated, and this was becoming a twentieth-century condition for others as well. Slowly this understanding went into my work after that, and by now I can say that kind of protagonist interests me more than characters who are firmly rooted.

Let me see if I can take this further: Before *The Naked and the Dead* was published, I didn't know whether I could make a success of writing. Maybe I couldn't. Time would tell. Then came startling success. *The Naked and the Dead* was number one on the best-seller list for several months and, to repeat, I was totally unprepared. I felt as if I were secretary to someone named Norman Mailer, and to meet him, people had to say hello to me first. It took a long time to realize that this same celebrity, which had so unhorsed me in the beginning, was now an acquired appetite. As the Marquis de Sade once said, "There is no pleasure greater than that obtained from a conquered repugnance." I began to want more. Fame not only makes you realize that you are amputated from normal life, but also offers a sense of how delicate and unstable is identity. And so my new experience finally became interesting to me. I could now write about the interior life of people who had gained power and had to put up, therefore, with the new person they had become. Be it noted that this new person can be full of surprises: bold where one was once timid yet vulnerable in places that once seemed secure, even hard-edged.

Moreover, there's an irony to fabricating an alternate self. A surprising amount of choice is involved. When I wrote *Advertisements for Myself,* I realized that one could literally forge one's career by the idea you instilled of yourself in others. That is, impersonate the person you might have some reasonable chance of arriving at in a couple of years and soon enough you are lifting yourself by your bootstraps. It is an unbelievably demanding task—as profound a game as a criminal lawyer plays by cutting himself off forever, perhaps, from any clear notion of what his own morality might be.

One unhappy aspect is that people who have never even met you begin to tell exaggerated stories about your person. Soon you are the inheritor of a legend as long as a dinosaur's tail, and it's *false* legend—it never existed even on the day it was created. Twenty years later, you're still using your best efforts to drag the tail around. One relief to getting older is that I no longer have to square my shoulders every time I go into a bar.

On the other hand, others can even aid and abet your legend. Here is my recollection of a dialogue that took place something like fifty years ago:

A CASUAL FRIEND: Norman, I have a confession to make. I was at an Upper East Side party last night, and I didn't know anyone. So I told this good-looking girl that I was you. (pause) Then, I took her home. We got into the sack. I hope you're not mad that I used your name.

MAILER: Were you good with her?

FRIEND: Yeah. It was a good one. Real good.

MAILER: Then I'm not mad.

James Jones was also shot out of a cannon. But Jones had gone through more than I had before he wrote *From Here to Eternity*. By the time he'd arrived, he was ready to enjoy his success. I was a dependable pain in the ass to a great many people, because all through the first year I'd keep saying, "Oh, now I will never know the experience of other people." Jones didn't give a damn. He knew he had brought home the game, and he wanted to eat it. But I kept wanting to go back to what seemed like a sweet past when only a few people knew that I had talent. A young writer, if he is unknown, can be at a party and watch what everyone is doing. If he has a marvelous ear for dialogue, he can wake up the next morning and remember all that was said and how it was said. He is a bird on a branch. Sees like a bird and writes books that can be extraordinarily well observed. But once you are successful, especially if it happens quickly, it's as if the bird is now an emu. It cannot fly. It's big and grows haunches and fore shoulders and a mane: Lo and behold, it is a lion. And everyone is looking at the lion, including the birds. But it is a lion with the heart of a bird and the mind of a bird. So there is a terrible period when the transmogrified emu is trying to live like a lion and has small gifts for it. Then the beast begins to experiment. When it runs, it now sees other animals scamper. It takes a while—often years—to get to appreciate your effect on others and even longer to begin to understand human beings again. In the old days, you could write about friends, enemies, and strangers by intuition, by induction; now, by deduction. Of course, you do have more material on which to work your deductions.

I've always been fascinated with spies and their spiritual associates—actors. The latter can, of course, not be wholly equated to spies, but they do have the experience of embodying a false life for the duration of a given role, and that characterization can become more real than their own identity. The few times I've acted, I've been struck by how alive you can feel during the impersonation, sometimes more real than in your own life. When a spy feels friendship for someone he is going to betray, the friendship is still real. The average journalist is, in that sense, a spy.

LIVING IN THE WORLD

————

Since good novelists have to be brave on the one hand but prudent on the other, we make up a delicate species. More sensitive than others in the beginning, we have to develop the will, the stamina, the determination, and the insensitivity to take critical abuse. A good writer, therefore, does well to see himself as a strong, weak person, full of brave timidity, sensitive and insensitive. In effect, we have to learn how to live in the world with its bumps and falls and occasionally startling rewards while protecting the core of what once seemed a frightfully perishable sensitivity.

If you start a novel before you're ready, it's exactly as if you are a young athlete out in a contest with professionals who are far beyond you. Not ready, you get clobbered. You receive a painful lesson in identity. One does well to build up a little literary experience before trying a long piece of work. On the other hand, if you can accept in advance the likelihood of ending in failure, a young writer can learn a good deal by daring to embark on the long voyage that is a novel.

I've virtually said as much before, but it is so worth repeating. I tend to look at my contemporaries in the way an athlete looks at rival athletes. You try to have a state of mind where you see everything they do that's better than what you can bring off, yet you certainly look to remain aware of those of your skills that are superior to theirs. Good athletes look at their peers in that manner. After all, they have to face each other.

Of course, this is not often true for authors. But we act as if it is. That's because if we are good enough, our games can have their conclusions a hundred years after we are gone.

The energy I put into my public, performing self probably helped my mind and hurt my work. I believe it gave me an understanding of the complexity of the world that I would not have had if I'd stayed at home. I would have tended then to have a much more paranoid vision of how sinister things are. They can be, but not in the way I used to think. That is one of the better tests of the acumen of the writer. How subtle, how full of nuance, how original, is his or her sense of the sinister?

City life produces caustic wit. In New York and Chicago, it serves as a tonic. It even functions as a bridge to others, one of the essences of a city. But if you live in the country, such readiness for confrontation can get you hurt. People who live in the country have one similarity to convicts. All too often they have nothing to think about but the occasional insult they have received. That is one good reason city and country people do tend to make each other nervous.

In the world, you have to learn how to live with deceit. Trotsky once made the incisive remark that the only way you can tell the truth is by a comparison of the lies. While you may never be able to find out who is lying more, you can come close to the relations between two liars. Especially if they are married. We may even be able to say with some certainty, "They hate each other," or, "Isn't it extraordinary how they love each other despite all?"

You also have to learn to live with the possibility of violence. The few times in my life I've been associated with real danger stay with me and remain a *source* for writing. I have a theory concerning crucial experiences that I've expressed from time to time but it might be worth stating again. Certain events, if they are dramatic or fundamental to us, remain afterward like crystals in our psyche. Those experiences should be preserved rather than written down. They are too special, too intense, too concentrated to be used head-on. Whereas if you project your imagination through the crystal, you can end up with an imaginative extrapolation of the original events. Later, coming from another angle, you may obtain another scenario equally good and altogether different from the same crystal. It is there to serve as a continuing source so long as you don't use it up by a direct account of what you felt.

Actors, in their way, may use the same primal experiences to fuel many an emotional aspect of many a role. Sometimes, in the long run of a play, they can use up such a source and have to find another.

I think Hemingway got into trouble because he had to feel equal to his heroes. It became an enormous demand. He could not allow a character in his books to be braver than he was in his private life. It's a beautiful demand, and there's honor in forcing oneself to adhere to such a code, but it does cut down on the work you can get out. While it's legitimate to write about a man who's braver than yourself, it is better to recognize him quickly as such. I believe I could put a heavyweight champion of the world into a novel and make him convincing, even enter his mind without having to be the best old fighter-writer around. I would look to use one or another of the few crystals I possess that are related to extraordinary effort.

Hemingway's death was cautionary to me. His suicide was as wounding as if one's own parent had taken his life. I keep thinking of John Gardner's unforgettable remark that when a father commits suicide, he condemns his son to the same end. Well, of course, you can go to suicide by more ways than killing yourself. You can rot yourself out with too much drink, too many failures, too much talk, too many wild and unachieved alliances—Hemingway was a great cautioning influence on all of us. One learned not to live on one's airs, and to do one's best to avoid many nights when—thanks to Scott Fitzgerald's work—one knew it was three o'clock in the morning.

All the same, many of us also knew what it was to come home after a dull, ugly party, full of liquor but not drunk, leaden with boredom, angry, a little sick, on the edge of what might legitimately be called despair. Sometimes, it was so bad, one tried to put down a few words about it. But writing at such a time is like making love at such a time. Hopeless. It desecrates one's future, yet one does it anyway because at least it is an act. The premise is that what comes out might be valid because it is the record of a mood. What a mood. Full of vomit, self-pity, panic, paranoia, megalomania, *merde*, whimpers, and excuses. The bends of Hell. If you purge it, if you get to sleep and tear it up in the morning, you hope it did no more harm than any other debauch.

Few good writers come out of prison. Incarceration, I think, can destroy a man's ability to write. The noise in prison is tremendous. Plus the paranoia—you do have to fear or distrust too many of the people you are among. The tension of past events is always there: You hassled someone three weeks ago when you were feeling strong; today, you are weak and the other guy is in the yard working out with weights. You get his bad looks. Then there is the daily injustice, which is inevitable—some guards have a hard-on just for you.

Most convicts may not have a very good sense of the rights due others, but they have a close to absolute sense of what is due them. They're not getting their rights most of the time. And injustice breeds obsession. In turn, obsession blots out the power to write well. Obsession is like a magnetic field. You keep being pulled back into a direction you have not chosen. All this militates against writing with clarity. It kills nuance! Given the variety of people in prison, you'd think that writers would ferment like yeast, but they don't. Only the best survive to be able to write once they get out.

One of the hardest things about being a young writer is that every day you spend writing is the day you don't meet this fabulous woman who will be the best heroine in American fiction—at least in your willing hands. Now I'm happily removed from all that. Work used to be the great stone on one's back. Today, it's the opposite. I can't quite carry the analogy out to say that the boulder has become a lighter-than-air balloon, but, I confess, work now nourishes me as much as it wears one down.

The literary world is a dangerous place to inhabit too frequently if you want to get serious work done. It's almost necessary to take on airs in order to protect oneself. And these airs have to be finely tuned if they are to do the job. Capote had a wonderful set and walked around like a little fortress. Hemingway committed suicide working on his airs. He took the literary world much too seriously. His death is there now as a lesson to the rest of us: Don't get involved at too deep a level or it will kill you and—pure Hemingway—it will kill you for the silliest reasons: for vanity, or because feuds are beginning to etch your liver with the acids of frustration. Hemingway did his best to eschew much of that world, but he established a fief with a royal court of followers. He may have worked as hard on that as on his books. I would repeat: His airs killed him.

A writer, no matter how great, is never altogether great; a small part of him is seriously flawed. Tolstoy evaded the depths that Dostoyevsky opened; in turn Dostoyevsky, lacking Tolstoy's majestic sense of the proportions of things, fled proportion and explored hysteria. A writer is recognized as great when his work is done, but while he is writing, he rarely feels so great. He is more likely to live with the anxiety of "Can I do it? Should I let up? Will dread overwhelm me if I explore too far? Or depression deaden me if I do not push on? Can I even do it?" As he writes, the writer is reshaping his character. He is a better man and he is worse, once he has finished a book. Potentialities in him have been developed, other talents have been sacrificed. He has made choices on his route and the choices have shaped him. By this understanding, a genius is a man of large talent who has made many good choices and a few astounding ones. He has had the wit to discipline his cowardice and he has had the courage to be bold where others might cry insanity. Yet no matter how large his genius, we can be certain of one thing—he could have been even greater.

The example is extreme. Just so. There is a kind of critic who writes only about the dead. He sees the great writers of the past as simple men. They are born with a great talent, they exercise it, and they die. Such critics see the mastery in the work; they neglect the subtle failures of the most courageous intent and the dramatic hours when the man took the leap to become a great writer. They do not understand that for every great writer, there are a hundred who could have been equally great but lacked the courage. The writer, particularly the American writer, is not usually—if he is interesting—the quiet master of his craft; he is rather a being who ventured into the jungle of his unconscious to bring back a sense of order or a sense of chaos; he passes through ambushes in his sleep and, if he is ambitious, he must be ready to engage the congealed hostility of the world. If a writer is really good enough and bold enough he will, by the logic of society, write himself out onto the end of a limb that the world will saw off. He does not go necessarily to his death, but he must dare it. And some of us do go into death; Thomas Wolfe most especially, firing the passions which rotted his brain on those long paranoid nights in Brooklyn when he wrote in exaltation and terror on the top of a refrigerator. And Hemingway, who dared death ten times over and would have had to dare it a hundred more in order to find more art, because each time he passed through death the sweet of new creativity was offered.

Well, few of us dare death. Most of us voyage out a part of the way into our jungle and come back filled with pride at what we dared and shame at what we avoided, and because we are men of the middle and shame is an emotion no man of the middle can bear for too long, we act like novelists, which is to say that we are full of spleen, small gossip, hatred for the success of our enemies, envy at the fortunes of our friends, ideologues of a style of fiction which is uniquely the best (and is invariably our own style), and so there is a tendency for us to approach the books of our contemporaries like a defense attorney walking up to a key witness for the prosecution. At his worst, the average good novelist reads the work of his fellow racketeers with one underlying tension—find the flaw, find where the other guy cheated.

One cannot expect an objective performance therefore when one novelist criticizes the work of other novelists. It is better to realize that a group of men who are to a degree honest and to another extent deceitful (to the reader, or to themselves, or to both) are being judged by one of their peers, who shares in the rough their proportions of integrity and pretense and is likely to have the most intense vested interest in advancing the reputation of certain writers while doing his best to diminish others. But the reader is at least given the opportunity to compare the lies, a gratuity he cannot always get from a good critic writing about a novelist, for critics implant into their style the fiction of disinterested passion when indeed *their* vested interest, while less obvious, is often more rabid, since they have usually fixed their aim into the direction they would like the art of the novel to travel, whereas the novelist by the nature of his endeavor is not only more ready to change but by the character of the endeavor itself is obliged to be ready for a new approach.

Virtually every writer, come soon or late, has a cramped-up love affair which is all but hopeless. *Of Human Bondage* could be the case study of half the writers who ever lived. But the obsession is opposed to art in the same way a compulsive talker is opposed to good conversation. The choice is either to break the obsession or enter it. The compulsive talker must go through the herculean transformation of learning to quit or must become a great monologuist. As did Henry Miller!

When it comes to being judged on a moral scale, good novelists are usually in the middle: not too good, and preferably not too evil. The evil, after all, do see more advantages to telling lies than truth. Not a good practice for a novelist. Fiction is the only overriding lie you are permitted.

On the other hand, if your character is awfully decent, you are, to a degree, estranged from humanity. So it helps if your character is average lousy but with striking contrasts and excellent elements. Then the contradictions in your moral makeup will work for you.

MIND AND BODY,
EGO AND WORK

It may be that part of the ability to remain a writer is to learn how to protect your ego through the years. One does ring oneself around with ego protections, the first of which, unhappily, is prudence. The price: Inspiration does not manage to blow the door open as often. Still, you do carry out the main brunt of your projects. That, of course, is exactly the major function of the ego—this dogged, determined, and often ugly servant of civilization itself.

If we think of all the attitudes we take on to fortify the ego or plug holes in it, blind patriotism is probably the most expensive. That is why we will look long and far before we find a good writer who is also a blind patriot. A reasonably dependable ego is crucial to a hardworking author, but an ego that is much more powerful than our literary needs is a superhighway straight into mediocrity. A good many best-selling authors can line up for that one.

Only another writer can know how much damage writing a novel can do to you. It's an unnatural activity to sit at a desk and squeeze words out of yourself. Various kinds of poisons—essences of fatigue—get secreted through your system. As you age, it grows worse. I believe that is one of the reasons I've been so interested in prizefighters. I think often of the aging boxer who has to get into shape for one more fight and knows the punishment it will wreak on his body. No wonder it puts him in gloom. What characterizes every older fighter I have seen training for a fight is the bad mood that hangs over him and his camp. The only good thing likely to come out of it will be money. For the rest is close to a foregone conclusion. Even if he wins the fight—even if he wins it well—he is not going to get a new purchase on life out of a dazzling success, not in the way he did as a young fighter. That's also true in my profession. Often, you have to make grave decisions: Am I going to attempt this difficult venture or not? At a certain point, you must believe that the work will yet prove truly important. Or else why suffer the slow self-destruction it will entail? Writing a novel over two or three years of the hardest work sometimes does the kind of damage to the body that is equal to obliging someone who has never smoked before to consume two or three packs a day for months. In reaction, I think, I've become an interested amateur about medicine; when you are a writer, you are, in a certain sense, doctor to yourself. You can always feel tensions and ailments creeping into you. It goes with the territory. Your factory is yourself. You are always examining the mill for potential breakdowns, anticipating troubles, and so you become alert to the relation not only between yourself and other people but between yourself and your body. Writing impinges on that body; writing depends ultimately on that body. Proust, with his asthma, was like an important industrialist who manages to get out an extraordinarily consistent product even if one wing of the plant is notoriously subject to breakdown.

Writing can also be a way of using up a large and uncomfortable presence in yourself. It's famously known, for instance, that pornographers end up impotent. That's probably a myth with a certain amount of predictability. If you work a muscle hard, it tends to develop; overworked, it can break down. I think something of the same is true of imagination. Force it too far, and it can cease to return anything. We write novels out of two cardinal impulses (other than to make a living and the desire to be famous). One is to understand ourselves better, and the other is to present what we know about others. Of course, it is often impossible to comprehend anyone else until one has plumbed the bottom of certain preoccupations about oneself. That is why the writer is always at risk of using his or her talent for therapy—which can be closer to creative inanition than to art.

Since we are often obliged to write in a state of ignorance about our real motives, one way to tell whether we are engaged only in therapy is that the work engages no risk or, to the contrary, is so wild that it will find no public and no publisher. Therapy, taken by its bottom line, is always self-indulgence, self-absorption.

There is always fear in trying to write a good book. That is one reason why there are many more people who can write well than do. And, of course, many can't take the meanness of the occupation. There's nothing so very attractive about going into a room by yourself each day to look at a blank piece of paper (or monitor) and make calligraphic marks. To perform that act decade after decade punishes through the very monotony of the process. The act of writing itself, taken as a physical act, is less interesting, for example, than painting or, certainly, sculpture, where your body is more exercised in the doing.

Like all occupations, writing also presents its unique elements of risk. In the case of the novelist, it is to his ego. You really don't want to get into a theme where you take no real chances, especially if it is a long book. How to dignify the time it uses up?

I'm always a little uneasy when my work comes to me without much effort. It seems better to have to forge the will to write on a given day. I find that on such occasions, if I do succeed in making progress against resistance in myself, the result is often good. As I only discover days or weeks later. (*The Armies of the Night,* for example, was written in the face of considerable resistance and gloom!) With all else, I was talking about myself in the third person. While it seemed interesting up to a point to speak of a protagonist named Norman Mailer, it was, on the other hand, damned odd. I was halfway into the book before I got used to it. It is even a dislocating way to regard oneself. Yet by the time I was done, I missed this character of Norman Mailer so much that I brought him back for book after book. It never worked as well again. The commitment has to be there. In *The Armies of the Night,* I was a true protagonist of the best sort—half-heroic, three-quarters comic.

—

Usually, on an average working day, you try to raise yourself to a level where you can pick up your story again. You have to pass through a peculiar hour or two, getting yourself in shape for the daily stint. That is equal to saying you have to face yourself each morning. While every salesman, teacher, executive, fireman, or cop does exactly that one way or another on many a morning (and many a pickpocket as well!), the writer must do it alone, day after day after day, a matter of brooding and drifting, and possibly getting into what's bothering you, or even just unwinding a bit. Since you are ready, however, as a novelist to sit in judgment on others, you are obliged to look sooner or later each morning on everything in yourself that's weak or second-rate or irrelevant.

When I'm writing, therefore, I am rarely in a good mood. A part of me prefers to work at a flat level of emotion. Day after day, I see hardly anyone. I'll put in eight or ten hours, of which only three or four will consist of words getting down on the page. It's almost a question of one's metabolism. You begin, after all, from a standing start and have to accelerate up to a level of cerebration where the best words are coming in good order. Just as a fighter has to feel that he possesses the right to do physical damage to another man, so a writer has to be ready to take chances with his readers' lives. If you're trying for something at all interesting or difficult, then you cannot predict what the results of your work will be. If it's close enough to the root, people can be psychically injured reading you. Full of heart, he was also heartless—a splendid oxymoron. That can be the epitaph for many a good novelist.

Today, most of my ideas are less involved with new exploration than with occupying thematic territories I reconnoitered years ago. If you no longer have the pleasure of enjoying your mind in the way you could when young, you have, at least, more worldly knowledge to work with. In 1972, while interviewing Henry Kissinger, I asked him if he enjoyed the intellectual stimulation of his White House work, and he said in effect, "I am working with ideas I formed at Harvard years ago. I haven't had a new idea since I've been on this; I just work with the old ones." By now, I know what he meant. There are just so many new thoughts you can have. There comes a time in your life when you have no choice but to implement them. To quote from *The Deer Park:* ". . . for experience when it is not communicated to another must wither within and be worse than lost." One owes the reader a fee when quoting oneself, but here the tariff feels acceptable.

I can sit with an empty mind. If I do think of something, then all right, I think of it. But a tired brain is happy to contemplate nothing.

On the other hand, our continuing existence as novelists often depends on lively hypotheses. They fructify one's fiction. For example, it is likely that one of the covert motives of jealousy is that it always offers a powerful hypothesis. The moment a husband or wife does not trust the mate, his or her life may become painful, but it is undeniably interesting. Let's say the husband comes in after work and by the way he puts his hat and coat away, the wife can think, Yes, yes, he's feeling guilty. So she can keep the hypothesis going—at least so long as new evidence does not absolutely refute the premise. Then, perhaps, she finds out that the woman she is convinced he is having an affair with has been teaching in China for the last half-year. All right, thereby ends this hypothesis. Now the wife either has to find a new mistress out there or reassess her acumen.

The above, you might say, is a private chart of reality. We also keep world-size charts. A huge geographical and/or philosophical map. The West is in decline—a large hypothesis. Depending on the character of one's mind, one can have an immensely complicated worldview or a narrower and most restricted map, where all you can say is, "I know this region well. Let the rest remain uncharted." Very few of us have a reasonably filled-in vision of the world. We tend to develop only those areas we are interested in.

As a perfect example, how many Americans had Afghanistan anywhere on their chart until September 11? Now we are picking up bits and tidbits about Islam. A flurry! A superficial but lively work-in-progress is proceeding.

To dignify this notion, let me propose that indeed we do try to use these charts, whether good or superficial, to serious purpose. For we are all navigating through life. That is one reason why good novels have a quality that other forms of communication do not offer. It's very hard to think of an interesting protagonist who is not always moving between choices. And you, as the writer, have to monitor these decisions. When your characters come alive for you, which is one of the more agreeable if undeniably eerie aspects of serious novel-writing—when you find yourself having dialogues with them or at the least thinking about how they might react in certain situations that have nothing to do with your novel—then they do bear comparison to a prominent and troublesome friend.

A specific example: At one point in the middle of *Harlot's Ghost,* I thought it would be interesting to send my protagonist—who was a young man in the CIA (and very much under the tutelage of a very high CIA official called Harlot)—to Israel. Why? Because Harlot is in competition with the gray eminence of the CIA, James Jesus Angleton. Harlot feels Angleton not only has too much of a hegemony in the CIA but is also on the inside track with the Mossad. So Harlot decides to send over his subaltern. Perhaps the young man will be able to submarine Angleton just a bit.

That appealed to me. And I thought: Do I dare? Then realized: Can't be done. The research will take a year. I'll have to go over to Israel. Never having been in Israel before, that'll be another book, probably, and I'll have to find out about the Mossad. My chart was no help there. All I had was a blank area that said "Truly major intelligence organization." Learning about the Mossad would be even more difficult than picking up on the CIA. I deliberated for all of a restless week before I was ready to tell myself, "You could wreck this book by sending Harry Hubbard to Israel. At best, you'll lose much too much time." Instead, I had him do something less bold. But that is the way we make such novelistic decisions. Very much as we do in life.

GENDER, NARCISSISM,
MASTURBATION

___

If you believe in fiction, if you believe in the power of the novelist, then all subjects are possible. Of course, certain choices present more obstructions than others. It would be harder, as an example, for a male novelist to learn about the small irritations of a woman's day than to imagine what her sex would be like. A novelistic element in sex, after all, is the feeling of nearness to the Other. It's one of the compelling reasons for sex precisely because such sentiments live almost entirely outside formal sacraments and private codes. It may be indeed why pious people so often feel driven to break their own deepest sexual prohibitions. It's because the experience of meeting the Other is incomparable. Which is why I say it's easier—if you are going to write about those of the opposite gender—to limn them sexually than attempt to get into the nitty-gritty of their daily life.

Another word on gender. Women certainly have every right to create men at war, but I think it might be recognized that it's likely to be less comfortable for them. War, after all, is essentially a male invention. How often have women shown the same inventiveness and hellishness that men have at war? How can they approach that near-psychotic mix of proportion and disproportion which is at the heart of mortal combat? On the other hand, if we ask whether men and women can write equally well about bravery, I would say yes. How are we to define bravery, after all? Take a woman who is awfully timid—let's say she was terrorized through her childhood. She has an all-too-acute awareness of how bad things can come upon you suddenly. When she's an old lady and every bone in her body is aching, it may be an act of courage for her to cross a busy street all by herself. She doesn't know if she can make it across before the lights change, yet she has to do it. For her own honor, if you will. And she does it. That may be more brave, given the relative situation, than the bold act of a soldier who's been trained to be courageous, who is bonded to the soldiers he is with, who lives with the idea that there's no disgrace in life worse than not being up to the military occasion. You can't speak of true bravery in combat for such a good soldier until he has exhausted his code to that point where he feels, Yes, I may lose—I may lose my heart, my dignity, my honor. I'm scared. I'm terrified. I can't move. If, at this point, he still proceeds to press himself forward, then his behavior is courageous.

In a certain sense, we all know this—we know what constitutes brave action. So a woman can certainly write about brave soldiers, even though she's not the least bit brave, not at that level. Of course, she has to have an immense talent. I've often thought that Joyce Carol Oates, who is a very talented woman, will often, on the basis of a small bit of experience, write a six-hundred-page novel. I think she's an arch example of someone who does almost all of it through talent. She's willing to dare terrible humiliation. The irony is that she is rarely attacked. I expect she arouses a fundamental if somewhat bemused respect in many a mean spirit.

The narcissist suffers from too much inner dialogue. The eye of his consciousness is forever looking at his own action. Yet—let us try to keep the notion clear. A narcissist is not only a study in vanity and self-absorption. One part of the self is always immersed in studying the other part. The narcissist is the scientist and the experiment in one. Other people exist, have value to the narcissist, because of their particular ability to arouse one role or another in himself. And are valued for that. May even be loved for that. Of course, they are loved as an actor loves his audience.

Since the amount of stimulation we can offer ourselves is, obviously, limited, the underlying problem of the narcissist is boredom. So there are feverish, even violent attempts to shift the given. One must alter that drear context in which one half of the self is forever examining the stale presence of the other. That is one reason why narcissists are forever falling in and out of love, jobs, places, and addictions. Promiscuity is the opportunity to try a new role. The vanity gained from a one-night stand is an antidote to claustrophobia. That is, if the gamble of the one-night stand turns out well! Henry Miller complains to Anaïs Nin of his dear beloved's lack of center, the incapacity of June to tell the truth or even recognize it. "I want the key," he says, "the key to her lies." Blind to himself—does not every artist have to live in partial and self-induced blindness, or he could never find a foundation for his effort?—Henry Miller does not want to recognize that the key may be simple. Every day is a scenario for June. On the best of days, she creates a life into which she can fit for a few hours. She can feel real love and real hate for strangers, and thereby leave the circle of her self-absorption. Through scenarios, she can arrive in an hour at depths of emotion that other people voyage toward for years. Of course, the scenario once concluded, so too is the love for the day. That passing actor she played with for a few hours is again a stranger to her. It is useless to speak of whether she loves or does not love Miller. It depends on where he dwells in her scenario for that day. So it is also useless to speak of her lies. They are no more real to her than yesterday's lies. It is today's scenario that is her truth and her life—that is liberation from the prison cell of the narcissist.

Of course, it is not all that bad. Part of Miller's continuing literary obsession with June is due to the variety of her roles. Each, after all, offers a new role for Miller. He does play opposite the leading lady. If for one day she turns him into a detective and on the next a thief, that keeps interest in his own personality alive.

Narcissists, after all, induce emotion in each other through their minds. It is not their flesh which is aroused so much as the vibrancy of the role. Their relations are at once more electric and more empty, more perfect and more hollow. But the hollow seems never to fill. So, narcissism may be a true disease, a biological displacement of the natural impulse to develop oneself by the lessons of one's experience—narcissism, therefore, could bear the same relation to love that onanism does to copulation or a cancer to the natural growth of tissue. Can we come a little nearer to the recognition that there may be a base beneath all disease, an ultimate disease, a psychosomatic doom, so to speak, against which all the other illnesses, colds, fevers, infections, and deteriorations are bulwarks to protect us against a worse fate? Which is what? Perhaps an irreversible revolt of the flesh or the mind into cancer or insanity. That is psychosomatic doom—to follow the growth of the flesh or the mind into terminal anomaly. But if that is the case, how can we not suppose that for the narcissist—always so aware that something is wrong within—there is a constant unconscious terror: His or her isolation, if unrelieved, will end in one arm or the other of the ultimate disease.

The paradox is that no love can prove so intense, therefore, as the love of two narcissists for each other. So much depends on it. Each—the paradox turns upon itself—is capable of offering deliverance to the other. To the degree that they tune each other superbly well, they begin to create what before had been impossible: They begin to acquire the skills that enable them to enter the world. (For it is not love of the self but dread of the world outside the self which is the seed of narcissism.) Narcissists can end, therefore, by having a real need of each other. That is, of course, hardly the characteristic relation. The love of most narcissists tends to become comic. Seen from the outside, their suffering manages to be equaled only by the rapidity with which they recover from suffering. Is it hundreds or thousands of such examples that come to us from Hollywood?

The reality, of course, is more painful. Given the delicacy of every narcissist and the timidity that created their detachment, we can see again that the highest intensity of their personal relations is, for good cause, with themselves. For their own self-protection, they need an excess of control over external events. (Not too removed in analogy is that excess of control which technology is forever trying to exact from nature.)

To the degree, however, that narcissism is an affliction of the talented, the stakes are not small, and the victims are playing a serious game right in the midst of their scenarios. For if one can break out of the penitentiary of self-absorption, then there may be artistic wonders to achieve.

Henry Miller could have been playing, therefore, for the highest stakes. He had the energy, the vision, the talent, the outrageous individuality to have some chance of becoming the greatest writer in America's history, a figure equal to Shakespeare. (For Americans.) Of course, to invoke such contrasts is to mock them. A writer cannot live too seriously with the idea that (as Hemingway once boasted) he will or will not beat Tolstoy. He contains, rather, some sense of huge and not impossible literary destiny in the reverberations of his own ambition; he feels his talent as a trust, and his loves seem evil when they balk him. He is living, after all, with his own secret plot. He knows that a writer of the largest dimension can alter the nerves and marrow of a nation. No one, in fact, can measure what whole and collective loss would have come to the English people if Shakespeare had not lived to write. (Or, for that matter, conceive of how the South would be strikingly less interesting without Faulkner. It certainly is now.)

In those seven years with June, Miller was shaping the talent with which he would go out into the world. It is part of the total ambiguity of narcissism (despite the ten thousand intimate details he offers of his life) that we do not know by the end of *The Rosy Crucifixion* whether June breathed a greater life into his talent or exploited him. We do not know if Miller, if he had never met her, could have become capable of writing about tyrants and tycoons (instead, repetitively, of his own liberation) or—we are left wide open—if the contrary is the true possibility and he might never have written nearly as well if he had not met her. All we know is that after seven years of living with June, he went off to Paris alone and learned to live by himself, having come into a confluence of his life where he could extract an overpowering and unforgettable aesthetic from ogres and sewers. It is kin to the nightmare of narcissism that we are left with this question and no answer.

A corollary of narcissism is, of course, masturbation. An author is forever consulting his mind, even as the hand will query the penis. So follow a few remarks from an interview done almost forty years ago in *The Realist*. Rereading it, I find it still valid. The act of writing is so close to the psychic character of masturbation that if we are going to discuss the world of the writer, then we ought to deal with this as well. It is the unspoken subtext behind the epithet *scribbler.*

PAUL KRASSNER: Do you think you're something of a puritan when it comes to masturbation?

NORMAN MAILER: I think masturbation is bad.

PK: In relation to heterosexual fulfillment?

NM: In relation to everything—orgasm, heterosexuality, to style, to stance, to being able to fight the good fight. I think masturbation turns people askew. It sets up a bad and often enduring tension. Anybody who spends his adolescence masturbating generally enters his young manhood with no sense of being a man.

PK: Is it possible you have a totalitarian attitude toward masturbation?

NM: I'm saying it's a miserable activity.

PK: Well, we're getting right back to absolutes. You know—to some, masturbation can be a thing of beauty.

NM: To what end? Who is going to benefit from it? Masturbation is bombing oneself.

PK: I think there's a basic flaw in your argument. Why are you assuming that masturbation is violence unto oneself? Why is it not pleasure unto oneself? And I'm not defending masturbation—well, I'm defending masturbation, yes, as a substitute if and when—

NM: All right, look. When you make love, whatever is good in you or bad in you goes out into someone else. I mean this literally. I'm not interested in the biochemistry of it nor in how the psychic waves are passed back and forth. All I know is that when one makes love, one changes a woman slightly and a woman changes you slightly—

PK: Certain circumstances can change one for the worse.

NM: But at least you have gone through a process which is part of life. One can be better for the experience, or worse. But one has experience to absorb, to think about, one has literally to digest the new spirit that has entered the flesh. The body has been galvanized for an experience of flesh, a declaration of the flesh.

If one has the courage to think about every aspect of the act—I don't mean think mechanically about it—but if one is able to brood over the act, to dwell on it, then one is *changed* by the act. Because in the act of restoring one's harmony, one has to encounter all the reasons one was jangled.

So finally, one has had an experience which was nourishing. Nourishing because one is able to *feel* one's way into more difficult or more precious insights as a result of it. One's able to live a tougher, more heroic life if one can digest and absorb the experience.

But if one masturbates, all that happens is, everything that's beautiful and good in one goes up the hand, goes into the air, is *lost*. Now, what the hell is there to *absorb*? One hasn't tested oneself. You see, in a way, the heterosexual act lays questions to rest and makes one able to build upon a few answers. Whereas if one masturbates, the ability to contemplate one's experience is disturbed. Fantasies of power take over and disturb all sleep.

If one has, for example, the image of a beautiful, sexy babe in masturbation, one still doesn't know whether one can make love to her in the flesh. All you know is that you can have her in your *brain*. Well, a lot of good that is.

But if one has fought the good fight or the evil fight and ended with the beautiful, sexy dame, then whether the experience is good or bad, your life is changed by it. One knows something of what happened. One has something real to build on.

The ultimate direction of masturbation always has to be insanity—the ultimate direction, mind you, not the immediate likelihood.

I was asked whether these remarks apply to women, and realized that I did not know the answer. It strikes me that masturbation, for a variety of reasons, does not affect the female psyche as directly.

A male friend of mine remarked, "Since you've been married all your adult life, you don't know the true extent of the problem."

THE UNCONSCIOUS

I n the course of fashioning a character, as you search into his
or her existence, there invariably comes a point where you
recognize that you don't know enough about the person you are
trying to create. At such times, I take it for granted that my unconscious knows more than I do. As we go through life, we do,
after all, observe everyone, wittingly and unwittingly. Perhaps,
out of the corner of your eye, you glimpse someone in a restau-
rant who represents a particular inspiration or menace or possibility, potentially a friend or foe—and the unconscious goes to
work on that. It needs very little evidence to put together a comprehensive portrait because, presumably, it has already done
most of that labor. To use an unhappy analogy, it's as if the unconscious is a powerful computer that does not often need much
in the way of new data to fashion a portrait, considering how
much material has already been stored away.

On the other hand, the unconscious can often feel violated by
what we demand, by what, indeed, we manage to extract from it.
Perhaps a great deal of the material it is now supplying was originally filed away for its own purposes. Suppose the unconscious
has a root in the hereafter that our conscious mind does not. If
so, it will have deeper notions about death than we do. Let us

then dare to surmise that the unconscious is on close, even familial, terms with that most elusive presence in the conscious mind—our soul. If that is the case, the unconscious can feel exploited by the push of the novelist to extract so much of his product from its resources.

Suppose the relation of the unconscious to the conscious is analogous to that of a cultivated Greek slave in service to an overbearing Roman master. If we use this notion as a working premise, we can assume that our unconscious is full of the trickiest kinds of resistance. All the writer receives is a sense of dull, edgy resentment. Perhaps the unconscious is not ready to plumb into the material requested. The acute form of this is writer's block. But, for that matter, there is a touch of writer's block in almost every working day. It is part of the experience of writing. At a certain point we are going well for a page or two, perhaps even as many as four or five. On happy days, one is writing as if it's all there, a gift. You don't even seem to have much to do with it. You're only around to transcribe what's coming up. Then comes the moment when our ambition orders us to keep going: "Three pages away from the end of the chapter. You can't stop now, not with this marvelous streak." At this point, so often, the sentences begin to strain, and you feel, no, we've got to pack it in for now—dammit, dammit—now tomorrow morning will be lost, but, no, don't try to finish now, you're going to wreck it. That's what you learn over time. Because in the early years of writing, you do force it, and what happens, of course, is equal to blowback. From its point of view, the unconscious has done its job. It's damned if it's going to give you any more right now. If you insist, flatness of affect will be your reward—*nothingness,* the dread antagonist. It's there. One of the most painful elements in the act of writing is to live so much of the day with little but that. It is why many talented men and women do a good book or two, then stop. To deal on a daily basis with *nothingness* is vitiating. Writers who have been at it for decades often do not keep as vital an inner life. They remain professional enough to take what is potentially exciting in their concept and put it on paper. But the inner landscape shows its flats. That may be due to our violation of the frustrated desire of the unconscious to be left alone on those occasions when we nonetheless insist on hard-working its vein. So our ambition ends by contributing to the *nothingness* that besets us. The irony is that so often it is our fear of living with an inner void that makes us ambitious in the first place.

Part of the art of being a novelist is to play that delicate game of obtaining experience without falsifying it by the act of observation. Generally speaking, it's easier to take in such knowledge when you are part of an event that is much larger than yourself—like the fall of the Twin Towers.

There must be five hundred young writers in New York who had a day of experience that was incomparable—nothing remotely like that had ever happened before in their lives. And it's likely that some extraordinary work will come out of it. Hopefully, not all of it about 9/11. If you never write about 9/11 but were in the vicinity that day, you could conceivably, in time to come, describe a battle in a medieval war and provide a real sense of such a lost event. You could do a horror tale or an account of a plague. Or write about the sudden death of a beloved. Or a march of refugees. All kinds of scenes and situations can derive ultimately from 9/11. What won't always work is to go at it directly. That kind of writing can be exhausted quickly. And the temptation to drive in head-on is, of course, immense—the event was traumatic to so many.

Unhappily, a large part of writing serves this eliminatory process. The worst thing that can be said about literary work is that it can reduce itself all too easily to self-expression that is all too close to psychic excretion. Ideally, you are there to bring wealth to others. Wealth of observation, of perception, the riches of a philosophical attitude that is to a degree new, insights into psychology the reader hasn't had before—all these are on the selfless side of writing. On the other hand, there is ego, vanity, and need—the desire, finally, to advance oneself as a writer. People don't become authors solely to benefit humanity. They're in the same position as priests. Part of them wants to be good to others; the other self wants, one way or the other, to have some acquaintance with power. Which is often hugely at odds with the first notion. Generosity vies with acquisition; compassion is besieged with greed. Not surprising, then, if such tension pushes one toward accomplishing neither, but converting it all into reduction of stress, therapy through the act of writing and more writing until such logorrhea exhausts one's unrest to some degree. In such cases, it is the loss of good writing that pays for the draining of all that unrest.

——

I've found that I can't do serious writing without getting into a mild depression. (Note! I am not speaking of a clinical depression.) An ongoing bad mood can be, however, a vital part of the process, because to begin with, it's perilous to fall in love with what you're doing. You lose your judgment. And for the simplest reason—the words, as you are writing them, stir up your feelings too much. Odds are, if they excite you disproportionately, they may do much less to others. (This accounts for the bewilderment of novice writers when a story they have written that charged them up to the heights appears to have little impact on others.)

With veteran writers, a mild working depression is not always simple to explain. The deeper your theme and the more material you are bringing up from your unconscious to support it, the more you may be exhausting the possibilities of other themes-in-waiting. So gloom can descend. Certain large possibilities won't get written about after all. No book I wrote kept me in a more sustained bad mood (while doing it) than *The Armies of the Night*. I was putting so much in, and at so fast a rate—the first three-quarters of the book was written for *Harper's* magazine over a stretch of eight weeks—that I was probably uprooting all sorts of possibilities for future projects. Gloom descends when you have wounded too many psychic tissues in your determination to achieve one urgent goal.

Sometimes, the only way you can be certain you are attracted to a new subject is that you know so little about it and yet are drawn toward it. Perhaps you possess one deep insight into the subject—a special kind of purchase that will accelerate your comprehension as you proceed. It's more amusing, for instance, to read a mystery novel if early on you have an idea who did it, a feeling that you and the author share something. In such happy condition, you are going, right or wrong, to get more out of the book than others. I think something of the sort can also occur in historical research. Reading about ancient Egypt, I felt I knew something about burial customs that the average Egyptologist didn't—not more about the details, which I hadn't learned as yet, but more about the underlying reason for some of the practices. That was enough to fire up the wish to pursue it a long way further.

—

I've always had the feeling that it doesn't make much sense to take on a subject if others can do it as well. As an instance, I never felt my childhood was so unique to me that it was worth recording. On the other hand, I conceal, sometimes from myself, what there is to write about those years. It can be wasteful to plunge into what you have to say on a subject before you're ready to give your full commitment.

This may sound odd to people who do not write. They usually have not come in contact with the authority of the unconscious to resist one's conscious will. Over and over again, I discover that my unconscious is going to disclose to me what it chooses, when it chooses. You can, to a limited degree, force it to respond, but that rarely occasions much happiness on either side. Sometimes I think you have to groom the unconscious after you've used it, swab it down, treat it like a prize horse who's a finer animal than you.

Practically, how do you go about this? How do you groom the unconscious? I don't have a conscious clue. The trouble with relying on metaphors is that they too can desert you just as quickly as anyone or anything else.

Over the years, I've found one rule. It is the only one I give on those occasions when I talk about writing. It's a simple rule. If you tell yourself you are going to be at your desk tomorrow, you are by that declaration asking your unconscious to prepare the material. You are, in effect, contracting to pick up such valuables at a given time. Count on me, you are saying to a few forces below: I will be there to write. The point is that you have to maintain trustworthy relations. If you wake up in the morning with a hangover and cannot get to literary work, your unconscious, after a few such failures to appear, will withdraw.

It is likely that your unconscious is never all that much in love with you. The battle between the ego and the unconscious is, I think, a war of some dimension. In many people it's equal to an unhappy marriage, and marriages depend, after all, upon trust. Unhappy marriages depend immensely on what little mutual trust there is. So, you have to establish decent relations with your working depths, and you might as well recognize that this procedure is possibly as difficult to achieve as any far-reaching union with someone outside your skin.

The unconscious presence within may have as many interests, aspects, principalities, chasms, terrors, underworlds, other-worlds, and ambitions as yourself. Your unconscious may even have ambitions that are not your own. For practical purposes, it may be worth thinking of it as a separate creature. If you are ready to look upon your unconscious as a curious and semi-alienated presence in yourself with whom you have to maintain decent relations—if you are able to see yourself as some sort of careless general (of the old aristocratic school) and picture the unconscious as your often unruly cohort of troops—then, obviously, you wouldn't dare to keep those troops out in the rain too long; certainly not at the commencement of any serious campaign. On the contrary, you make a pact: "Work for me, fight for me, and I will honor and respect you."

To repeat: The rule is that if you say to yourself you are going to write tomorrow, then it doesn't matter how badly you're hungover or how promising is a sudden invitation in the morning to do something more enjoyable. No, you go in dutifully, slavishly, and you work. This injunction is wholly anti-romantic in spirit. But if you subject yourself to this impost upon yourself, this diktat to be dependable, then after a period of time—it can take weeks, or more—the unconscious, nursing its disappointments, may begin to trust you again.

This is a burden on young writers who are not only ambitious but wild enough to feel that their wildness is part of their talent. They hate to submit to the heavy hand (that awful, severe, unbending demand for moderation) and obey the rule that you have to show up.

On the other hand, you can sometimes say to yourself, "I'm not going to work tomorrow," and the unconscious may even by now be close enough in accord not to flood your mind with brilliant and all-too-perishable material. That is also important. Because in the course of going out and having the lively day and night you're entitled to, you don't want to keep having ideas about the book you're on. Indeed, if you are able on your day off to avoid the unpleasant condition of being swarmed with thoughts about a work-in-progress when there is no pen in your hand, then you've arrived at one of the disciplines of a real writer.

—

The rule in capsule: If you fail to show up in the morning after you vowed that you would be at your desk as you went to sleep last night, then you will walk around with ants in your brain. Rule of thumb: Restlessness of mind can be measured by the number of promises that remain unkept.

PHILOSOPHY

PRIMITIVE MAN,
ART AND SCIENCE,
EVIL AND JUDGMENT

Since the primitive had senses that were closer to the animal, he also had fears not unlike the animal. Those fears, obviously, were intense. Anyone who has ever felt dread in any real way knows it's a near to unendurable experience; one will do almost anything to avoid it. One is tempted to advance the notion that civilization came out of human terror at having to face dread as a daily condition. So we worked to elaborate a civilization that would insulate us from the exorbitant demands of existence. I'm not speaking now of those early and unbelievably pressing concerns of growing crops or killing enough game to be able to live. I'm conceiving of a greater terror, where the trees virtually spoke to one and the message one took in from the rustling of the leaves and the swaying of the branches was accurate: the storm they were ready to tell you about—the terrible storm that was coming in a few weeks—would wash the river over its banks and flood your settlement. That warning proved to be prophetic. Small wonder if man did everything he could to remove himself from such intimacy with nature. He even escalated the costs of tribal war in order to found large nations— anything to avoid a daily existence filled with dread. Carnage ensued and philosophy developed. Is it possible that at the heart of Divinity, Irony is well installed? Carnage walks the aisles of history hand in hand with philosophy. If there is no afterworld where the contest continues, then existence is indeed absurd.

Primitive man had to see himself surrounded by a circle of forces—demons, gods, friendly forces, impersonal forces. If I think of a primitive walking through a forest, I expect his movement to be different from ours. If we pass through the woods on an easy trail, we walk; if it's not open, we bushwhack. But the primitive may have stopped before a certain tree and bowed. Before another, he may have lain prostrate, even abject, on the ground; where there was familiarity with a relatively modest divine force, just a nod of the head as he passed by. That was no more than was required unless the tree gave an indication that it was annoyed. How did it speak? By many shades of distinction in the rustling of its leaves.

If we accept these suppositions, then consciousness had to be more intense for the primitive. He was always a protagonist. His day was heroic or ghastly. For what does it mean to be a hero? It requires you to be prepared to deal with forces larger than yourself. Terrified and heroic, it is no wonder that the life span of primitive man was shorter than ours.

By pagan times, of course, societies as developed as the Romans' were ready to rely on rituals and special relation to their gods. Earlier, among the Egyptians, amulets could even be the equal in value of estate holdings. If you are trying to form and maintain a society, you can't have people going off every moment to propitiate forces on their own. You do well to get them believing there is a central force, society itself, which offers the best approach to propitiation of the gods. Can one go so far as to suggest that there is a buried element in many talented writers that unconsciously expects their work to serve not only literature but as acts of conjuration or propitiation? What, when you get down to it, was Joyce, as one mighty example, trying to show us in *Finnegans Wake*?

The artist seeks to create a spell. Today, of course, the artist is no primitive man; he is all but completely insulated from the senses primitive man once had. By now, the artist usually acts as a mediator between magic and technology. But no matter how technologized he becomes, his central impulse is to create a spell equivalent to the spell a primitive felt when he passed a great oak and knew something deeper than his normal comprehension was reaching him. Perhaps the primitive felt close to what we feel when we see a great painting on a museum wall. We are near then to something we can't even call knowledge. It's larger, less definable, and certainly more resonant.

While the physicist is stirred, if uncomfortably, by feeling the presence of magic in his experiment and the artist is often drenched in statistical detail (since he has to deal with a world that grows more and more technical and difficult to comprehend), at bottom their interests are opposed. Finally, the physicist is trying to destroy the fundament of magic, and the artist is trying to undermine the base of technology. The artist believes (and this is the greatest generalization I can make) that all cosmic achievement is attainable within the human frame—that is, if we lead lives witty enough and skillful enough, bold enough and, finally, illumined enough, we can accomplish every communication and reach every vault within the cosmos that technology would attempt to take by force: telepathy rather than telephony.

An equation sign can also be seen as a statement of metaphor. When you say: "y equals x to the 2nd power," you are in effect establishing a metaphor. Or, the obverse: An artist in a gallery, looking at a painting, says, "I see God in the yellow." All right, that can be stated mathematically. The yellow of this painting is a function of God. Either way, artist or physicist is trying to penetrate into the substance of things. In that sense, the physicist and the artist are closer to one another than the artist and the gallery owner, or the physicist and the engineer.

I've long had the notion that when highly charged people have a confrontation—Shakespearean characters, for example—coincidences will occur. Indeed, if there is any order in the cosmos, it should not be so exceptional that this is so. If a general, let us say, is getting ready for battle and there are gods and devils surrounding him, they are certainly involved in the outcome. Whether the general wins or loses the contest on that day will have an effect on the fortunes of these gods. So they're going to be paying attention, are they not? In turn, the general is going to be aware of them—at least insofar as he has sensitivity to their presence. Such a man is not necessarily foolish or psychotic if he spends his last ten minutes in bed debating whether he should first put his left foot down on the floor or choose the right. Perhaps he is calling on the left or right echelon of his gods. We can also assume that these gods will be doing their best to create startling coincidences. A coincidence, after all, excites us with the livid sense that there's a superstructure about us, and in this superstructure are the agents of a presence (or a spiritual machine) larger than our imagination. When a warlike general bends his knee in prayer, it is as likely that he is calling upon a demon as invoking Jesus Christ. Of course, he may be thinking that he calls on the Lord. Doubtless he has never encountered Kierkegaard's dictum that when we feel most saintly, we could be working for the devil.

J. MICHAEL LENNON: Many of your characters over the years have carried on negotiations with evil—Marion Faye, D.J., Rojack—I take it that you would not agree with Hannah Arendt on the essential banality of evil?

NORMAN MAILER: I wouldn't agree with Hannah Arendt at all, not at all. Of course, she can make a case. There are any number of prodigiously evil people who have, from the writer's point of view, disappointing exteriors. Eichmann, superficially speaking, was a little man, an ordinary man in appearance, and vulgar and dull, but to assume therefore that evil itself is banal strikes me as exhibiting a prodigious poverty of imagination. You know, one of the paradoxes I always found in the liberal temperament is that they are immensely worshipful of Freud—even though most of his ideas are antipathetic to the notion of liberalism itself. But liberals do go to Freud as if he is their umbilical cord for cerebral nourishment. The reason is simple: Freud's stance is reductive, and liberals don't like to believe in the vast power of the unconscious or the evil of true murderousness residing in the most ordinary people. To accept the surface for the reality is to perform the fundamental liberal reflex. In effect, liberals are near to saying, "I don't see God, so why do you assume God exists?" Talk of the devil is off the charts. Out of that has come, I think, their present bankruptcy. Liberalism has no exciting ideas to offer anymore. I think this enervation comes because it has not been able to deal with the most haunting question of the twentieth century, which is not Communism but Nazism. Liberalism can't come near to understanding this incredible phenomenon that took over a country of the most decent, hardworking, and *clean* people in the world, this incredible phenomenon of a fascism that went far beyond the bounds of totalitarianism into the most despicable and extraordinary extermination of vast numbers of people. And this, coming out of a nation that had always been exceptionally— even comically—law-abiding, suggested that the unconscious was truly a place of hideous ambushes and horrors. Liberals, unable to weave that thought into their philosophy, were happy to welcome Hannah Arendt's phrase. But I think to speak of the banality of evil is precisely to point us further in the wrong direction. Evil has dimensions. Evil is mysterious. It can be palpable or invisible. It can appear to be banal or, equally, can show itself as intensely dramatic. September 11 does come to mind.

Back to Kierkegaard. He was ready to suggest that at the moment we're feeling most saintly, we may in fact be evil. And that moment when we think we're most evil and finally corrupt, we might, by the startling judgments of God, be considered saintly. The value of this notion is that it strips us of the fundamental arrogance of assuming that at any given moment any of us has enough centrality—that is, possesses a *seat* from which we can expound our dogma or determine our own moral value. I may have a fairly well formed *cloud* of intuitions about the nature of the good, and, like a cloud, it has, to a certain degree, its structure; yet the form is capable of altering quickly. A cloud changes shape over a few moments, but it remains a cloud. It's not just simply an unformed chaos. That, I would propose, is as close as we get to any moral truth. This is why I love the novel. It is, I would repeat, the form best suited for developing our moral sensitivity—which is to say our depth of understanding rather than our rush to judgment. Given the complexity of the last century and the surrealistic knockdowns of the first two years of this century, quick judgment has become a need analogous to the kind of all-consuming hunger that is ready to eat grass and dirt to fill the void. Or, go to McDonald's.

The moment you moralize in your novel, your book is no longer moral. It has become pious. Piety not only corrodes morality but consorts with corruption. Piety and corruption go together like hot dogs and mustard. They have to. No one can fulfill the demands of piety; as a daily demand, it is inhuman. So it inspires its opposite—just for the sheer health of the body, if not the soul. Whereas morality, when subtle, brings proportion to human affairs. Tolstoy is a great writer—maybe he is our greatest novelist—because no other can match his sense of human proportion. We feel awe supported by compassion when we read Tolstoy. A remarkable achievement. We are in the rare presence of moral evaluations that are severe yet ultimately tender.

I've used this example before, but it bears repeating: Anyone who worries about whether he is going to hurt somebody's feelings by his work is no more a writer than a surgeon who says to himself, "In making this incision, I am going to give this young woman a scar on her belly that could injure her love life for the next thirty years." The surgeon just makes the cut. He may be right or wrong in the need for the operation, but he keeps a necessary insensitivity to the rest of the context. Writers also have their own kind of restricted vision. They cannot afford to say to themselves, "This portrait is going to scar my good friend." Or my father. Or my sister. If they feel such sentiments, they can't write. Indeed, a great many young writers think of all the people they're going to hurt or, worse, those they're going to make enemies of, and, full of funk, begin to brood on the retribution that will ensue. So there has to be something a bit maniacal about a young man or woman who would be an exciting writer. He or she has to be willing to get that book out no matter how many psychic casualties are left in its passage. On the other hand, a good young writer does well not to take an immediate advantage over people he dislikes by dumping on them in his pages. It's a bad habit to cash such easy checks. Ergo, the moral vision of the young writer is on a tightrope.

I may not be a good intellectual, but my avocation is, nonetheless, to create intellections. I put them on like adhesive plasters. In the case of Gary Gilmore, however, I had to pull them off. As I explored deeper into what Gilmore's nature might be, I decided that every concept I had about him was inadequate. So I wanted the reader of *The Executioner's Song* to confront the true complexity of one human. That state of perception will always

arise by studying any person close enough. That he was a murderer made my task simpler, because we are all fascinated by
killers. But any person studied in depth will prove fascinating. It
is certainly the yeast in any good marriage. Take any soul alive,
and he or she can prove exceptional provided you get to know
him or her well enough. Of course, if we are dealing with a sad
case, the exceptional element is more likely to be found in the
canyons of their horrendous bad luck or in the contortions of an
ongoing cowardice. Or both. Bad luck feeds fear; the obverse
may be equally true.

ATTACKS ON REALITY

———

Readers often have a problem when an author mixes real and fictional characters. I've never been bothered by that. As far as I'm concerned, it's all fiction. Let's say for the purpose of argument there are a thousand large and small details necessary for a particular historian to capture a given moment in time—Napoleon's return from Elba or the rise of Robespierre. Whatever is chosen, the historian has to decide which of those details are most relevant. He can't use them all. More important, he can't obtain them all. Let's say he selects a few hundred pieces of information that adhere to his various assumptions on what probably happened within the event. These pieces of detail are usually called *facts*.

Should the novelist come in, also ready to write about the same happening, he or she is not nearly as good, doubtless, at research and comes up with only forty or fifty details that seem vital. Nonetheless, I would argue that the historian and the novelist are both engaged in writing fiction. The difference is that the historian uses more facts, although they can never be numerous enough to enclose the reality. Moreover, the historian usually writes in a more pedestrian style. But there they are both doing fiction. The real point is that each, the novelist and the historian, is making an attack on the possible nature of reality. Such attacks are the fundamental element in good fiction whether the mode of assault is history or the novel.

I've always been drawn more toward realism than fantasy, because it seems to me realism is endlessly interesting and finally indeterminable. Realism is a species of fantasy that's much more integrated and hard-core than fantasy itself. If you are ready to come to grips with the inevitable slipperiness of most available facts, you come to recognize that realism is not a direct approach to the truth so much as the most concentrated form of fantasy.

Borges has a magical ability to put plots through metamorphoses. So, he poses the difficulty of comprehending reality. He shows us that every time we think our mind is approaching reality, we have only been writing a scenario to comprehend it. The scenario is the equivalent of a hypothesis that seems correct until new evidence subverts it. In the course of this subversion, however, we learn a good deal. The revised hypothesis, ideally, should be superior. Reading Borges, you live in this highly diverting and not always agreeable business of seeing elaborate hypotheses destroyed by the one event that is able to turn them inside out. Borges is always teaching us that it is not enough to live with Aquinas's dictum, Trust the evidence of your senses. Rather, trust them until they are dramatically revealed as inadequate, tricked, or downright betrayed—then refine them. Borges is not the least bit easy.

Paranoia? It is either the center of one's sanity or the edge of one's psychosis. You never know when it's devoted to your safety or to your ultimate breakdown.

There is a famous story that Shelley rushed up to a mother, seized her infant, held it aloft, and cried out: "Babe, speak! Reveal your immortal truth!" Like Plato—a great Platonist at that point, was Shelley—he believed that the education you begin to receive when young obfuscates the instinctive knowledge with which you're born. Then you spend the rest of your life trying to unmake that education.

   Well, I too am able to believe we're born with a profound appreciation of the universe and do lose it in the first few years of our life (not to mention the first few weeks!) and then spend the rest of our time trying to gain it back. By the time we are six, the school system makes certain we lose it. I don't think this is so awful. It is rather in the nature of things. It was intended that way. We're supposed to lose it and regain it. I think it is impossible to conceive of any real achievements in knowledge without that fall. Because if knowledge is something we receive merely by opening ourselves to it, well—in the West, we can't conceive of that. Most of us find something a hint repellent about Hindu philosophy. It's the idea that you receive wisdom without a Faustian effort. We react against the assumption that the more you give yourself to the universe, and the more passive, therefore, you become, the nearer you will be to the secrets of existence. This thought is, of course, antipathetic to the Western mind. We feel you only get to the kernel of real secrets by smashing the shell. That's the way we want it. It's what we were built to do. If this doesn't have something to do with novel-writing, then I don't know what this book is about.

The twentieth-century artist who conceivably had the most influence on my work was not a writer but Picasso. He kept changing the nature of his attack on reality. It's as if he felt there is a reality to be found out there but it's not a graspable object like a rock. Rather, it is a creature who keeps changing shape. And if I, Picasso, have been trying to delineate this creature by means of a particular aesthetic style and have come only this far, then I am going to look for another style altogether. And off Picasso goes into a new mode of attack on reality. It's as if you have to work your way up the north face of the mountain, come back and do the south face, the southwest face, so forth.

In line with Picasso, what I find most interesting in writing at this point is to keep making a new attack on the nature of reality. It's as if reality has some subtle desire to protect itself. If we keep pushing forward in the same direction, reality is able to handle us or evade us and may even do it in the way organisms become resistant to various antibiotics and pesticides.

We tell ourselves stories in order to make sense of life. Narrative is reassuring. There are days when life is so absurd, it's crippling—nothing makes sense, but stories bring order to the absurdity. Relief is provided by the narrative's beginning, middle, and end. Without an end, you have an obsession, a constant circling around a fact or situation that cannot be put in place. The danger, therefore, in recognizing the insubstantiality of fact is that one is all too ready to welcome the art of the absurd. That is one good reason why so many are obsessive (and endlessly boring) in their recitation of supposedly well-seated facts.

SOCIAL VISION

The great economists pondered the interchanges of human energy. They looked for those means and ways that such energy could be augmented institutionally or dissipated or even destroyed. In that sense, *Das Kapital* is a phenomenological novel, with commodities serving (and experiencing an extraordinarily vital life) as protagonists. The commodities gain and lose energy just as humans do in novels. Perhaps in future years we will read some magnificent writer, probably not yet born, who will transcend the categories and write a work to marry those visions of society that have to do with how we offer human energy to each other, and steal it from one another, develop it, divert it.

Obviously, Freud brought off a revolution in our consciousness of the human psyche. But it may be wise to restrict his insights to the nineteenth century. I expect that his final importance in intellectual history will be that he gave us more insight into the underside of that century than anyone but Marx. Freud is the key to understanding how people put up with the psychic weight of the lives they led in the 1880s, 1890s, and early 1900s: locked up, terribly overstuffed, yet still existing with a considerable amount of power, energy, and pressure. In those days the psyche was analogous to a plumbing system. People were accustomed to living under high pressure and finding ways, no matter how bizarre, to open the steam valve. That's not what we have now. Today we know a world in which people not only act out many of their anxieties but work to find reassuring explanations of their conduct, which is often overtly contradictory rather than repressed.

Marx, for vastly more complex reasons, is also not adequate any longer. First imperialism, then corporate capitalism, made their end runs around him. So I don't try to create a bridge in my mind from Marx to Freud, not anymore. But when I wrote "The White Negro" back in the Fifties, I was ready to see that everything in society—from the largest institutions to private and intimate personal moments—might yet be connected as parts of a new and vast social vision. In a limited sense, I'm still trying. Of course, I grew up under the shadow of both men. I was nothing if not intellectually ambitious when I was young, and wanted to present a comprehensive vision of existence. By now I've come to realize that I have neither the intellectual discipline nor the scholarly retentiveness to begin to do anything of that sort. Still, it is important to connect up what one can. Until we understand how we are obliged to lead our lives in ways we don't particularly enjoy ("The mass of men enter into social and productive relations independent of their will."—Marx), until we understand more of those reasons why so many of us feel dead inside so much of the time, yes, until we recognize how much of that is not due solely to our lack of imagination or the grinding confines of a responsible life, but is also the product of vast institutional systems of greed, injustice, and manipulation that we are schooled to perceive as relatively benign manifestations, we have arrived nowhere. The only way I can tell something terrible is going on is that I feel a little duller than I ought to. Very often that's at the end of a long chain, you might say, of social processes designed to keep us malleable, amenable, and short on such powerful emotions as outrage at injustice. In that sense, I still try to find the ultimate indictment against all that's awful and, yes, evil in society—all the awfuls: plastic, high-rises, mall architecture, static, interruptions for commercials, making money out of money, and—certainly not least—the highly developed structures of injustice. They're all there if one can find the grid on which to locate them. A devil's grid.

MORAL VISION

_____

Back in 1959, Ralph Ellison and I were out at the University of Iowa on a literary symposium gotten together by *Esquire*. We had a lively audience, and the show went on for several intense days. At the end, it seemed a little strange to me that we had really worked that hard, gotten into so many discussions with students and attendant academics, and even argued with each other as lively as hell. When it was over, there was even a bit of sadness. Something that had become just a bit exceptional was done. So I said to Ellison, "Why the hell do we do it? Why did we work so hard?" He said, "Man, we're expendable." I've always liked that remark.

One's work is just that—expendable. If any of my ideas can succeed in changing the mind of someone who's more intelligent than myself, fine. If you advance a thought as far as you can and it's overtaken and improved by someone who will argue on the opposite side, then in effect you have improved your adversary's mind. We can, however, feel the confidence that someone will come along who will take your opponent's improvement of your idea and lift it higher on your side. Democracy is the throbbing embodiment of the dialectic—thesis, antithesis, and synthesis ready to become the new thesis.

You cannot have a great democracy without great writers. If

great novels disappear, as they are in danger of doing, and our storytelling is co-opted by television and journalism, then I think we will be that much farther away from a free society. Novels that reinvigorate our view of the subtlety of moral judgments are essential to a democracy. Americans were affected for decades by *The Grapes of Wrath*. Some good Southerners even developed a sense of the tragic by reading Faulkner.

I don't like to say to myself, "I want to get this idea across." Rather, I try to arouse a state of consciousness in the reader that will accommodate the material I am presenting. My hope is that my work will change their minds. Be it understood! I don't want to change everybody's mind in one direction—that's equal to propaganda. Rather than move all my readers ten degrees to the left, I would be happier if I nudged some there while others were swinging to the right. My fundamental belief about a good society is that the cops get better and so do the crooks.

I feel that the final purpose of art is to intensify—even, if necessary, to exacerbate—the moral consciousness of people. In particular, I think the novel at its best is the most moral of the art forms. You are exploring the interstices of human behavior—which is the first approach to religious experience for many of us, especially since the organized religions don't begin to offer sufficient account of the terrible complexities of moral experience and its dark sibling, moral ambiguity. The wisest rule of thumb for the would-be moralist is: There are no answers. There are only questions.

The logic of reincarnation, it seems to me, is that it may enable God to go back to certain projects, just as an artist sometimes wishes to improve his or her first attempt, work it further, go to the point where he can do better, or, if not, know at least that he has failed and can abandon a particular notion. Some human souls may represent some of the more poignant notions of God. You see, there's an extraordinary beauty in the potential of most human relations if we're willing to assume that under all the absurdities, the spleen, the waste, the brutality, there was, indeed, a blocked aesthetic conception.

Speaking at the MacDowell Colony once, I found myself saying, "There is no reason to believe the novelist is not better equipped to deal with the possibilities of a mysterious and difficult situation than anyone else, since he or she is always trying to discover what the nature of reality might be. It's as if the novelist is out there, sprung early, with something most people never contemplate—which is 'How and what is the nature of this little reality before me?' The novelist is the first to ask, 'Do I love my wife? Does she love me? What is the nature of love? Do we love our child? How do we love? Would we die for our child? Or do we let the child die for us?' The novelist has to deal with these questions because living with them is the only way to improve his or her brain. Without improving that brain, without refining the edge of one's perception, it's almost impossible to continue to work as a writer. Because if there is one fell rule in art, it is that uninspired repetition kills the soul. So the novelist is out there early with a particular necessity that may become the necessity of us all. It is to deal with life not as something given us as eternal and immutable but rather as half-worked, because it is our human destiny to enlarge what we were given, to forge (I might have said to *clarify*) a world which was always before us in a manner different from the way we had seen it the day before."

I'm right and I'm wrong so often that I have no interest in convincing others to think the way I do. I'm interested, rather, that we all get better at thinking. If a book is good enough, you cannot predict how your readers are going to react. You shouldn't be able to. If it is that good, it is not manipulative, and everyone, therefore, can voyage off in a different direction.

Yes, it is no ordinary human business to say you are going to write a novel. You are planning to create a world. This God-like presumption may be intoxicating, but it can never be comfortable. Nor should it be. To come up with a vision that can give us some notion of the Lord's mind—that partakes of beauty. When we read Proust or Stendhal or Joyce, any, indeed, of the great novelists, Tolstoy, Mann, or Faulkner, or on occasion Hemingway, they do give us the idea that one special side of God's mind is not alien to the *style* of their mind.

I go back again and again to Dostoyevsky dying in despair because he could not write the novel about the great saint he envisioned.

To us, now, it seems, "Why despair? Look at the great books you did write." But Dostoyevsky, given his unique intuitions, may have sensed that Russia was heading toward a prodigious catastrophe that he could not quite name. Nonetheless, he felt he could help avert this oncoming disaster if he could create in his pages a saint who would be believable enough to the Russian people to inspire them.

This is not as impossible a mission as it seems today. In Russia, in that time, a few novelists were revered like gods—or, if not a god, Tolstoy certainly was regarded by his readers as a major, virile, powerful saint. In turn, Dostoyevsky may have been looked upon as a mad genius, but absolutely a genius. It was taken for granted that you could learn more about life by reading their novels than from your own personal experience. The Russians paid just this exceptional attention to their novelists. So from Dostoyevsky's point of view, if he could only make that marvelous saint in his mind come to life in a book, then he could help to save Russia. All right, slightly demented, as was so much of Dostoyevsky, but it was not wholly unbalanced. He had one chance in a hundred, one real chance in a hundred. That's all a genius ever looks for—one live chance in that hundred. Geniuses, we do well to remind ourselves, are people who take those hundred-to-one shots because they see how strange is the luminescence in the flicker of the solitary candle.

Writers aren't taken seriously anymore, and a large part of the blame must go to the writers of my generation, most certainly including myself. We haven't written the books that should have been written. We've spent too much time exploring ourselves. We haven't done the imaginative work that could have helped define America, and as a result, our average citizen does not grow in self-understanding. We just expand all over the place, and this spread is about as attractive as collapsed and flabby dough on a stainless steel table.

If I could give one maxim to a young writer, I'd say live with your cowardice. Live with it every day. Hate it or defend it, but don't try to slough it off. Cowardice is a prime cause; literary apathy or overt writer's block is all too often the effect.

BEING AND
NOTHINGNESS

———

The reader will be aware by now that I have some obsession
with how God exists. Is He an essential or an existential
God? Is He all-powerful or is He, like us, an embattled existential presence who may succeed or fail in His vision? I think this
obsession began to show itself while I was doing the last draft of
The Deer Park. Then it continued to grow as a private theme during all the years I was smoking marijuana. One's condition on
marijuana is always existential. One can feel the importance of
each moment and how it is changing one. One feels one's being.
One becomes aware of the enormous apparatus of nothingness—the hum of a hi-fi set, the emptiness of a pointless interruption. One becomes aware of the war between each of us, how
the nothingness in each of us seeks to attack the being of others,
how our being in turn is attacked by the nothingness of others.

I'm not speaking now of violence or the active conflict between one being and another. That still belongs to drama. But
the war between being and nothingness is the underlying illness
of the twentieth century. Boredom slays more of existence than
war. I'd hardly read anything by Sartre at this time and nothing
by Heidegger. I've read a bit since and I have to admire their
formidable powers, but I suspect they are no closer to the buried

continent of existentialism than were medieval cartographers near to a useful map of the world. The new continent that shows on our psychic maps as intimations of eternity is still to be discovered.

I've never felt close to Beckett and haven't read his novels. Friends tell me the best of his literary substance is there. I am, however, familiar with *Waiting for Godot, Krapp's Last Tape,* and *Endgame,* and I've always been fascinated by how he has done something that no writer ever did before. When it comes to the presence of *being* and *nothingness,* Beckett said in effect, "*Nothing* is half of life and it is the half I know about. I am going to dwell on that." The trouble, however, is that we have to live with the words in English, where the reverberation on the ear is not as agreeable as *être* or *néant* can be to the ear in French.

Nothingness is, after all, anathema to most writers. We take it for granted that we will have to spend a good part of our lives accepting *nothing* as the price to pay in order to feel a resonant opposite: *being.* On days when one's mind is not alive, one goes through hours where boredom itself can be close to dread. It is, after all, a state that offers no sensual affect and so feels vaguely sinister in ways you cannot name. It's as if in boredom you come to the wrong kind of rest, a pause that does not restore. *Nothingness* invariably suggests *endless* nothingness.

Yet here we have Beckett, lively and witty as he travels into these subtly fetid caves of virtual non-existence. I always saw such states as the price you pay in order to command a grasp of existence, of being. So in advance, my initial reaction to Beckett was disapproval. I was bothered in those years—the late Fifties—at how people were so ready to welcome the art of the absurd.

I detest this art. When, for instance, I see a college play (and, given the number of my children, I've seen my share), invariably the drama department has opted for a play that celebrates the art of the absurd. Their reason is clear: You cannot judge the merit of the production too closely. Professors of drama at these schools do not rush to be measured. It's unfailing how often they choose García Lorca, Ionesco, Artaud—name twenty difficult and talented playwrights of the absurd and then set college kids to try to do something with it. They can't win and they can't lose, because the actors are going to get laughs. Whenever an audience is not able to follow a non sequitur, an automatic laugh comes up. Especially from parents, roommates, relatives, and friends. If you have an actor say, "The situation is getting kind of boborigymous," the audience will not only roar at the fecal cacophony of the sounds but will look to cover over their ignorance of the exact meaning. A horde of fail-safes is always available in plays when they are dedicated to the absurd.

About the time Beckett arrived on Broadway, therefore, I was certain, given the advance publicity, that he would be the worst of all. Seeing *Godot,* I had to recognize that something profound was going on, but I couldn't like it. I felt all too familiar with such states of existence. Marriage, after all, is filled with comparable situations—the rigamarole of marriage, the routine, the dreadful repetitions—nothingness pitted against nothingness—except that Beckett added to it an acute sense of despair. *Godot* had dimension, resonance, vibrancy. Beckett's despair was sinister and joyful at once, as if he were saying, "Once you feel this kind of woe, nothing will ever be that bad again." Never as bad again.

There was, inarguably, this remarkably quality in Beckett. Nonetheless, he was putting the emphasis upon nothingness. My outrage became sententiousness: What if *being* is in trouble? We don't have a clue any longer to what it might be—there is such misuse of *being*. For a daily example, every time you become interested in a narrative on television, a commercial comes on and you are jacked over abruptly from pleasure to nothingness. The impact is there even though the commercial may be lively, noisy, even on occasion amusing. But your concentration has been broken at an instant when you weren't prepared for that.

Philosophically, Beckett seemed to be saying, "*Nothingness* is at least one half of existence, so let's study it, let's attempt to enjoy it." The assumption that it could be enjoyed was the irritant. If fiction depends on how life moves from *being* to *nothingness* and back again, Beckett chooses to stay in *nothingness*. He's Mozartian, however, in the variations he can play on the theme. He is one of the very few writers in the second half of the twentieth century who prompts you to speak of his genius. He took a deserted road and went far with it. But he never entered the dialectic between *nothingness* and *being*. Let me try to exemplify what I am saying.

I have always felt that *The Old Man and the Sea* was one of Hemingway's failures. He wanted to bring off a short novel about a fine man who worked with his hands, a fisherman. Looking to write a novel of affirmation about just such a man, Hemingway had him row out to sea in his dinghy again and again. But after many days of poor fishing, the old man finally hooks into the biggest fish he's ever had. He hangs on, and the contest goes for hour after hour after hour—the fish tows him for miles—yet the old man succeeds in wearing the beast out, and gaffs him. Since the catch is too heavy to bring on board, he lashes it to the side of his dinghy and starts to row back to shore. Then the sharks come and devour his prize. He's left with nothing. The critics all agreed this was Hemingway's view of the literary world—sharks out to destroy a beautiful work.

The critics, however, decided near unanimously (and Hemingway went along) that he had written a novel of human affirmation because the protagonist never gave up. But then there is never a moment in the telling when the man said to himself, "I'm suffering too severely. I'm going to cut the rope." Because if the old fisherman had weakened, then Hemingway would have had to have a serious affirmation. Which is: *Why* doesn't the fisherman cut the fish loose? What remains in him to war with that temptation? Instead, the old Cuban was never tempted. So Hemingway never had to find a reason for the fisherman to say, "I'll hold on." Not enough of a character had been created to answer such a question.

I think the same fault in considerably more elaborated form is present with Beckett. He never enters a situation where any of his people might try to break out of whatever trap they are in. They can be ensconced in garbage cans or talking to a tape recorder, which, speaking of traps, is no mean example. But there is never an arduous attempt to escape whatever trap they are in. Of course, one can argue that Beckett dared to try something no one else had ever attempted and so was reaffirming *being*. Daring is, after all, a vital element in *being*. But we are not able to enjoy this daring nearly so much as we are obliged to feel the ongoing possibilities of more *nothingness*, and so the final impact of his plays is obsessive rather than haunting.

In parallel, the essence of all that hubris in corporate advertising may be its well-founded fear of *nothingness*. For good cause. The corporates are always pouring their presentations into our minds. To which I would reply that filling such essentially empty forms as commercials is a direct species of *nothingness*. Whenever you do not fill the aesthetic you set yourself, you are purveying just that. By now, many if not most television commercials, no matter how spiked with clash and color, give, nonetheless, little attention to the item they are there to sell. The intent of the advertisers comes down to the premise that if you entertain your audience, if you pay them, in effect, for the interruption by getting them to laugh during the commercial, it's not inconceivable that a fraction of these viewers may even remember the name of the product—that's all the advertiser needs. Far better than to have someone speak directly of the sterling virtues of the brand. Who would believe them? No, advertisers work to overcome the onus of *nothingness* that the TV commercial inserts into our nervous system.

MISCELLANY:
PORNOGRAPHY, PICASSO,
AND APHORISMS

————

I can see some reasonably deep moral questions about whether people should be free to create hard-core pornography. I'd vote yes, but let's not assume no damage is taking place. For some, it would be a curse; to others, a perverse blessing. But you could be playing with your soul. Let's say the moral shadings are not without their parallel to men doing their best to take each other out in the ring while other men and women cheer them on. Note that I put it this way even though boxing is my favorite sport to watch.

You can tell a lot about every stage of sex—before, during, and after—by odor. One is often aware of one's own spiritual condition through one's scent. Just so, as one enters a house, one knows the happiness or the misery of its people by the smell one encounters. This faculty, therefore, can become unendurable at times. You walk in on old friends and realize that something's going to go bust with them—not yet, maybe, but it's there, maybe a month or two away, a year or two away. The odor speaks unmistakably of stale miseries that will yet exact their payment. Or, at least, all this was true in the years when I still had a vivid sense of smell.

—

One can say that if Picasso had been braver at certain points in his life, he might have been a more generous artist. Some of the cruelty might have gone out of his work. Something grand might have come in. He had enormous talent; he was, arguably, the greatest painter since Michelangelo. With generosity, maybe Picasso would have been nobler, but the odds are that he would have been less. Because the selfishness of the artist is often there to protect the part that is generous. To the degree that artists give of themselves to all people, they don't want to give anything at all in other ways. There's an economy to generosity. And very often, the people who are the most generous are not the most talented. I think the inner sanction that artists give themselves is that they've got to be selfish—absolutely!—or nothing will get done.

Such thoughts are not happy, but the evidence—if the biographies of artists and writers are at all reliable—does support the notion that it is best to revere painters, poets, and novelists for their talent rather than their character.

A great many artists are narcissists—certainly writers. In Picasso's case, narcissism is too small a word. I think he saw himself as an intermediary between humankind and the forces that created the world and kept it in upheaval. I think he saw himself as a demiurge. That is, a demiurge with half of himself. The other half was a modest man who spoke French badly and was five feet three inches tall.

I've always felt that there was a good deal of compatibility between La Rochefoucauld and Gore Vidal. I say this critically. One of the largest arguments I have with Vidal and his mind and his work is that they represent the end of an intellectual tradition that began with La Rochefoucauld. Many of Vidal's remarks stand up, I think, in comparison. He can put his finger on many a boil. For example: "Whenever a friend succeeds, a little something in me dies." No one can accuse Gore of not being able to step forth with a good line. What I would argue, however, is that his particular tradition has become inadequate to our needs. The world is growing so genuinely complex (and perplexed) that it's limiting to enclose it with aphorisms, no matter how brilliant. One has to qualify them.

For example: Not everything wilts in me when another novelist succeeds. There is also admiration—unwanted, it is true, but then whoever insisted that we are absolutely without treachery to ourselves?

Which opens a useful exercise for novelists: It is to take on a few of the better maxims, adages, insights, and sayings of the celebrated, and see if you can work them further. There is that whole remark of Tolstoy's: *"It is amazing how complete is the delusion that beauty is goodness."* Agreed. At the least, a temporary, if successful, collaboration between good and evil may well be going on—which could be why Tolstoy distrusted it so, and why we react with fear, wonder, avidity, and, yes, distrust when we encounter a beautiful woman.

But now that I have commenced this, I cannot stop:

Voltaire once said: *"Common sense is not so common."* He could have gone on to remark that the greatest abuse of common sense is generally perpetrated by those people who are forever proclaiming the value of that virtue in themselves.

Abraham Lincoln: *"Most of us are just about as happy as we make up our minds to be."* Sometimes, one doesn't decide to be happy, because the likelihood is that upcoming events will be dire. Which suggests that the fall will come from a greater height.

"Merit envies success and success takes itself for merit."—Jean Rostand
    Success is so confident that it is possessed of merit that merit, to its horror, comes to respect success more than its own merit.

One good reason for indulging this exercise is to remind young writers never to hitch their minds to a wise saying. A wiser one can usually be built upon it, or, at least, one ought to make the attempt.

Example:
    "The whole problem with the world is that fools and fanatics are always certain of themselves, and wiser people so full of doubts."
                                                            —Bertrand Russell

172 · THE SPOOKY ART

This is because stupidity is not a liability but an asset if all you care about is getting your way. Before obstinate fools, we are all weak.

"Rudeness is the weak man's imitation of strength."—Eric Hoffer

Half-true, no more. Rudeness can lead to a fight the rude man would be wise not to get into. Usually, however, the instigator of any harsh discourtesy has sensed already who is weaker at the moment than himself. Like many another foul art, rudeness has gifted practitioners.

PART II

GENRE

GENRE

———

Genre, as used here, is an excursion into a few of the art forms available to the novelist other than non-fiction or literary criticism. Where the average good novelist is content to stick to his or her last—certainly that is tricky enough—still, it is hard by now to be good at our trade without feeling attracted to such other venues as journalism, television, studies of the occult, and, for a few of us, forays into art criticism.

Certain human relations are comparable to literary forms. For instance, the one-night stand is like a poem, good or bad. The affair that does not go on forever is equal to a short story. By this logic, marriage is a novel. In a short story, we're interested in the point that's made. In a novel, we usually follow the way people move from drama to boredom back to drama again, and, of course, marriage is the paradigm for that. Our interest is not so much in the understanding that is arrived at on a given night but in the way the new sensibility is confirmed or eroded over the weeks or months that follow. The narrative line of wedlock is, in that sense, good days and bad ones. And most people seem to prefer to live in this form—just as there are people who prefer to live in the space of the short story. Psychopaths, in their turn, have lives that consist of poems, mostly bummers.

Journalism is another matter. For that, we will need other metaphors.

Centuries from now, the moral intelligence of another time may look in horror on the history implanted into twentieth-century people by way of newsprint. A deadening of the collective brain has been one consequence. Another is the active warping of consciousness in any leader whose actions are consistently in the papers, for he has been obliged to learn how to speak only in quotable and self-protective remarks. He has also had to learn not to be too interesting, since his ideas would then be garbled and his manner criticized. Some men never could learn, Eugene McCarthy for one, and so their careers did not prosper in proportion to their courage and their wit. Of course, those stalwarts who learned how to respect the limitations of the reporter may never have had a serious thought again. In order to communicate with the communicators, they gave up any hint of private philosophy.

I began my forays into journalism with prejudices on how the materials of history were gathered. I also possessed the large advantage that I had weeks to ponder over what I had seen and nearly enough days in which to do the writing. I also had a literary heritage to remind me that the world is not supposed to be reassembled by panels of prefabricated words. Rather, I was a novelist. It was expected of me to see the world with my own eyes and my own words. See it by the warp or stance of my character. Which if it could collect some integrity might be called a style. I enlisted then on my side of an undeclared war between those modes of perception called journalism and fiction. When it came to accuracy, I was on the side of fiction. I thought fiction could bring us closer to the truth than journalism, which is not to say one should make up facts when writing a story about real people. I would endeavor to get my facts as scrupulously as a reporter. (At the least!) The difference would be found elsewhere. Journalism assumes the truth of an event can be found by the use of principles that go back to Descartes. (A political reporter has a fixed view of the world; you may plot it on axes that run right to left on the horizontal and down from honesty to corruption on the vertical.) Indeed, the real premise of journalism is that the best instrument for measuring history is a faceless, even a mindless, recorder. Whereas the writer of fiction is closer to the moving world of Einstein. There, the velocity of the observer is as crucial to the measurement as any object observed, since we are obliged to receive the majority of our experience at second hand through parents, friends, mates, lovers, enemies, and the journalists who report it to us. So our best chance of improving those private charts of our own most complicated lives, our un-admitted maps of reality—our very comprehension, if you will, of the way existence works—seems to profit us most if we can have some little idea, at least, of the warp of the observer who passes on the experience. Fiction, as I use the word, is then that reality which does not cohere to anonymous axes of fact but is breathed in through the swarm of our male and female move-ments about one another, a novelistic assumption, for don't we perceive the truth of a novel as its events pass through the per-sonality of the writer? By the time we have finished a story, we tend to know, in our unconscious at least, where we think the au-thor is most to be trusted and where in secret we suspect he is more ignorant than ourselves. That is the flavor of fiction. We observe the observer. Maybe that is why there is less dead air in fiction and usually more light. It is because we have the advan-tage of seeing around a corner, and that is aesthetically compa-rable to a photograph of a range of hills when the sunset offers its backlighting to the contours. Be certain the journalistic flash-bulb is better for recording the carnage of an auto crash. But little else.

The excerpt that follows is part of a piece written for *Esquire* in 1961 and so, of course, is out of date, but, I will avow, inter-estingly so. The surface details have gone through a metamor-phosis. The noise in one pressroom of a hundred working typewriters is no longer present, since computers and laptops are silent. Large events no longer have long banks of telephones for the assembled journalists—cell phones substitute. The hotels no longer smell like cigars, or armpits, or feet. They are usually glitzy. Las Vegas set the new tone. And the reporters are much better dressed. The deadlines are now in many a case more ex-tended and the daily writing has improved. Yet in one funda-mental way, nothing has changed in the profession: The inner death of the soul is still with us.

Remember the old joke about the three kinds of intelligence: human, animal, and military? Well, if there are three kinds of writers—novelists, poets, and *reporters*—there is certainly a gulf between the poet and the novelist. Quite apart from the kind of living they make, poets invariably seem to be aristocrats, usually spoiled beyond repair; and novelists—even if they make a million or have large talent—look to have something of the working class about them. Maybe it is the drudgery, the long, obsessive inner life, the day-to-day monotony of applying themselves to the middle of the same continuing job, or perhaps it is the business of being unappreciated at home—has anyone met a novelist who is happy with the rugged care provided by his wife?

Now, of course, I am tempted to round the image out and say reporters belong to the middle class. Only I do not know if I can push the analogy: Taken one by one, it is true that reporters tend to be hardheaded, objective, and unimaginative. Their intelligence is sound but unexceptional, and they have the middle-class penchant for collecting tales, stories, legends, accounts of practical jokes, details of negotiation, bits of memoir—all those capsules of fiction which serve the middle class as a substitute for ethics and/or culture. Reporters, like shopkeepers, tend to be worshipful of the fact that wins and so covers over the other facts. In the middle class, the remark "He made a lot of money" ends the conversation. If you persist, if you try to point out that the money was made by digging through his grandmother's grave to look for oil, you are met with a middle-class shrug. "It's a question of taste whether one should get into the past" is the winning reply.

In his own person there is nobody more practical than a reporter. He exhibits the same avidity for news which a businessman will show for money. No bourgeois will hesitate to pick up a dollar, even if he is not fond of the man with whom he deals: So a reporter will do a nice story about a type he dislikes or a bad story about a figure he is fond of. It has nothing to do with his feelings. There is a logic to news—on a given day, with a certain meteorological drift to the winds in the mass media, a story can only ride along certain vectors. To expect a reporter to be true to the precise detail of the event is kin to the sentimentality which asks a fast-revolving investor to be faithful to a particular stock in his portfolio when it is going down and his others are going up.

But here we come to the end of our image. When the middle class gather for a club meeting or social function, the atmosphere is dependably dull, whereas ten reporters come together in a room for a story are slightly hysterical, and two hundred reporters and photographers congregated for a press conference are as void of dignity, even stuffed-up, stodgy, middle-class dignity, as a slew of monkeys tearing through the brush. There is reason for this, much reason; there is always urgency to get some quotation which is usable for their story and, afterward, find a telephone. The habitat of a reporter, at its worst, is identical to spending one's morning and evening transferring from the rush hour of one subway train to the rush hour of another. In time, even the best come to remind one of the rush hour. An old fight reporter is a sad sight. He looks like an old prizefight manager, which is to say he looks like an old cigar butt.

Nor is this true only of sports reporters. They are gifted with charm compared to political reporters, who give off an effluvium that is unadulterated cancer gulch. I do not think I exaggerate. There is an odor to any Press Headquarters which is unmistakable. One may begin by saying it is like the odor in small left-wing meeting halls except it is worse, far worse, for there is no poverty to put a guilt-free iron into the nose; on the contrary, everybody is getting free drinks, free sandwiches, free news releases. Yet there is the unavoidable smell of flesh burning quietly and slowly in the service of a machine. Have any of you ever been through the smoking car of an old coach early in the morning when the smokers sleep and the stale air settles into congelations of gloom? Well, that is a little like the scent of Press Headquarters. Yet the difference is vast, because Press Headquarters for any big American event is invariably a large room in a large hotel, usually the largest room in the largest hotel in town. Thus it is a commercial room in a commercial hotel. The walls must be pale green or pale pink, dirty by now, subtly dirty like the toe of a silk stocking. (Which is, incidentally, the smell of the plaster.) One could be meeting bureaucrats from Tashkent in the Palace of the Soviets. One enormous barefaced meeting room, a twenty-foot banner up, a proscenium arch at one end, with high Gothic windows painted within the arch—almost never does a window look out on the open air. (Hotels build banquet rooms on the *inside* of their buildings; it is the best way to fill internal space with revenue.)

The room is in fever. Two hundred, three hundred, I suppose even five hundred reporters get into some of these rooms, there to talk, there to drink, there to bang away on any one of fifty standard typewriters, provided by the people in Public Relations, who have set up this Press Headquarters. It is like being at a vast party in Limbo—there is tremendous excitement, much movement, and no sex at all. Just talk. Talk fed by cigarettes. One thousand to two thousand cigarettes are smoked every hour. The mind must keep functioning fast enough to offer up stories. (Reporters meet as in a marketplace to trade their stories—they barter an anecdote they cannot use about one of the people in the event in order to pick up a different piece, which is usable by their paper. It does not matter if the story is true or altogether not true—it must merely be suitable and not too mechanically libelous.) So they char the inside of their bodies in order to scrape up news which can go out to the machine, that enormous machine, that intellectual leviathan which is obliged to eat, each day, tidbits, gristle, gravel, garbage cans, charlotte russe, old rubber tires, T-bone steaks, wet cardboard, dry leaves, apple pie, broken bottles, dog food, shells, roach powder, dry ballpoint pens, grapefruit juice. All the trash, all the garbage, all the slop, and a little of the wealth go out each day and night into the belly of that old American goat, our newspapers.

So the reporters smell also of this work, they smell of the dishwasher and the pots, they are flesh burning themselves very quietly and slowly in the service of a machine which feeds goats, which feeds The Goat. One smells this collective odor on the instant one enters their meeting room. It is not a corrupt smell, it does not have enough of the meats, the savory, and the vitality of flesh to smell corrupt and fearful when it is bad—no, it is more the smell of excessive respect for power, the odor of flesh gutted by avidities that are electric and empty. I suppose it is the bleak smell one could find on the inside of one's head during a bad cold, full of fever, badly used, burned out of mood. The physical sensation of a cold often is one of power trapped corrosively inside, coils of strength being liquidated in some center of the self. The reporter hangs in a powerless power—his voice directly, or via the rewrite desk indirectly, reaches out to millions of readers; the more readers he owns, the less he can say. He is forbidden by a hundred censors, most of them inside himself, to communicate notions which are not conformistically simple, simple like plastic is simple, that is to say monotonous. Therefore a reporter forms a habit equivalent to lacerating the flesh: He learns to write what he does not naturally believe. Since he did not start, presumably, with the desire to be a bad writer or a dishonest writer, he ends by bludgeoning his brain into believing that something which is half-true is in fact—since he creates a fact each time he puts something into a newspaper—nine-tenths true. A psyche is debauched—his own; a false fact is created. For which fact, sooner or later, inevitably, inexorably, the public will pay. A nation which forms detailed opinions on the basis of detailed fact which is askew from the subtle reality becomes a nation of citizens whose psyches are skewed, item by detailed item, away from *any* reality.

So great guilt clings to reporters. They know they help to keep America slightly insane. As a result perhaps, they are a shabby-looking crew. The best of them are the shabbiest, which is natural if one thinks about it—a sensitive man suffers from the prosperous life of lies more than a dull man. In fact the few dudes one finds among reporters tend to be semi-illiterates, or hatchet men, or cynics on two or three payrolls, who do restrained public relations in the form of news stories. But this is to make too much of the extremes. Reporters along the middle of the spectrum are shabby, worried, guilty, and suffer each day from the damnable anxiety that they know all sorts of powerful information a half-hour to twenty-four hours before anyone else in America knows it, not to mention the time clock ticking away in the vault of all those stories which cannot be printed or will not be printed. It makes for a livid view of existence. It is like an injunction to become hysterical once a day. Then they must write at lightning speed. It may be heavy-fisted but true, it may be slick as a barnyard slide, it may be great, it may be fill—what does it matter? The matter rides out like oats on a conveyor belt, and the unconscious takes a ferocious pounding. Writing is of use to the psyche only if the writer discovers something he did not know he knew in the act itself of writing. That is why a few men will go through hell in order to keep writing—Joyce and Proust, for example. Being a writer can save one from insanity or cancer; being a bad writer can drive one smack into the center of the plague. Think of the poor reporter, who does not have the leisure of the novelist or the poet to discover what he thinks. The unconscious gives up, buries itself, leaves the writer to his cliché, and saves the truth, or the part of it the reporter is yet privileged to find, for his colleagues and his friends. A good reporter is a man who must tell you the truth privately; he has bright, harsh eyes and can relate ten good stories in a row standing at a bar.

Still, they do not quit. The charge of adrenaline once a day, that hysteria, that sense of powerless power close to the engines of history—they can do without powerless power no more than a gentleman junkie on the main line can do without his fix. You see, a reporter is close to the action. He is not *of* the action, but he is close to it, as close as a crab louse to the begetting of a child. One may never be President, but the photographer working for his paper has the power to cock a flashbulb and make the eyes of JFK go blink!

However, it is not just this lead-encased seat near the radiations of power that keeps the reporter hooked on a drug of new news to start new adrenaline; it is also the ride. It is the free ride. When we were children, there were those movies about reporters; they were heroes. While chasing a lead, they used to leap across empty elevator shafts, they would wrestle automatics out of mobsters' hands, and if they were Cary Grant, they would pick up a chair and stick it in the lion's face, since the lion had the peculiar sense to walk into the editor's office. Next to being a cowboy or a private eye, the most heroic activity in America was to be a reporter. Now journalism has become an offshoot of the welfare state. Every last cigar-smoking fraud of a middle-aged reporter, pale with prison pallor, deep lines in his cheeks, writing daily pietisms for the sheet back home about free enterprise, is himself the first captive. It is the best free ride anyone will find since he left his family's chest. Your room is paid for by the newspaper, your trips to the particular spots attached to the event—in this case, the training camp at Elgin, Illinois, for Patterson, and the empty racetrack at Aurora Downs for Liston— are by chartered limousine. Who but a Soviet bureaucrat, a British businessman, a movie star, or an American reporter would ride in a chartered limousine? (They smell like funeral parlors.) Your typing paper is free if you want it; your seat at the fight, or your ticket to the convention, is right there, under the ropes; your meals if you get around to eating them are free, free sandwiches only, but then a reporter has a stomach like a shaving mug and a throat like a hog's trough: He couldn't tell steak tartare from guacamole. And the drinks—if you are at a big fight—are without charge. If you are at a political convention, there is no free liquor. But you do have a choice between free Pepsi Cola and free Coca-Cola. The principle seems to be that the reporting of mildly psychotic actions—such as those performed by politicians—should be made in sobriety; whereas a sane estimate of an athlete's chances are neatest on booze. At a fight Press Headquarters, the drinks are very free and the mood can even be half-convivial. It's like being in an Army outfit everyone's forgotten. You get your food, you get your beer, you get your pay, the work is easy, and leave to town is routine. You never had it so good—you're an infant again: You can grow up a second time and improve the job.

That's the half and half of being a reporter. One half is addiction, adrenaline, anecdote shopping, deadlines, dread, cigar smoke, lung cancer, vomit, feeding The Goat; the other is Aloha, Tahiti, old friends, and the free ride to the eleventh floor of the Sheraton-Chicago, Patterson-Liston Press Headquarters, everything free. Even your news free. If you haven't done your homework, if you drank too late last night and missed the last limousine out to Elgin or Aurora this morning, if there's no poop of your own on Floyd's speed or Sonny's bad mood, you can turn to the handouts given you in the Press Kit. No need to do your own research. The Kit is part of the free list, an offering of facts with a little love from the Welfare State.

It is so easy, so much is done for you, that you remember those days with nostalgia. When you do get around to paying for yourself, it is a joy to buy your own food, an odd smacking sensation to spring for a drink. It is the Welfare State which makes the pleasure possible. When one buys all one's own drinks, the sensation of paying cash is without much joy, but to pay for a drink occasionally—that's near bliss. Ah, journalism!

The problem of going out and searching for experience is, I think, true for very young writers who just don't have enough to write about. There comes a point where you say, "I want to be a writer. I feel all the urgings of a writer, I feel the penetrating intelligence of a writer in myself, but I don't really know enough." This is where journalism rears its ugly head. It's very hard to enter strange places and learn a lot about them unless you have clout. Kids get into journalism because the moment they flash a card that says they're a bona fide reporter, people often start talking to them. Of course it's a false experience. Hopefully, you develop a sense of how to filter this experience and correct it, re-fract it into what experience might have been like if you hadn't had the peculiar advantage of being a reporter.

I discovered this at the beginning of the Sixties, when I started doing journalism and realized it was a marvelous way for me to work. It was vastly easier than trying to write novels, and I was discouraged with the difficulty of writing fiction at that point. I had run into the business of trying to tell a good story and yet say exceptional things about the nature of the world and society, touch all the ultimates, and still have it read like speed. I always had a terrible time finding my story in the novel. My sto-ries were always ending up begrounded. There I'd be in the middle of the dunes, no gas in the tank. I loved journalism for a little while because it gave me what I'd always been weakest in—exactly that, the story. Then I discovered that this was the hor-ror of it. Audiences liked it better. They'd all been following the same events you'd been seeing up close, and they wanted inter-pretation. It was those critical faculties that were being called for rather than one's novelistic gifts. I must say I succumbed, and spent a good few years working at the edge of journalism be-cause it was so much easier.

During sports events and political conventions, reporters get to-gether in the evening to exchange stories. In effect, the average reporter gives away the stories that his paper is not likely to print and gets other stories that other newspapers or magazines are not interested in. In this media marketplace, everybody winds up using everybody else's stuff to some degree. What is worse, however, is that everybody usually arrives at the same general interpretation. To wit, Jack Kennedy is a lightweight, Nelson Rockefeller is a wonderful guy. Whatever the interpreta-tion is for that week—count on it—it will come out as gospel. So much political wisdom is a consensus of this journalistic market-place. At my end, possessing the confidence of a novelist, I found it was easy to take the larger step of thinking that, yes, the way in which I see this event is likely to be closer to the real story than the way they are seeing it. You can go a long way on that confidence. It's banal to make the remark that all you have to do is look at what is going on, but the trick is to be able to look. That is not easy for the average journalist, whose vision is curtailed by the unrelenting impositions, limitations, and urgencies of his job.

Almost always a reporter must give a false impression of an

event. That is because journalists cannot afford to have too much interest in the mood of an occasion, particularly if it is a political meeting. Invariably, there is an a priori decision that certain elements of the event must be recorded as literally as possible. If a man is giving a speech, his topic is of cardinal importance, and whatever quotations are taken from the speech had best be given accurately; although if you don't know the tone of the speaker—peremptory, fumbling, thundering, hesitant, forthright, uneasy, etc.—you really know very little. The journalistic assumption is that the additional stuff—all those nuances!—are not as crucial as the preordained tenets one is programmed to obey. The long-term tendency is to deaden future history into a gargantuan fact machine. One reason it would be dreadful if the novel died is that it is one of the few forms of Western civilization that attempts to deal with the notion of whole experience.

One of the elements I knew was wrong is that all events had to be boiled down to somewhere between three hundred and three thousand words. I thought the trick was to expand, use twenty thousand words, capture the human wealth of the event. I also began to feel that the personality of the narrator was probably as important as the event. Not that the narrator would be important in his own person; it was not that I, Norman Mailer, could be a balance weight to the Democratic Convention of 1960 but rather that I did come in with a set of prejudices. You, as the reader, couldn't begin to understand this event unless you knew enough about me to reflect upon my bias. Then the reader could say, "Oh well, Mailer is impossibly romantic," or, "Norman is outrageously nihilistic," or, "He sure is a fool." With that sense of superiority, the reader could thus relax sufficiently to enjoy his interpretations of what I reported. It also occurred to me that that is the way we read. We are always saying to ourselves, "Well, John Irving or Updike or Vonnegut"—or whoever it is— "is very good here, but not so good on that." It brought me to a large but obvious conclusion: Objective reporting is a myth. The reader is entitled to be aware of the bent of the man or woman pretending to be that quintessential impostor, the fair and accurate journalist.

On the other hand, journalism is easier to live with than a novel. Give me the events that history put in order for me and I'm content—all I've got to do then is tell the tale. The difficulty of bringing off a truly impressive novel is equal to asking a singer of the stature of Pavarotti to compose his own music. Journalism makes opera singers of novelists. We've got the story, now all we've got to do is go in and show our vocal cords.

In a novel, you've got to decide whether your character turns left or right on a given street. And you have to keep making those decisions through the book. One major decision gone wrong can ruin the job. What makes journalism easy is, I repeat, that you are given the story. If I'd written *The Fight* as a novel, I'd have had to decide: Does Foreman win or Ali? I'd lose six months deciding. So, you know, there it is; Ali won. A marvelous story.

JOURNALISTIC
RESEARCH

———

I t is painful to admit that study of the CIA may not lead to exposure of facts so much as to the epistemology of facts. We will
not get the goods so quickly as we will learn how to construct a
model that will tell us why we cannot get the goods.

EPISTEMOLOGICAL MODEL I

If half the pieces in a jigsaw puzzle are missing, the likelihood is
that something can still be put together. Despite its gaps, the picture may be more or less visible. Even if most of the pieces are
gone, a loose mosaic can be arranged of isolated elements. The
possibility of the real picture being glimpsed under such circumstances is small but not altogether lost. It is just that one would
like to know if the few pieces left belong to the same set.

EPISTEMOLOGICAL MODEL II

Maybe it is the splinters of a mirror rather than the scattered
pieces of a jigsaw that provide a superior ground for the model.
We are dealing not with reality, after all, but that image which
reaches the surface through the cracked looking glass of the
media.

—

A novelist ought to be able to pick up a good bit about a subject just by going into a room. If, for example, you visit an auto-sales showplace with the idea you might buy a car, you could end by deciding to write about the people who work there. One difficulty—you don't know a great deal about the milieu. All the same, you have an insight that feels as if it is your private insight, no one else's. In this good state, it is not that hard to pick up collateral material. Everything you witness is illumined by this private perception. Sometimes, however, you really have to do the research. If it's a large subject, you can spend ages reading related books.

Ancient Evenings, a novel about ancient Egypt, took over a decade to finish. In the beginning, all I knew was that I had certain instincts about death—these intimations had curious similarities to Egyptian notions. The ideas of the ancient Egyptians were certainly not identical with mine, but one element was near. In death, believed the Egyptians (and so did I), you entered upon a second set of adventures, which brought you to a better place or a worse one. That was stimulating. But I had to learn just about everything else on the subject. It's a hell of a way to spend all those years. In fact, I was unfaithful, because, believe me, if you become a serious novelist—dare I say it?—it's almost easier to steal a march on your beloved than on your manuscript. The real question is who or which is more unforgiving, the book or the lady? It can well be the book. In the case of *Ancient Evenings* —and I do speak of that work as a creature—*she* ended up being immensely forgiving. I left her for two years to write *The Executioner's Song.* And it's as if when I came back, she only said, "Hmmm, you look tired. Do your feet hurt? Here, I'll wash them." And there I was right back in Egypt. But often, if you desert a big project, that's the end. It does not come back to you.

There's an enormous commitment to writing a long novel. If you take on something that's larger than yourself, you can end up seriously beached. It's more agreeable to work on a subject about which other authors have already written well. Part of the difficulty of doing my opus was that most Egyptologists had just the sort of style you would expect, and so you not only had to absorb reams of fact but also delouse your literary synapses from the style of the worst and heaviest scholars (who, half the time, were the most essential to read).

That's the worst, this cleaning-out. It is kin to the problem young writers face after they have grown up with bad prose in books and in *newspapers*. They, too, have to pick themselves clean of second-rate texts.

Larry Schiller, who is justly famous for getting people to agree, despite all objections, to interviews, was collaborating with me on research in Russia when I was doing *Oswald's Tale*. We spent most of our time in Minsk, because there were still about thirty people living in the city who had known Lee Harvey Oswald well. (He had lived there for more than two years.) These putative witnesses had never spoken to any reporter about him. For good cause. Right after the assassination, the primal reaction of the KGB, given their mind-set, was that President Kennedy had probably been assassinated by American powers on high and Oswald had been framed because the United States wanted to start a war with Russia. Oswald would, indeed, have been the perfect American for such a purpose. He was in the Soviet Union from 1959 to 1962 and had gone over as a self-declared Communist. So the KGB spread the word to anyone in Minsk who had known him: Don't say a word about Oswald. And for thirty years, no one had spoken. Schiller and I, there in 1992 and 1993, discovered that the Russians who had spent time with him in 1960, '61, and '62 made wonderful witnesses to what Oswald had been like. They hadn't opened their mouths since then, so he was minted in their memory.

The point I'm working toward, however, is that Schiller would sometimes, for a variety of reasons, have trouble obtaining an interview. Then he would pull out all the stops. He would say to the person who did not wish to meet with us, "You *must* be interviewed by Norman Mailer! He is our American Tolstoy!" Astonishingly, that worked when all else failed. As a good Russian, one cannot refuse to speak to Tolstoy—even when he is a pale American reflection.

One time, a very nice middle-class woman, a teacher, was being interviewed by us. But when two interrogators are doing an interview and each is working in a different direction on that day, then each gets infuriated. The interview is going in the wrong direction. We'd interrupt each other at critical moments. Before long, we were roaring at each other, "You're asking the wrong question." "Go screw!" The poor woman was sitting there saying to herself, *This* is the American Tolstoy?

TELEVISION

———

Already there have been a number of remarks made in this book (nearly all derogatory) about television, but there was a time in the early Fifties when I watched it religiously, and the piece that follows underlines the intensity of the adverb attached to "watched." In any event, the piece sets up a nice contrast between the black-and-white TV of that period and the big color palette of the present. Television has changed so much. Intrinsically it remains the same. In fact, the piece from which this extract is taken is titled "Of a Small and Modest Malignancy, Wicked and Bristling with Dots."

In the years before he ever went on TV himself, he used to watch it religiously; after a while, sacrilegiously. It started in the winter he was first smoking marijuana. He smoked it with all the seriousness of what was then his profoundly serious heart. It was 1954, and the drug was more important than any love affair he had ever had. It taught him more. Making love to different women, he would attempt to find that place where marijuana had last left him. It was the arena of the particular sensation he chased, as though he had been given a lovely if ineluctable emotion while watching a bullfight, and so went to the Plaza the following week to look for the same emotion—it did not matter altogether who the bullfighter was.

Since he was then in the opening-out of a career that would later provide a false legend of much machismo, he was still timid. Being deep in pot, and relatively full of life, certainly full of every intimation about himself, he was nonetheless too timid to go out late at night and see what the bars would provide. Since his second wife, not unlike himself in her jangled relations to bravery and cowardice, had usually and prudently gone to bed, he would be up alone at night, his mind teeming, and he would watch TV till the stations shut down. In those days, he made monumental connections on pot. He had to see no more than one animated spiral inserted by a commercial into the guts of a washing machine, a lively spiral that would tunnel right up the tube, and he would try to explain to his friends next day that the advertising agency was promoting the idea that their washing machine was congenial to a housewife's cunt. His friends thought him mad. He examined automobile commercials by the same light and saw that they were no longer selling the car by way of the pretty girl sitting on the fender as once they did; now, they were selling the car itself. The car was the fuck. "Dynaflow does it in oil," the announcer would say of an automatic transmission. So, he would tell his friends. His friends would think him mad and try to dissuade him from smoking too much pot. Marijuana was regarded differently in those days; it offered echoes of *Reefer Madness*.

He would watch Ernie Kovacs and Steve Allen late at night and would recognize that they knew what he knew. They saw how the spiral worked in the washing machine commercial, and why Dynaflow did it in oil. Years later, when Motivational Research was presented to the world, and everybody was ready to tell everybody at a party that an automobile was not used by a man to get a mistress but was the mistress, and a housewife liked to identify the health of her washing machine with her own genito-urinary harmonies—speak no ill of the bowels!—Mailer was merely glad that Vance Packard had done the job. He was behind on too many of his own jobs. Marijuana had flung the separate parts of his brain into too many vivid places. In those days he had perceptions on every subject; was convinced, on the consequence, that he was a genius. He was getting very little writing done.

Still, he clung to his set. It explained the world to him. He was getting hip to everything, and the beauty was that he did not have to venture out.

It would not occur to him until six years later, when he would stab his wife, that it was not timidity which had been his first vice, but violence, a murderous nest of feeling so intransigent that he did not dare to go out at night for good cause, and did not know how to sleep at night without Seconal for even better cause—there was too much hatred at the distance between what he wished to do and what he was able to accomplish. Since his wife, faced with the choice of going to sleep early or entering on a claustrophobic quarrel, would, of course, go to sleep, he would sit by himself from midnight until two in the morning, when the last show would go off the air, the flag would ripple in the wind, and "The Star-Spangled Banner" would be played. In those days, he got to hate "The Star-Spangled Banner." It sounded like the first martial strains of that cancer he was convinced was coming on him, and who knows? If he had not stabbed his wife, he might have been dead in a few years himself—our horror of violence is in its unspoken logic.

So, through those early mornings in the middle of the night when television was his only friend, he knew already that he detested his habit. There was not enough to learn from watching TV. Some indispensable pieces of experience were missing. Except it was worse than that. Something not in existence was also present, some malignancy to burn against his own malignancy, some onslaught of dots into the full pressure of his own constricted vision. Often, when the stations would go off the air and no programs were left to watch, he would still leave the set on. The audio would hum in a tuneless pullulation, and the dots would hiss in an agitation of strange forces. The hiss and the hum would fill the room and then his ears. There was, of course, no clamor—it was nearer to anti-noise dancing in eternity. And watching the empty video, he would recognize it was hardly empty. Bands of gray and lighter gray swam across the set, rollovers swept away dots, and something like sun-spots crackled forth. Then the set went back to the slow scan of the waves and the drone of the audio. He discovered at last that such use of TV was a species of tranquilizer and could deaden the rawest edge of his nerve. Blunted, impalpably bruted by a half-hour of such odorless immersion, he would with the aid of his Seconal be a little more ready to go to sleep.

A few years later, when McLuhan would torment the vitals of a generation of American intellectuals with the unremovable harpoon that "the media is the message," Mailer could give his agreement. The message of TV was the scan of gray on gray and the hum of the sound when there was neither music nor a voice. Much later, in the fall of '72, he would set out to make audiences laugh by comparing President Nixon's then featureless but disturbing personality to a TV screen that is lit when nothing is on the air. Nixon was there, he would remark, to deaden the murderous mood of the Republic. Indeed, it was the best explanation for why a man so unpopular was going to win by so great a majority. If Nixon did not make anyone very happy, neither did the TV set. Its message was equal to Nixon's: I am here to deaden you—you need it!

Maybe America did need it. Brooding over America of the Sixties, that insane expanding America where undercover FBI men were inspiring (wherever they were not committing) the most violent acts of the Left, brooding on that rich and powerful country where puritanism was still as alive as every Baptist, that corporate land with no instinctive response to aesthetics engaged now in the dissemination throughout the world of the worst applied aesthetics in the history of the world, its superhighways the highest form of strip mining, its little office buildings kin to shoeboxes, its big buildings scaled to the module of one cardboard carton set on top of another, the U.S. skyline thereby deserting the high needles of Manhattan for the Kleenex boxes of Dallas; that food-guzzling Republic that froze its food before it would overcook it, and liked to lick ketchup off French fries so soggy they dropped from your fingers like worms—the worst food in the history of the world!—that sex-revolutionary Republic where swinging singles were connecting up with like-units—every other Baptist!—that sadistically revolutionary Republic going into black leather, S-M, and knocking off gooks in rice paddies, defoliating the foliage, digging the hog-resonance of motors between one's legs, and flame-throwers and comic books, and Haight-Ashbury, hitting golf balls on the moon, yes, that America, full of dread, could certainly use TV— I am here to deaden you, you need it!

Those were legitimate feelings for 1972. One had spent a large fraction of a life by then watching TV, and one had long ago had the education of putting oneself on shows. Back in '53 and '54, however, stoned on pot, wafted up and down on Seconal, jammed with ambition, terror, and the common lust to learn the secrets of the world some easy way, the immersion into TV was profound. By it, one could study the world, and the tricks of the world.

So, for instance, would he examine people as strange to him as Igor Cassini, who had a show in those years for snobs and it was hard as fiberglass. TV proved to be more interesting then, for you could see a genuine article regularly, well-groomed, Republican, rich enough to own horses, sexy enough to marry up, and empty enough to find any topic of conversation amusing provided it was void of content. Those were Igor Cassini's guests. Mailer would on such occasions peer right into the tube to get a little nearer to the novelistic wealth.

Or: studying the tourist, he learned much about American fellatio. TV was scintillating for that. Next to the oil of Dynaflow and the spiral in the washing machine came the phallic immanence of the microphone. A twinkle would light up in Steve Allen's eye as he took the mike and cord down the aisle and in and out of impromptu interviews with his audience, snaking the rounded knob right up to the mouth of some starched skinny Middle West matron, lean as whipcord, tense as rectitude, a life of iron disciplines in the vertical wrinkles of the upper lip; the lady would bare her teeth in a snarl and show a shark's mouth as she brought her jaws around to face and maybe bite off that black dob of a knob so near to touching her tongue.

A high school girl would be next, there with the graduating class on a trip to New York, her folks watching back home. She would swoon before the mike. She could not get her mouth open. She would keep dodging in her seat, and Steve would stay in pursuit, mike extended. Two nights ago she dodged for two hours in the back seat of a car. My God, this was in public. She just wouldn't take hold of the mike.

A young housewife, liberal, sophisticated, happy to present her congenial point of view, compliments Mr. Allen on the quality of his show. "We watch you regularly, Steve, and like to think we're not too far behind the times up in Norfolk, Connecticut. That's right, Norfolk, not Norwalk." Her mouth, which has regular lips, is held a regular distance from the microphone. She has been ready to accept. She shows no difficulty with it, no more than she would have with a phallus; two fingers and a thumb keep the thing canted right. There can be nothing wrong, after all, in relations between consenting adults. So speaks her calm.

Then there is a big heavy-set man who owns a grain-and-feed store in Ohio. He prides himself on imperturbable phlegm, and some thrift with words. He is not quite aware of the mike. If a man came into his store and proceeded to expose himself, this proprietor would not see it right away. He might, after all, be explaining the merits and demerits of one feed-mix to another; since he chews no gum when he walks, neither does he offer attention to tangentia as he talks. Now, singled out from the audience to be interviewed, he is stiffnecked, and responds only from that side of his mouth adjacent to the cheek on which Steve is asking the questions; he allows, "New York is a good place to visit, but, yessir, I'll be glad to start up for home," then, bla-looh! he sees it, black blimp-like little object! he blinks, he swallows, he looks at Steve: "I guess I've had my say, Mr. Allen," he says, and shuts up shop. Later he will tell a pinochle partner about the crazy people in New York. "Yes," the friend will acknowledge.

"You bet, Steve," says the next fellow. "I'm awfully glad you selected me. I've always wanted to talk to you." He is fully aware of the mike and what it portends. "Yes, yes, I'm a male secretary, love the work." "It doesn't bother you," asks Steve, "if people say, 'What is that, a male secretary, isn't it supposed to be women's work?'" "Oh, Steve, that doesn't bother me a bit. Here," he says, reaching for the mike. "Do you mind? I'm much more comfortable when I hold it."

"Help yourself," says Steve.

"Oh, I intend to," says the guest. "Life is a feast, and I think we should all get what we can, don't you?"

FILM

———

The making of my first underground movie probably had a good bit to do with the decision many months later to treat myself as the third-person protagonist of *The Armies of the Night*. When I sat down to write the book, I had already edited *Wild 90*, in which I was the leading character. Since there had been way too much of me in the rushes, I had come to see myself as a piece of yard goods about which one could ask "Where can I cut this?" The habit of looking at myself as if I were someone other than myself—a character ready to be described in the third person— had already been established. Parenthetically, I think it's also a way of getting your psychiatry on the cheap. I've never gone to an analyst—I always felt it was not wise to look for the taproot— but I have certainly been more balanced after the years it took in the editing room to extract one hundred minutes of under-ground movie film from forty-five hours of sound-on-film— *Maidstone*, my failed cinematic masterpiece!

Movies are more likely than literature to reach deep feelings in people. Movies are more primitive, or so I would argue. Film delves into deeper states of consciousness. People who can't read are quite able to reach profound reactions in the dark of a theatre. I would also say that to the degree film reaches us in a precise way, it's not very good. Film is best when ambiguous. A truly good film will affect two people profoundly, but often, they will argue for hours over the message. For one, it's a satire, to the other, a tragedy. That's as it should be. Film should reach so far inside the psyche that one person will react in horror even as another is laughing his head off. That's good film. Bad film is when everybody laughs on cue, for then they are being manipulated. They have entered the engines of manipulation of the power-trip institutions.

Time is your money in a film—literally, it's your money. If you, as the director, don't finish a scene scheduled to be done by lunch, then you are going to come back after lunch and possibly lose not half an hour or an hour but two hours. So you're gambling to finish the scene before the break, even if you're not wholly satisfied with the result. Then you find out in the dailies if your gamble was too costly. The scene brought in before lunch needed one more setup. Making movies, you're absolutely in the world. You're a gambler. Whereas in literature, you withdraw from the world in order to perceive it. So movie directing uses another, even opposite, side of yourself from writing. I think you can get closer to your soul in a book, but you come to appreciate the effective or ineffective working of your psyche with a movie. Let me amplify this if I can. In writing a book, there are exceptional moments when you feel as if you're beaming a flood lamp down into the abyss of your soul. By the light of your intuition, you do, in the course of writing a novel, get out to some astonishing places. But when you are making a film, particularly after you've shot it and start editing it, you have to look at the same scene over and over in order to clean out little dead spots. Makes you feel like a surgeon. What it also involves is your taste, and your concentration. Seeing one piece of film over and over, you must still keep your taste alive even as you exercise your ability to concentrate again and again upon the same material. Since I am the one who wrote "Repetition kills the soul," I thought of that remark more than once while working with the movie editor. Of course, it was not meaningless repetition. Rather, I was altering the given a little each time.

———

All this is easy. Much too easy. What is more to the point is that you can lose your mind looking for the point. When it comes to understanding film, we can feel with some justice that we are still at the edge of an aesthetic continent all but uncharted.

The piece that follows, taken from an exposition of my motives in trying to make *Maidstone,* is, I believe, as good as anything I've done in criticism. If your reaction on reading it comes down to "Why is he making it so complicated? I just want to enjoy movies," then let us salute each other and part on mutual terms, since I am obviously not the writer for you.

———

Perhaps a thousand actors and two thousand films can be cited where the movie frame comes alive and there is no dip at the foot of consciousness because something is false at the root. Nonetheless any such appearance of talent was close to magic. The conventional way of making most films usually guaranteed its absence. For there was an element which interfered with motion pictures as much as the blurring of print would hinder the reading of a book, and this flaw derived from the peculiar misapprehension with which the silent film gave way to sound, the supposition that sound-and-film was but an extension of the theatre, even as the theatre was but an extension of literature. It was assumed that movies were there to tell a story. The story might derive from the stage or from the pages of a book or even from an idea for a story, but the film was asked to issue from a detailed plan, which would have lines of dialogue. The making of the movie would be a fulfillment of that script, that literary plan; so each scene would be shaped like a construction unit to build the architecture of the story. It was one of those profoundly false assumptions which seem at the time absolute common sense, yet it was no more natural than to have insisted that a movie was a river and one should always experience, while watching a film, emotions analogous to an afternoon spent on the banks of a stream. That might have been seen instantly as confining, a most confining notion; but to consider the carry-over of the story from literature to the film as equally constricting—no, that was not very evident.

For few people wished to contemplate the size of the job in transporting a novelist's vision of life over to a film; indeed, who in the movie business was going to admit that once literary characters had been converted over to actors, they could not possibly produce the same relation to other actors that the characters once had to each other? Interpretations had to collide. If each actor had his own idea of the dialogue he committed to memory, be certain the director had a better idea. And the producer! Lifetimes of professional craft go into halving such conceptual differences. The director gives up a little of his interpretation, then a little more, then almost all of it. The actor is directed away from his favorite misconceptions (and conceptions). Both parties suffer the rigor mortis of the technical conditions— which are not so close to a brightly lit operating theatre as to a brightly lit morgue. Then the scriptwriter has dependably delivered the scenario with his own private—and sometimes willful— idea buried in it (and if the work is an adaptation, odd lines of the novelist are still turning over). The coherence of the original novel has been cremated and strewn. Now the film is being made with conflicting notions of those scattered ashes. Of course the director is forced back willy-nilly to his script. It is all he can finally depend upon. Given the fundamental, nay, even organic, confusion on a movie set over what everybody is really doing, the company has to pool all differences and be faithful to the script even when the script has lost any relation to the original conception, and has probably begun to constrict the real life which is beginning to emerge on the set. No wonder great novels invariably make the most disappointing movies, and modest novels (like *The Asphalt Jungle*) sometimes make very good movies. It is because the original conception in modest novels is less special and so more capable of being worked upon by any number of other writers, directors, and actors.

Still, the discussion has been too narrow. The film, after all, is fed not only by literature but by the theatre, and the theatre is a conspicuous example of how attractively a blueprint can be unfolded. In fact, the theatre is reduced to very little whenever the collaboration between actors and script is not excellent. Yet the theatre has had to put up with many a similar difficulty. Can it be said that something works in the theatre which only pretends to work in the film? If the first error perpetrated upon movies has been to see them as an adjunct of literature, perhaps the second is the rush to make film an auxiliary of the theatrical arts, until even movies considered classics are hardly more than pieces of filmed theatre.

Of course a film lover could counter by saying that he was not necessarily thinking only of such monuments as *Gone with the Wind* when he used the term *classic*. In fact, he would inquire about *A Night at the Opera* or *The Maltese Falcon*.

The difficulties had obviously begun. The Marx Brothers, for example, stampeded over every line of a script and tore off in enough directions to leave concepts fluttering like ticker tape on the mysterious nature of the movie art. Certainly, any attempt to declare *The Maltese Falcon* a piece of filmed theatre would have to confess that *The Maltese Falcon* was more, a mysterious ineffable possession of "more" and that was precisely what one looked for in a film. It was a hint to indicate some answer to the secrets of film might begin to be found in the curious and never quite explained phenomenon of the movie star. For Humphrey Bogart was certainly an element of natural film, yes, even *the* element which made *The Maltese Falcon* more than an excellent piece of filmed theatre. Thinking of the evocative aesthetic mists of that movie, how could the question not present itself: Why did every piece of good dramatic theatre have to be the enemy of the film? It was unhappily evident that any quick and invigorating theses on the character of movie stars and the hidden nature of the movie might have to wait for a little exposition on the special qualities of theatre.

A complex matter. You might, for instance, have to take into account why people who think it comfortable to be nicely drunk at the beginning of a play would find it no pleasure to go to a movie in the same condition. Pot was more congenial for a film. If the difference for most hardworking actors between movies and theatre seemed hardly more than a trip across a crack, the split to any philosopher of the film was an abyss, just that same existential abyss which lies between booze and the beginnings of the psychedelic.

Existentially, theatre and film were in different dominions (and literature was probably nearer to each of them than they were to each other). The theatre was a ceremony with live priests who had learned by rote to pool their aesthetic instincts for a larger purpose. So theatre partook of a near obscene ceremony: It imitated life in a living place, and it had real people as the imitators. Such imitation was either sacrilege to the roots of life, or a reinforcement of them. Certainly, sentiments called re-

ligious appeared ready to arise whenever a group of people attended a ceremony in a large and dimly lit place. But in fact
anyone who has ever experienced a moment of unmistakable
balance between the audience, the cast, the theatre, and the *manifest* of the play, an awe usually remarked by a silence palpable as
the theatrical velvet of an unvoiced echo, knows that the foundation of the theatre is in the church and in the power of kings,
or at least knows (if theatre goes back to blood sacrifices performed in a cave—which is about where the most advanced theatre seems ready to go) that the more recent foundations were
ecclesiastical and royal. Theatre, at all of its massive best, can be
seen as equal to a ceremony, performed by noblemen who have
power to chastise an audience, savage them, dignify them, warm
them, marry their humors, even create a magical forest where
each human on his seat is a tree and every sense is vibrating to
the rustle of other leaves. One's roots return then to some lost
majesty of pomp and power. Of course, theatre is seldom so
good. None of us have had a night like that recently. Still, theatre has its minutes. While the actor is engaged in an emotional
transaction which is false by its nature (because he knows by
heart the lines of apparently spontaneous passion he will say
next), still he has to be true to the honest difficulty of not knowing whether the audience will believe him or not. His position
on stage is existential—he cannot know in advance if his effort will succeed or not. In turn, the audience must respect
him. For he is at the least brave enough to dare their displeasure. And if he is bad enough . . . well, how can he forget old
nightmares where audiences kill actors? So the actor on stage is
at once a fraud (because he pretends to emotion he cannot by
any Method feel absolutely—*or he would be mad*) and yet is a true
man engaged in a tricky venture, dangerous in its potentialities
for humiliation. That is the strength of the theatre. A vision of
life somewhat different each night (because each audience is different) comes into existence between the actors and the theatre-
goers. What has been lost in the playwright's vision is sometimes
transcended by the mood of a high theatrical hearth.

We are speaking of course only of the best and freshest plays.
Even in a good play something dies about the time an actor rec-
ognizes that he can be mediocre in his performance and survive.
The reputation of the play has become so useful that the audience has become a touch mediocre as well; at this point in the

season the actor inevitably becomes as interesting as a whore in a house after her favorite client has gone for the night.

Nonetheless, it is still reminiscent of orgy to have relations with two worlds of sentience at once, and when fresh, theatre is orgy. On stage, the actor is in communion with the audience and up to his neck in relations with other actors (if they are all still working together). A world of technique supports them. There are ways and means to live and act with half-thought-out lines of dialogue and errors of placement by the director, ways to deal with sentiments which have no ring and situations one knows by heart and still must enter with a pretense of theatrical surprise. An actor's culture exists, after all, for the working up of the false into the all-but-true; actors know the audience will carry the all-but-true over into the real and emotionally stirring if given a chance. So actors develop a full organ of emotional manifests. Large vibrant voices, significant moves. It all works because the actor is literally alive on a stage and therefore can never be false altogether. His presence is the real truth: He is at once the royal center of all eyes, and a Christian up before lions. So his theatrical emotion (which bears the same relation to real emotion that veneer of walnut bears to walnut) is moved by the risk of his position into a technique which offers truth. A skillful actor with false gestures and false emotions elicits our admiration because he tries to establish a vault under which we can seize on the truth since, after all, he has told the lie so well. Why, then, must that be an emotional transaction light-years of the psyche away from the same transaction carried over to film?

It is because the risk in film is of other varieties. No audience is present other than the director, the script girl, the producer, the cameramen and the union grips. And that is a specific audience with the prejudices and tastes of policemen. Indeed the grips usually dress like cops off duty and are built like cops (with the same heavy meat in the shoulders, same bellies oiled on beer), which is not surprising, for they are also in surveillance upon a criminal activity: People are forging emotions under bright lights.

But it is no longer false emotion brought by technique to a point where it can be breathed upon and given life by audiences who do not know the next line. No, now the crew is a set of skills and intelligences. They are as sophisticated to the lines of the scene as the actors themselves. Like cops they see through every fake move and hardly care. The camera must move on cue, ditto the sound boom, lights are to be shifted and the walls slid apart —the action is easily as complex as a professional football team running through the intricacies of a new play or preparing a defense against it.

In fact, the actor does not usually address himself to the technicians. It is the director whose intelligence he will feel first, a charged critical intelligence knowing more of the scene than himself, a center of authority altogether different from a theatrical audience's authority (which is ready to relax with every good sound the actor makes). The movie director, however, does not relax then. The good sound of the actor can turn the plot inside out. No, here, the actor must work into a focus of will. The real face he speaks to, whether a step or ten steps to the side of the director, is a circle of glass as empty of love as an empty glass. That lens is his final audience. It takes precedence over the director and even over the actors he plays with. In the moment of his profoundest passion, as he reaches forward to kiss the heroine with every tenderness, his lips to be famous for their quiver, he is of course slowly and proficiently bringing his mouth up to the erogenous zone of the lens.

On stage, an actor, after twenty years of apprenticeship, can learn to reach the depths of an audience at the moment he is employing the maximum of his technique. A film actor with equivalent technique will have developed superb skills for revealing his reaction to the circle of glass. He can fail every other way, disobey the director or appear incapable of reacting to his direction, leave the other actors isolated from him and with nothing to react to, he can even get his lines wrong, but if he has film technique he will look sensational in the rushes, he will bring life to the scene even if he was death on the set. It is not surprising. There is something sinister about film. *Film is a phenomenon whose resemblance to death has been ignored for too long.* An emotion produced from the churn of the flesh is delivered to a machine, and that machine and its connections manage to produce a flow of images which will arouse some related sentiment in those who watch. The living emotion has passed through a burial ground—and has been resurrected. The living emotion survives as a psychological reality; it continues to exist as a set of images in one's memory which are not too different, as the years go by, from the images we keep of a relative who is dead. Think of a favorite uncle who is gone. Does the apparatus of the mind which flashes his picture before us act in another fashion if we ask for a flash of Humphrey Bogart next? Perhaps it does not. Film seems part of the mechanism of memory, or at the least, a most peculiar annex to memory. For in film we remember events as if they had taken place and we were there. But we were not. The psyche has taken into itself a whole country of fantasy and made it psychologically real, made it a part of memory. We are obviously dealing with a phenomenon whose roots are less defined than the power and glory of king and church. Yes, movies are more mysterious than theatre; even a clue to the undefinable attraction of the movie star is that he remains a point of light in that measureless dark of memory where other scenes have given up their light. He has obviously become a center of meaning to millions, possessed of more meaning than the actor next to him who may be actually more attractive, more interesting—definition of the phenomenon frays as we try to touch it. But has the heart of the discussion been sounded? Does it suggest that movie stars partake of the mysterious psychic properties of film more than other actors? that something in them lends itself to the need of memory for images of the past one can refer to when the mind has need to comprehend something new before it? We have to be careful. It is perhaps not so simple as that. The movie star may also suggest obsession, that negative condition of memory, that painful place to which we return over and over because a fundamental question is still unresolved: Something happened to us years ago which was important, yet we hardly know if an angel kissed us then or a witch, whether we were brave or timid. We return to the ambiguity with pain. The obsession hurts because we cannot resolve it and so are losing confidence in our ability to estimate the present.

Obsession is a wasteful fix. Memory, when it can be free of obsession, is a storehouse to offer up essences of the past capable of digesting most of the problems of the present; memory is even the libido of the ego, sweetening harsh demands of the will when memory is, yes, good. But the movie star seems to serve some double function: The star feeds memory *and* obsession— one need only think back to one's feelings about Marilyn Monroe! The movie star is welcoming but mysterious, unavailable yet intimate, the movie star is the embodiment of a love which could leave us abject, yet we believe we are the only soul the movie star can love. Quintessence of the elusive nature of film, the movie star is like a guide to bring us through the adventures of a half-conscious dream. It is even possible the movie star gives focus to themes of the imagination so large, romantic, and daring that they might never encounter reality: How can an adolescent have any real idea whether he will ever have sex with a beautiful woman or fight for his life? Events so grand need years of psychic preparation. It is therefore possible that the dream life of the film exists not only to provide escape but to prepare the psyche for apocalyptic moments which most likely will never come.

Some differences of film from theatre may then have been noted. Theatre works on our ideas of social life and our understanding of manners. At its most generous theatre creates a communion of bodies and a savory of the emotions—it becomes a feast and a fuck. But film speaks to the lost islands of the mind. Film lives somewhere in that underground river of the psyche which travels from the domain of sex through the deeps of memory and the dream, on out into the possible montages of death—we need only think of any man who was rescued from drowning after he thought he was on the last trip down. Does he ever relate the experience without speaking of the sensation that his life became a film running backward? *It is as if film has an existence within the brain which may be comparable to memory and the dream,* be indeed as real as memory and the dream, be even to some degree as functional. It was as if the levels of that existential river which runs into ultimate psychic states would no longer read as perhaps once it did: sex—memory—dream—death; but now it flows through a technological age and so has to be described by way of sex—memory—*film*—dream—death. Theatre has to be in the world of manners, but film is in the physiology of the psyche. For that reason, perhaps, film comes nearest to a religion as the movie houses are empty; it speaks across all the lonely traverses of the mind; it is at its most beautiful in precisely those places it is least concrete, least theatrical, most otherworldly, most ghostly, most lingering unto death—then the true experience of the film as some Atlantis of the psyche will manifest itself, and directors like Antonioni and Bergman will show us that the film inhabits a secret place where the past tense of memory and the future intimations of the dream are interchangeable, are partners in the film: There is an unmistakable quality to any film which is not made as filmed theatre but rather appears as some existence we call film. That existence runs through Chaplin and *Sunset Boulevard* and *Persona*—it runs through home movies. It was Warhol's talent to perceive that in every home movie there is a sense of Time trying to express itself as a new kind of creation, a palpability which breathes in the *being* of the film. The best of works and some of the worst of film works have this quality. One can even find it for flashes in cranky old battered films of the purest mediocrity late at night on TV, B-films without an instant of talent, yet the years have added magic to what was once moronic—Time is winking her eye as we look at the film. Time suddenly appears to us as a wit.

Of course, there are movies which have delivered huge pleasures to millions and never were film at all, just celluloid theatre convertible to cash. Some were good, some very good, some awful, but the majority of motion pictures, particularly the majority of expensive ones, have always labored against the umbilical antipathy of film for theatre. They were, no matter how good as filmed theatre, never equal to theatre at its best—rather, scaled-down repasts for the eye and ear. They had a kind of phlegmatic tempo and all-too-well-lit color which rarely hindered them from reaching lists for the Ten Best Pictures of the year. They were pictures like *Oklahoma!, South Pacific, The Sound of Music, Mary Poppins,* and *The Best Years of Our Lives.* They were even such critical favorites as *Marty, Born Yesterday, Brief Encounter,* and *The Seven Year Itch,* or *Anne of the Thousand Days,* add *Lust for Life, All About Eve, Around the World in Eighty Days, West Side Story.* All that celluloid was super-technique for audiences who had not necessarily ever seen a play but were constantly nourished in the great cafeteria of the American Aesthetic. To the owners of that cafeteria there was something obscene in the idea that one should not be able to translate a book into a play, film, or TV series. So, the categories remained apart, and the difference between the movies just named and films like *Zabriskie Point, Belle de Jour, Limelight, Diabolique, 8½, The Bicycle Thief, The 400 Blows, High Noon, Easy Rider,* and *Weekend* was as the difference between crud and sustenance for that needy if ghostly part of the psyche the film was supposed to enrich.

Very well. There was film and filmed theatre, there were relatively pure movies, and there were money-making motion pictures, which had almost nothing to do with movies or memory or dream but were filmed circus for the suckers who proceeded to enjoy them enormously, suckers who loved them for their binding glue, and the status of seeing them, and the easy massage such pictures gave to emotions real theatre might have satisfied more. These motion pictures, made for no motive more in focus than the desire for money, were derived from plays, or were written and directed as filmed plays, they composed three-quarters to nine-tenths of the motion pictures which were made, and they might yet be the terminal death of Hollywood, for they were color television on enormous screens and so failed more often than they succeeded.

Of course the best films were just as often watched in empty theatres. Such films provided experiences which were later as pure in recollection as splendid or tragic days in one's life, they were not unlike the memory of some modest love which did not survive but was tender in retrospect for now it lived with the dignity of old love. Such films also changed as one remembered them, since they had become part of one's psychological life. Like love, they partook a little of some miracle, they had emerged from the abominable limitations of the script, yes, they had emerged out of some mysterious but wholly agreeable lack of focus toward that script in the intent of the director and/or the actor, they were subtly attached to a creative mist, they had the ambiguity of film. For if filmed theatre could sometimes be effective, sometimes be even as perfect and deserving of admiration as *Midnight Cowboy* or *On the Waterfront*, such pictures still had their aesthetic fired by the simpler communication of the theatre, where relations between actors usually produced a dramatic outcome as capable of definition as the last line of a family fight. "Go to an analyst" turned out to be the message, or "Lover, we'll get along," or "God bless us, we're unhappy, but we'll stick for the kids." If it is theatre so rich as *The Little Foxes*, it will say, "I am prepared to kill you, and I will." Since the need of a stage actor is to draw an audience together, his instinct is to simplify the play and concentrate it, give it a single crisp flavor. So theatre speaks. Powerfully or with banality, comically or in the botch of hysteria, it speaks, secretly it almost always speaks vulgarly, for almost always it says, "We're here to tell you something about life. We've got a piece of the meat for you." Of course if it is bad theatre, conceived in advance as a television series or any other form of Cafeteria, then it is only there to tell you something about public opinion and how that works at the lowest common denominator. But good or bad, theatre functions at its simple best when every resonance of the evening can collect about a single point—that place where the actors seduced the audience to meet the play.

Film, however, is shown to audiences who do not often react together. Some laugh, while others are silent, some are bored. Few share the same time. They have come in on the movie at different places. For film always speaks of death. Theatre rouses desires between the living audience and the living actors; film stirs suicide pacts where each individual in the audience goes over the horizon alone with the star; film speaks of the ambiguity of death—is it nothingness we go to, or eternal life? Is it to peace we travel or the perilous migrations of the soul? So the ambiguity of the movie star is essential, and it helps to understand that subtle emptiness which is usually present in the colors of their acting, that pause in the certainty of what they would say, that note of distraction and sorrows on the other side of the hill, that hint they are thinking of a late date they will meet after this guy is gone. Movie stars are caught in the complexity of the plot but they do not belong to it altogether, as stage actors do. It does not matter of whom we speak: whether it is Garbo or Harlow or Marilyn Monroe, Carole Lombard or Myrna Loy, even Dottie Lamour or Grable, the star is still one misty wink of the eye away from clear presentation. Even Cagney, phallic as a column of rock, had the hint of bells ringing in his head from blows some big brother gave him in years gone by, and Gable's growling voice always seemed to hint at one big hunk of *other* business he would have to take care of in a little while. The charisma of the movie star spoke of associations with tangential thoughts, with dissipations of the story point into ripples which went out wider and wider, out to the shores of some land only the waves of the movies could wash.

———

The first time one has a profound sexual act, there is, when it's all over, this shocked, stunned, incredible recognition: "Why, God; God exists." That usually happens in sex rather than in love because it's got to happen quickly, a sudden revelation. So there are certain advantages to one-night stands. One brings none of one's baggage to a one-night stand and that makes it possible to have, once in a while, extraordinary emotions. The average one-night stand is, after all, not necessarily a small disaster, but unless it's very good indeed, it can leave very little. All the same, one-night stands can be exceptional; and when that happens, one often has a sense of wonder that is not unlike religious sentiment. For the experience is separate from the person—you don't know the person—it comes from something in sex itself. Sex may be something that's outside of people, something out there.

Last Tango in Paris is, of course, built on this premise.

TANGO, LAST TANGO

To pay one's $5 and join the full house at the Trans-Lux for the evening show of *Last Tango in Paris* is to be reminded once again that the planet is in a state of pullulation. The seasons accelerate. The snow, which was falling in November, had left by the first of March. Would our summer arrive at Easter and end with July? It is all that nuclear radiation, says every aficionado of the occult. And we pullulate. Like an ant-hive beginning to feel the heat.

We know that the century required for a minor art to move from commencement to decadence is off the board. Whole fashions in film are born, thrive, and die in twenty-four months. Still! It is only a half year since Pauline Kael declared to the readers of *The New Yorker* that the presentation of *Last Tango in Paris* at the New York Film Festival on October 14, 1972, was a date that "should become a landmark in movie history—comparable to May 29, 1913—the night *Le Sacre du Printemps* was first performed—in music history," and then went on to explain that the newer work had "the same kind of hypnotic excitement as the *Sacre*, the same primitive force, and the same jabbing, thrusting eroticism. . . . Bertolucci and Brando have altered the face of an art form." Whatever could have been shown on screen to make Kael pop open for a film? "This must be the most powerfully erotic movie ever made, and it could turn out to be the most liberating movie ever made. . . ." Could this be our own Lady Vinegar, our quintessential cruet? The first frigid of the film critics was treating us to her first public *frisson*! Prophets of Baal, praise Kael! We had obviously no ordinary hour of cinema to contemplate.

Now, a half year later, the movie is history, has all the palpability of the historic. Something just discernible has already happened to humankind as a result of it, or at least to that audience who are coming into the Trans-Lux to see it. They are a crew. They have unexpected homogeneity for a movie audience, compose, indeed, so thin a sociological slice of the New York and suburban sausage that you cannot be sure your own ticket isn't what was left for the toothpick, while the rest of the house has been bought at a bite. At the least, there is the same sense of aesthetic oppression one feels at a play when the house is filled with a theatre party. So, too, is the audience at *Tango* an infarct of middle-class anal majesties—if Freud hadn't given us the clue, a reader of faces could decide all on his own that there had to be some social connection between sex, shit, power, violence, and money. But these middle-class faces have advanced their historical inch from the last time one has seen them. They are this much closer now to late Romans.

Whether matrons or young matrons, men or boys, they are *swingers*. The males have wife-swapper mustaches, the women are department-store boutique. It is as if everything recently and incongruously idealistic in the middle class has been used up in the years of resistance to the Vietnamese War—now, bring on the Caribbean. Amazing! In America, even the Jews have come to look like the French middle class, which is to say that the egocentricity of the Fascist mouth is on the national face. Perhaps it is the five-dollar admission, but this audience has an obvious obsession with sex as the confirmed core of a wealthy life. It is enough to make one ashamed of one's own obsession (although where would one delineate the difference?). Maybe it is that this audience, still in March, is suntanned, or at the least made up to look suntanned. The red and orange of their skins will match the famous "all uterine" colors—so termed by the set designer—of the interiors in *Last Tango*.

In the minute before the theatre lights are down, what a tension is in the house. One might as well be in the crowd just before an important fight commences. It is years since one has watched a movie begin with such anticipation. And the tension holds as the projection starts. We see Brando and Schneider pass each other in the street. Since we have all been informed—by *Time* no less—we know they are going to take carnal occupation of each other, and very soon. The audience watches with anxiety as if it is also going to be in the act with someone new, and the heart (and for some, the bowels) shows a tremor between earthquake and expectation. Maria Schneider is so sexual a presence. None of the photographs has prepared anybody for this. Rare actresses, just a few, have flesh appeal. You feel as if you can touch them on the screen. Schneider has nose appeal—you can smell her. She is every eighteen-year-old in a mini-skirt and a maxi-coat who ever promenaded down Fifth Avenue in the inner arrogance that proclaims "My cunt is my chariot."

We have no more than a few minutes to wait. She goes to look at an apartment for rent, Brando is already there. They have passed in the street, and by a telephone booth; now they are in an empty room. Abruptly Brando cashes the check Stanley Kowalski wrote for us twenty-five years ago—he fucks the heroine standing up. It solves the old snicker of how do you do it in a telephone booth?—he rips her panties open. In our new line of *New Yorker*–approved superlatives, it can be said that the cry of the fabric is the most thrilling sound to be heard in World Culture since the four opening notes of Beethoven's Fifth.* It is, in fact, a hell of a sound, small, but as precise as the flash of a match above a pile of combustibles, a way for the director to say, "As you may already have guessed from the way I established my opening, I am very good at movie making, and I have a superb pair, Brando and Schneider—they are sexual heavyweights. Now I place my director's promise upon the material: You are going to be in for a grave and wondrous experience. We are going to get to the bottom of a man and a woman."

So intimates Bertolucci across the silence of that room empty of furniture, as Brando and Schneider, fully dressed, lurch, grab, connect, hump, scream, and are done in less than a minute, their orgasms coming on top of one another like refuse cans tumbling down a hill. They fall to the floor, and fall apart. It is as if a hand grenade has gone off in their entrails. A marvelous scene, good as a passionate kiss in real life, then not so good, because there has been no shot of Brando going up Schneider, and since the audience has been watching in all the somber awe one

---

*John Simon, as predictable in his critical reactions as a headwaiter, naturally thought *Last Tango* was part of the riff-raff. Since it is Simon's temper to ignore details, he not only does not hear the panties tearing (some ears reside in the music of the spheres) but announces that Schneider, beasty abomination, is wearing none.

214 · THE SPOOKY ART

would bring to the first row of a medical theatre, it is like seeing an operation without the entrance of the surgeon's knife.

One can go to any hard-core film and see fifty phalluses going in and out of as many vaginas in four hours (if anyone can be found who stayed four hours). There is a monumental abstractedness about hard core. It is as if the more a player can function sexually before a camera, the less he is capable of offering any other expression. Finally, the sexual organs show more character than the actors' faces. One can read something of the working conditions of a life in some young girl's old and irritated cunt, one can even see triumphs of the human spirit—old and badly burned labia which still come to glisten with new life, capital! There are phalluses in porno whose distended veins speak of the integrity of the hardworking heart, but there is so little specific content in the faces! Hard core lulls after it excites, and finally it puts the brain to sleep.

But Brando's real cock up Schneider's real vagina would have brought the history of film one huge march closer to the ultimate experience it has promised since its inception (which is to re-embody life). One can even see how on opening night at the Film Festival, it did not matter so much. Not fully prepared for what was to come, the simulated sex must have quivered like real sex the first time out. Since then we have been told the movie is great, so we are prepared to resist greatness, and have read in *Time* that Schneider said, " 'We were never screwing on stage. I never felt any sexual attraction for him . . . he's almost fifty you know, and'—she runs her hand from her torso to her midriff—'he's only beautiful to here!' "

So one watches differently. Yes, they *are* simulating. Yes, there is something slightly unnatural in the way they come and fall apart. It is too stylized, as if paying a few subtle respects to Kabuki. The real need for the real cock of Brando into the depths of the real actress might have been for those less exceptional times which would follow the film long after it opened and the reaction had set in.

Since *Tango* is, however, the first major film with a respectable budget, a superbly skilled young director, an altogether accomplished cameraman, and a great actor who is ready to do more than dabble in improvisation, indeed will enter heavily into such a near to untried filmic procedure, so the laws of improvisation are before us, and the first law to recognize is that it is next to impossible to build on too false a base. The real problem in movie improvisation is to find some ending that is true to what has gone before and yet is sufficiently untrue to enable the actors to get out alive.

We will come back to that. It is, however, hardly time to let go of our synopsis. Real or simulated, opening night or months later, we know after five minutes that, at the least, we are in for a thoroughgoing study of a man and a woman, and the examination will be close. Brando rents the empty apartment; they will visit each other there every day. His name is Paul, hers is Jeanne, but they are not to learn each other's names yet. They are not to tell one another such things, he informs her. "We don't need names here . . . we're going to forget everything we knew. . . . Everything outside this place is bullshit."

They are going to search for pleasure. We are back in the existential confrontation of the century. Two people are going to fuck in a room until they arrive at a transcendent recognition or some death of themselves. We are dealing not with a plot but with a theme that is open range for a hundred films. Indeed we are face to face with the fundamental structure of porno—the difference is that we have a director who by the measure of porno is Eisenstein, and actors who are as gods. So the film takes up the simplest and richest of structures. To make love in an empty apartment, then return to a separate life. It is like every clandestine affair the audience has ever had, only more so—no names! Every personal demon will be scourged in the sex—one will obliterate the past! That is the huge sanction of anonymity. It is equal to a new life.

What powerful biographical details we learn, however, on the instant they part. Paul's wife is a suicide. Just the night before, she has killed herself with a razor in a bathtub; the bathroom is before us, red as an abattoir. A sobbing chambermaid cleans it while she speaks in fear to Paul. It is not even certain whether the wife is a suicide or he has killed her—that is almost not the point. It is the bloody death suspended above his life like a bleeding torso—it is with that crimson existence before his eyes that he will make love on the following days.

Jeanne, in her turn, is about to be married to a young TV director. She is the star in a videofilm he is making about French youth. She pouts, torments her fiancé, delights in herself, delights in the special idiocy of men. She can cuckold her young director to the roots of his eyes. She also delights in the violation she will make of her own bourgeois roots. In this TV film she makes within the movie she presents her biography to her fiancé's camera: She is the daughter of a dead Army officer who was sufficiently racist to teach his dog to detect Arabs by smell. So she is well brought up—there are glimpses of a suburban villa on a small walled estate; it is nothing less than the concentrated family honor of the French Army she will surrender when Brando proceeds a little later to bugger her.

These separate backgrounds divide the film as neatly between biography and fornication as those trick highball glasses which present a drawing of a man or a woman wearing clothes on the outside of the tumbler and nude on the inside. Each time Brando and Schneider leave the room, we learn more of their lives beyond the room; each time they come together, we are ready to go further. In addition, as if to enrich his theme for students of film, Bertolucci offers touches from the history of French cinema. The life preserver in *L'Atalante* appears by way of homage to Vigo, and Jean-Pierre Léaud of *The 400 Blows* is the TV director, the boy now fully grown. Something of the brooding echo of *Le Jour Se Lève* and Arletty is also with us, that somber memory of Jean Gabin wandering along the wet docks in the dawn, waiting for the police to pick him up after he has murdered his beloved. It is as if we are to think not only of this film but of other sexual tragedies French cinema has brought us, until the sight of each gray and silent Paris street is ready to evoke the lost sound of the *Bal musette* and the sad near-silent wash of the Seine. Nowhere as in Paris can doomed lovers succeed in passing sorrow, drop by drop, through the blood of the audience's heart.

Yet as the film progresses with every skill in evidence, while Brando gives a performance that is unforgettable (and Schneider shows every promise of becoming a major star), as the historic buggeries and reamings are delivered, and the language breaks through barriers not even yet erected—no general of censorship could know the armies of obscenity were so near!—as these shocks multiply, and lust goes up the steps to love, something bizarre happens to the film. It fails to explode. It is a warehouse of dynamite and yet something goes wrong.

One leaves the theatre bewildered. A fuse was never ignited. But where was it set to go off? One looks to retrace the line of the story.

So we return to Paul trying to rise out of the bloody horizon of his wife's death. We even have some instinctive comprehension of how he must degrade his beautiful closet-fuck; indeed we are even given the precise detail that he will grease her ass with butter before he buggers her family pride. A scene or two later, he tricks forth her fear of him by dangling a dead rat, which he offers to eat. "I'll save the asshole for you," he tells her. "Rat's asshole with mayonnaise."* (The audience roars—Brando knows audiences.) She is standing before him in a white wedding gown—she has run away from a TV camera crew that was getting ready to film her pop wedding. She has rushed to the apartment in the rain. Now shivering, but recovered from her fear, she tells him she has fallen in love with somebody. He tells her to take a hot bath or she'll catch pneumonia, die, and all he'll get is "to fuck the dead rat."

No, she protests, she's in love.

"In ten years," says Brando looking at her big breasts, "you're going to be playing soccer with your tits." But the thought of the other lover is grinding away at him. "Is he a good fucker?"

"Magnificent."

"You know, you're a jerk. 'Cause the best fucking you're going to get is right here in this apartment."

No, no, she tells him, the lover is wonderful, a mystery . . . different.

"A local pimp?"

"He could be. He looks it."

She will never, he tells her, be able to find love until she goes "right up into the ass of death." He is one lover who is not afraid of metaphor. "Right up his ass—till you find a womb of fear. And then maybe you'll be able to find him."

"But I've found this man," says Jeanne. Metaphor has continued long enough for her. "He's you. You're that man."

In the old scripted films, such a phrase was plucked with a movie composer's chord. But this is improvisation. Brando's in-

---

*Dialogue from *Last Tango in Paris* was not entirely written in advance but was in part an improvisation. In other words, a small but important part of the screenplay has in effect been written by Brando.

stant response is to tell her to get a scissors and cut the fingernails on her right hand. Two fingers will do. Put those fingers up
his ass.

"*Quoi?*"

"Put your fingers up my ass, are you deaf? Go on."

No, he is not too sentimental. Love is never flowers, but farts
and flowers. Plus every superlative test. So we see Brando's face
before us—it is that tragic angelic mask of incommunicable anguish which has spoken to us across the years of his uncharted
heroic depths. Now he is entering that gladiator's fundament
again, and before us and before millions of faces yet to come she
will be his surrogate bugger, real or simulated. What an entrance into the final images of history! He speaks to us with her
body behind him and her fingers just conceivably up him. "I'm
going to get a pig" are the words which come out of his tragic
face, "and I'm going to have a pig fuck you"—yes, the touch on
his hole has broken open one gorgon of a fantasy—"and I want
the pig to vomit in your face. And I want you to swallow the
vomit. You going to do that for me?"

"Yeah."

"Huh?"

"Yeah!"

"And I want the pig to die while"—a profound pause—"while
you're fucking him. And then you have to go behind, and I want
you to smell the dying farts of the pig. Are you going to do that
for me?"

"Yes, and more than that. And worse than before."

He has plighted a troth. In our year of the twentieth century,
how could we ever contract for love with less than five hundred
pounds of pig shit? With his courage to give himself away, we
finally can recognize the tragedy of his expression across these
twenty-five years. That expression has been locked into the im-
possibility of ever communicating such a set of private thoughts.
Yet he has just done it. He is probably the only actor in the world
who could have done it. He is taking the shit that is in him and
leaving it on us. How the audience loves it. They have come to
be covered. The world is not polluted for nothing. There is
some profound twentieth-century malfunction in the elimina-
tion of waste. And Brando is on to it. A stroke of genius to have
made a speech like that. Over and over, he is saying in this film

that one only arrives at love by springing out of the shit in one-self.

So he seeks to void his eternal waste over the wife's suicide. He sits by her laid-out corpse in a grim hotel room, curses her, weeps, proceeds to wipe off the undertaker's lipstick, broods on her lover (who lives upstairs in the hotel), and goes through some bend of the obscure, for now, off-stage, he proceeds to disappear. We realize this as we see Jeanne in the empty rooms. Paul has disappeared. He has ordered her to march into the farts of the pig for nothing. So she calls her TV director to look at the empty apartment—should they rent it? The profound practicality of the French bourgeoisie is squatting upon us. She appreciates the value of a few memories to offer sauce for her lean marriage. But the TV director must smell this old cooking, for he takes off abruptly after telling her he will look for a better apartment.

Suddenly Brando is before her again on the street. Has he been waiting for her to appear? He looks rejuvenated. "It's over," she tells him. "It's over," he replies. "Then it begins again." He is in love with her. He reveals his biography, his dead wife, his unromantic details. "I've got a prostate like an Idaho potato but I'm still a good stick man. . . . I suppose if I hadn't met you I'd probably settle for a hard chair and a hemorrhoid." They move on to a hall, some near mythical species of tango palace where a dance contest is taking place. They get drunk and go on the floor. Brando goes in for a squalid parody of the tango. When they're removed by the judges, he flashes his bare ass.

Now they sit down again and abruptly the love affair is terminated. Like that! She is bored with him. Something has happened. We do not know what. Did his defacement of the tango injure some final nerve of upper French deportment? Too small a motive. Must we decide that sex without a mask is no longer love, that no mask is more congenial to passion than to be without a name in the bed of a strange lover?

There are ten reasons why her love could end, but we know none of them. She merely wants to be rid of him. Deliver me from a fifty-year-old may even be her only cry.

She tries to flee. He follows. He follows her on the Métro and all the way to her home. He climbs the spiraling stairs as she mounts in the slow elevator, he rams into her mother's apart-

ment with her, breathless, chewing gum, leering. Now he is all
cock. He is the memory of every good fuck he has given her.
"This is the title shot, baby. We're going all the way."

She takes out her father's army pistol and shoots him. He
murmurs, "Our children, our children, our children will remember . . ." and staggers out to the balcony, looks at the Paris
morning, takes out his chewing gum, fixes it carefully to the underside of the iron railing in a move that is pure broth of
Brando—culture is a goat turd on the bust of Goethe—and dies.
The angel with the tragic face slips off the screen. And proud
Maria Schneider is suddenly and most unbelievably reduced to
a twat copping a plea. "I don't know who he is," she mutters in
her mind to the oncoming *flics*. "He followed me in the street, he
tried to rape me, he is insane. I do not know his name. I do not
know who he is. He wanted to rape me."

The film ends. The questions begin. We have been treated to
more cinematic breakthrough than any film—at the least—since
I Am Curious, Yellow. In fact we have gone much further. It is hard
to think of any film that has taken a larger step. Yet if this is "the
most powerful erotic film ever made," then sex is as Ex-Lax. For
we have been given a bath in shit with no reward. The film, for
all its power, has turned inside out by the end. We have been
asked to follow two serious and more or less desperate lovers
as they go through the locks of lust and defecation, through
some modern species of homegrown cancer cure, if you will,
and have put up with their modern depths—shit on the face of
the beloved and find love!—only to discover a peculiar extortion
in the aesthetic. We have been taken on this tour down to the
prostate big as an Idaho potato only to recognize that we never
did get into an exploration of the catacombs of love, passion, in-
fancy, sodomy, tenderness, and the breaking of emotional ice,
instead only wandered from one onanist's oasis to another.

It is, however, a movie that has declared itself, by the power of
its opening, and so the measure of its success or failure is by the
same sexual aesthetic. Rarely has a film's value depended so
much on the power or lack of power of its ending, even as a fuck
that is full of promise is ready to be pinched by a poor end. So,
in *Tango*, there is no gathering of forces for the conclusion, no
whirling of sexual destinies (in this case, the audience and the
actors) into the same funnel of becoming, no flying out of the

senses in pursuit of a new vision, no, just the full charge into a blank wall, a masturbator's spasm—came for the wrong reason and on the wrong thought—and one is thrown back, shattered, too ubiquitously electrified, and full of criticism. Now the recollected flaws of the film eat at the pleasure, even as the failed orgasm of a passionate act will call the character of the passion into question.

So the walk out of the theatre is with anger. The film has been in reach of the greatness Kael has been talking about, but the achievement has only been partial. The performance by Brando has been unique, historic, without compare—it is just possible, however, that it has gone entirely in the wrong direction. He has been like a lover who keeps telling consummate dirty jokes until the ravaged dawn, when the girl will say, "Did you come to knit or to fuck?" He has come with great honor and dignity and exceptional courage to bare his soul. But in a solo. We are being given a fuck film without the fuck. It is like a Western without the horses.

Now the subtle sense of displacement that has hung over the movie is clear. There has been no particular high passion loose. Brando is so magnetic an actor, Schneider is so attractive, and the scenes are so intimate that we assume there is sexual glue between their parts, but it is our libido which has been boiling that glue and not the actors on the screen. If Kael has had a sexual liberation with *Tango,* her libido is not alone—the audience is also getting their kicks—by digging the snots of the celebrated. (Liberation for the Silent Majority may be not to attend a fuck but hear dirty jokes.) So the real thrill of *Tango* for $5 audiences becomes the peephole Brando offers us on Brando. They are there to hear a world-famous actor say in reply to "What strong arms you have"

"The better to squeeze a fart out of you."

"What long nails you have."

"The better to scratch your ass with."

"Oh, what a lot of fur you have."

"The better to let your crabs hide in."

"Oh, what a long tongue you have."

"The better to stick in your rear, my dear."

"What's this for?"

"That's your happiness and my ha-penis."

Pandemonium of pleasure in the house. Who wants to watch an act of love when the ghost of Lenny Bruce is back? The crowd's joy is that a national celebrity is being obscene on screen. To measure the media magnetism of such an act, ask yourself how many hundreds of miles you might drive to hear Richard Nixon speak a line like "We're just taking a flying fuck at a rolling doughnut," or, "I went to the University of the Congo; studied whale fucking." Only liberal unregenerates would be so progressive as to say they would not drive a mile. No, one could start mass migrations if Nixon were to give Brando's pig-and-vomit address to the test of love.

Let us recognize the phenomenon. It would be so surrealistic an act, we could not pass Nixon by. Surrealism has become our objective correlative. A private glimpse of the great becomes the alchemy of the media, the fool's gold of the century of communication. In the age of television we know everything about the great but how they fart—the ass wind is, ergo, our trade wind. It is part of Brando's genius to recognize that the real interest of audiences is not in having him portray the tender passages and murderous storms of an unruly passion between a man and a woman, it is rather to be given a glimpse of his kinks. His kinks offer sympathetic vibration to their kinks. The affirmation of passion is that we rise from the swamps of our diapers—by whatever torturous route—to the cock and the cunt; it is the acme of the decadent to go from the first explosive bout of love in *Tango* down to the trimmed fingernails up his rectum.

Then follows the murder. Except it does not follow. It has been placed there from the beginning as the required ending in Bertolucci's mind; it has already been written into the screenplay first prepared with Trintignant and Dominique Sanda in mind. But complications and cast changes occurred. Sanda was pregnant, et cetera. Brando appeared, and Schneider was found. Yet the old ending is still there. Since it did not grow convincingly out of the material in the original script, it appears, after Brando's improvisation, to be fortuitous altogether.

In the original screenplay, the dialogue is so general and the characters so vague that one has to assume Trintignant, Sanda, and Bertolucci planned to give us something extraordinary precisely by overcoming their pedestrian script. It is as if Bertolucci purposely left out whole trunklines of plot in order to discover them in the film. Only it was Brando who came along rather than Trintignant to make a particular character out of a general role, to "superimpose"—in accordance with Bertolucci's desire—his own character as Marlon Brando, as well as something of his life, and a good bit of his private obsessions. As he did that, however, the film moved away from whatever logic the script had originally possessed. For example, in the pre-Brando treatment, we would have been obliged to listen to the following:

LEON (alias Paul): I make you die, you make me die, we're two murderers, each other's. But who succeeds in realizing this is twice the murderer. And that's the biggest pleasure: watching you die, watching you come out of yourself, white-eyed, writhing, gasping, screaming so loud that it seems like the last time.

Oo la la! We are listening to a French intellectual. It is for good cause that Bertolucci wants to superimpose Brando's personality. Anything is preferable to Leon. And Brando most certainly obliterates this mouthy analysis, creates instead a character who is half noble and half a lout, an overlay drawn on transparent paper over his own image. Paul is an American, ex-boxer, ex-actor, ex-foreign correspondent, ex-adventurer, and now, with the death of his wife, ex-gigolo. He is that character and yet he is Brando even more. He is indeed so much like Brando that he does not quite fit the part of Paul—he talks just a little too much, and is a hint too distinguished to be the proprietor of a cheap flophouse at the age of fifty—let us say that at the least Paul is close enough to the magnetic field of Marlon for an audience to be unable to comprehend why Jeanne would be repelled. Who cares, if it is Marlon? On the other hand, he is also being Marlon the Difficult, Marlon the Indian from the Underworld, Marlon the shade of the alienated, Marlon the young star who when asked on his first trip to Hollywood what he would like in the way of personal attention and private creature comfort points to the nerve-jangled pet he has brought with him and says, "Get my monkey fucked."

Yes, he is studying whale-pronging in the Congo. He is the raucous out-of-phase voice of the prairie. Afterward, contemplating the failure, we realize he has been shutting Schneider off. Like a master boxer with a hundred tricks, he has been out-acting her (with all his miser's hoard of actor's lore), has been stealing scenes from her while she is nude and he is fully dressed, what virtuosity! But it is unfair. She is brimming to let go. She wants to give the young performance of her life and he is tapping her out of position here, tricking her there—long after it is over we realize he does not want the fight of the century but a hometown decision. He did not come to fuck but to defecate into the open-mouthed wonders of his audience and take his cancer cure in public. It is the fastest way! Grease up the kinks and bring in the pigs. We'd take a stockyard of pigs if he would get into what the movie is about, but he is off on the greatest solo of his life and artists as young as Schneider and Bertolucci are hardly going to be able to stop him.

So he is our greatest actor, our noblest actor, and he is also our national lout. Could it be otherwise in America? Yet a huge rage stirs. He is so great. Can he not be even greater and go to the bottom of every fine actor's terror—which is to let go of the tricks that ring the person and enter the true arena of improvisation? It is there that the future of the film may exist, but we won't find out until a great actor makes the all-out effort.

But now we are back to the core of the failure in *Last Tango*. It is down in the difficulty of improvisation, in the recognition that improvisation that is anything less than the whole of a film is next to no improvisation. It has diminished from the dish to a spice that has been added to the dish (usually incorrectly). Bertolucci is a superb young director, adventurous, steeped in film culture, blessed with cinematic grace. He gives us a movie with high ambition, considerable risk, and a sense of the past. Yet he plows into the worst trap of improvisation—it is the simple refusal of film makers to come to grips with the implacable logic of the problem. One does not add improvisation to a script that is already written and with an ending that is locked up. No matter how agreeable the particular results may be, it is still the entrance of tokenism into aesthetics: "You blacks may work in this corporation and are free to express yourselves provided you don't do anything a responsible white employee won't do." Stay true to the script. It reduces improvisation to a free-play period in the middle of a strict curriculum.

The fundamental demand upon improvisation is that the idea for the film and the style of improvisation ought to come out of the same thought. From the beginning, improvisation must live in the premise rather than be added to it. The notion is not easy to grasp, and in fact is elusive. It may even be helpful to step away from *Tango* long enough to look at another example of possible improvisation. An indulgence is asked of the reader—to think about another kind of film altogether, a distracting hitch to the argument, but it may not be possible to bring focus to improvisation until we have other models before us.

So the following and imaginary film is offered: Orson Welles to play Churchill while Burton or Olivier does Beaverbrook in the week of Dunkirk. Let us assume we have the great good fortune to find these actors at the height of their powers and have for *auteur* a filmmaker who is also a brilliant historian. To these beginnings, he adds a company of witty English actors and gives them the same historical material to study in order to provide a common denominator to everyone's knowledge. At this point the *auteur* and the company agree upon a few premises of plot. The *auteur* will offer specific situations. It will help if the episodes are sufficiently charged for the actors to lose their fear first of improvisation—which is that they must make up their lines.

Then a narrative action can begin to emerge out of the interplay of the characters, in much the way a good party turns out differently from the expectations of the hostess and yet will develop out of her original conception. With a script, actors try to convince the writer, if he is present, to improve their lines—with improvisation they must work upon their wits. Why assume that the wits of this company of intelligent English actors will have less knowledge of manner and history than an over-extended script writer trying to work up his remote conception of what Churchill and Beaverbrook might have been like? Why not assume Welles and Burton have a better idea? Are they not more likely to contain instinctive knowledge in their ambulating meat? Isn't the company, in its steeping as good British actors into their own history, able to reveal to us more of what such a week might have been like than any but the most inspired effort by a screenwriter?

We all contain the culture of our country in our unused acting skills. While Clark Gable could probably not have done an improvisation to save himself, since he had no working habits for that whatsoever, the suspicion still exists that Gable, if he had been able to permit himself, could have offered a few revelations on the life of Dwight D. Eisenhower, especially since Ike seems to have spent a good part of his life imitating Gable's voice. If violence can release love, improvisation can loose the unused culture of a film artist.

The argument is conceivably splendid, but we are talking about *historical* improvisation, where the end is still known and it is the details that are paramount. How simple (and intense) by comparison become the problems of doing a full improvisation for *Tango.* There we are given a fundamental situation, a spoiled girl about to be married, a distraught man whose wife is a suicide. The man and the girl are in the room to make love. We are back at the same beginning. But we can no longer project ahead! If the actors feel nothing for one another sexually, as Schneider has indicated in several interviews was the case for Brando and herself—she may even have been telling the truth—then no exciting improvisation is possible on sexual lines. (The improvisation would have to work on the consequences of a lack of attraction.) Actors do not have to feel great passion for one another to fulfill a role, but enough attraction must exist to provide a live coal for improvisation to blow upon. Without some kernel of reality to an improvisation only a monster can continue to offer interesting lines. Once attraction is present, there is nothing exceptional about the continuation of the process. Most of us, given the umbilical relation of sex and drama, pump our psychic bellows on many a sensual spark, but then most affairs are, to one degree or another, improvisations, which is to say genuine in some part of their feeling and nicely acted for the rest. What separates professional actors from all of us amateur masses with our animal instinct for dissembling, our everyday acting, is the ability of the professional to take a small emotion in improvisation and go a long distance with it. In a scripted piece of work, some professionals need no relation to the other actor at all; they can, as Monroe once said, "wipe them out" and substitute another face. But improvisation depends on a continuing life, since it exists in the no-man's-land between acting and uncalculated response; it is a *special* psychic state, at its best more real than the life to which one afterward returns, and so a special form of insanity. All acting is a corollary of insanity, but working from a script offers a highly controlled means of departing from one's own personality in order to enter another. (As well as the formal power to return.)

What makes improvisation fertile, luminous, frightening, and finally *wiggy* enough for a professional like Gable to shun its practice is that the actor is doing two things at once—playing at a fictitious role while using real feelings, which then begin to serve (rather than the safety of the script) to stimulate him into successive new feelings and responses, until he is in danger of pushing into emotional terrain that is too far out of his control.

If we now examine *Tango* against this perspective, the risks (once there is real sexual attraction between the man and the woman) have to multiply. They are after all not simply playing themselves but have rather inserted themselves into highly charged creatures, a violent man with a blood-filled horizon and a spoiled middle-class girl with buried tyrannies. How, as they continue this improvisation, can they avoid falling in love or coming to hate one another? With good film actors, there is even every real danger that the presence of the camera crew will inflame them further, since in every thespian is an orgiast screaming to get out.

So murder is the first dramatic reality between two such lovers in a continuing film of improvisation. They progress toward an end that is frighteningly open. The man may kill the woman, or the woman the man. For as actors, they have also to face the shame of walking quietly away from one another, a small disaster when one is trying to build intensity, for such a quiet ending is equal to a lack of inspiration, a cowardice before the potential violence of the other. Improvisation is profoundly wicked when it works; it ups the ante, charges all dramatic potential, looks for collision. Yet what a dimension of dramatic exploration is also offered. For the actors can even fall in love, can truly fall in love, can go through a rite of passage together and so reach some locked crypt of the heart precisely because they have been photographed fucking together from every angle, and still—perhaps it is thereby—have found some private reserve of intimacy no one else can touch. Let the world watch. It is not near.

So the true improvisation that *Tango* called for should have moved forward each day on the actors' experience of the day before; it would thereby have offered more aesthetic excitement. Because of its danger! There is a very small line in the last recognitions of the psyche between real bullets in a gun and blanks. The madness of improvisation is such, the intensities of the will become such, that one hardly dares to fire a blank at the other actor. What if he is so carried away by excitement that he will refuse to fall? Bring on the real bullet, then. Bite on it.

Of course, literal murder is hardly the inevitable denouement in improvisation. But it is in the private design of each actor's paranoia. Pushed further together in improvisation than actors have gone before, who knows what literal risks might finally have been taken. That is probably why Brando chose to play a buffoon at a very high level and thereby also chose to put Schneider down. Finally we laugh at those full and lovely tits that will be good only for playing soccer (and she will choose to lose thirty pounds after the film is done—a whole loss of thirty pounds of pulchritude). Brando, with his immense paranoia (it is hardly unjustified), may have concluded like many an adventurous artist before him that he was adventuring far enough. No need for more.

Still, he lost an opportunity for his immense talent. If he has been our first actor for decades, it is because he has given us, from the season he arrived in *Streetcar,* a greater sense of improvisation out of the lines of a script than any other professional actor. Sometimes he seemed the only player alive who knew how to suggest that he was about to say something more valuable than what he did say. It gave him force. The lines other people had written for him came out of his mouth like the final compromise life had offered for five better thoughts. He seemed to have a charged subtext. It was as if, whenever requested in other films to say script lines so bad as "I make you die, you make me die, we're two murderers, each other's," the subtext— the emotion of the words he was using behind the words— became "I want the pig to vomit in your face." That was what gave an unruly, all but uncontrolled, and smoldering air of menace to all he did.

Now, in *Tango,* he had nothing beneath the script, for his previous subtext was the script. So he appeared to us as a man orating, not improvising. But then a long speech can hardly be an improvisation if its line of action is able to go nowhere but back into the prearranged structures of the plot. It is like the aside of a politician before he returns to that prepared text the press already has in their hands. So our interest moved away from the possibilities of the film and was spent on the man himself, his nobility and his loutishness. But his nature was finally a less interesting question than it should have been, and weeks would go by before one could forgive Bertolucci for the aesthetic cacophony of the end.

Still, one could forgive. For, finally, Bertolucci has given us a failure worth a hundred films like *The Godfather*. Regardless of all its solos, failed majesties, and off-the-mark horrors, even as a highly imperfect adventure, it is still the best adventure in film to be seen in this pullulating year. And it will open an abyss for Bertolucci. The rest of his life must now be an improvisation. Doubtless he is bold enough to live with that. For he begins *Last Tango* with Brando muttering two words one can hardly hear. They are: Fuck God.

The unmanageable in oneself must now offer advice. If Bertolucci is going to fuck God, let him really give the fuck. Then we may all know a little more of what God is willing or unwilling to forgive. That is, unless God is old and has indeed forgot and we are merely out on a sea of human anality, a collective Faust deprived of Mephisto and turning to shit. The choice, of course, is small. Willy-nilly, we push on in every art and every technology toward the re-embodiment of the creation. It is doubtless a venture more demented than coupling with the pig, but it is our venture, our white whale, and by it or with it shall we be seduced. On to the Congo with sex, technology, and the inflamed lividities of human will.

I may as well confess (and indeed the preceding paragraph makes virtually no secret of it) that film seems a refined species of occult practice to me. Indeed, it sets up shop at the juncture of art, technology, and magic. So the themes to be presented next can be seen as a corollary to what has already been proposed.

THE OCCULT

———

M any a fiction writer lives with at least one sense cocked to
the possibility that some events are magical, and if so, how
do you write about it?

This portion of my preface to the book *Unholy Alliance*, by
Peter Levenda, will hardly answer the question, but it does give
a quick tour of the territory. In corollary, I can add that on very
good days, when your work is at its best and keeps revealing insights that you never knew were in you, it is not difficult to recognize that writing may also be a species of magic.

Sometimes, it is as if something larger than our educations, our
sense of good and evil, our lives themselves, seems to be moving
in upon our existence, and this anxiety illumines *Unholy Alliance*
like a night light in some recess of the wall down a very long corridor.

If magic is composed of a good many of those out-of-category
forces that press against established religions, so magic can also
be seen, in relation to technology at least, as the dark side of the
moon. If a Creator exists in company with an opposite Presence
(to be called Satan, for short), there is also the most lively possibility of a variety of major and minor angels, devils and demons,

good spirits and evil, working away more or less invisibly in our lives.

It is, therefore, a viable notion to some that magic is a presence and a practice that can exist, can even, to a small degree, be employed (if often with real danger for the practitioner). For such men and women, the proposition is assured—magic most certainly does exist as a feasible undertaking—even if the affirmative is obliged to appear in determinedly small letters when posed against technology: (How often can a curse be as effective as a bomb?)

Nonetheless, given the many centuries of anecdotal and much-skewed evidence on the subject, it is still not irrational to assume that phenomena of a certain kind can be regarded provisionally as magical in those particular situations where magic offers the only rational explanation for events that are otherwise inexplicable. Indeed, this is probably the common view. One explanation for the aggravated awe and misery that inhabited America in the days after the destruction of the Twin Towers was that the event was not only monstrous but brilliantly effected in the face of all the factors that could have gone wrong for the conspirators. The uneasy and not-to-be-voiced hypothesis that now lived as a possibility in many a mind was that the success of the venture had been fortified by the collateral assistance of magic. Few happenings can be more unsettling to the modern psyche than the suggestion that magic is cooperating with technology. It is equal to saying that machines have a private psychology and large events, therefore, may be subject to Divine or Satanic intervention.

So let us at least assume that magic may conceivably be present as an element in the very warp and woof of things. Anyone who is offended by this will not be interested in *Unholy Alliance*. Its first virtue, after all, is in its assiduous detail.

What augments the value of this work is the cold but understanding eye of the author. Since his knowledge of magic and magicians is intimate, one never questions whether he knows what he is writing about. Since he is also considerably disenchanted by the life practices of most of the magic workers, he is never taken in by assumptions of grandiosity or over-sweet New Age sentiments. He knows the fundamental flaw found in many occultists. It is the vice that brought them to magic in the first place—precisely, their desire to obtain power over others without paying the price. The majority of occultists in his pages appear to be posted on the particular human spectrum that runs from impotence to greed. All too often they are prone, as a crew, to sectarian war, all-out cheating, gluttony, slovenliness, ill will, and betrayal. Exactly. They are, at whatever level they find themselves, invariably looking for that gift of the gods—power that comes without the virtue of having been earned.

The irony, of course, is that most of them, in consequence, pay large prices in ill health, failure, isolation, addiction, deterioration of their larger possibilities, even personal doom. Goethe did not conceive of *Faust* for too little.

Peter Levenda captures this paradox. What he also gives us is a suggestion that cannot be ignored: The occultists on both sides in the Second World War (although most particularly Himmler and the Nazis) did have some real effect on its history—most certainly not enough to have changed the outcome but enough to have altered motives and details we have been taking for granted. What comes through the pages of *Unholy Alliance* is the canny political sense Hitler possessed in relation to the separate uses of magic and magicians. Levenda's dispassionate treatment of charged evidence is managed (no small feat) in a way to enable us to recognize that Hitler almost certainly believed in magic, and also knew that such belief had to be concealed in the subtext of his speeches and endeavors. Open avowal could be equal to political suicide.

Hitler was hell, therefore, on astrologers—and packed off many to concentration camps, especially after Rudolf Hess's flight to England in 1941, did his best (and was successful) in decimating the Gypsy population of Europe, sneered publicly at seers, psychic gurus, fortune-tellers, all the small fry of the occult movement. He saw them, clearly, as impediments to his own fortunes, negative baggage to his reputation. Yet he also gave his support to the man he made into the second most important Nazi in existence, Heinrich Himmler, an occultist of no modest dimension.

It was as if Hitler lived within Engels's dictum that "quantity changes quality." A little magic practiced by a small magician can prove a folly or a personal enhancement; a larger involvement brings on the cannibalistic practices to be expected of a magicians' society; and a huge but camouflaged involvement, the Nazi movement itself, with its black-shirted Knight Templars of

SS men, becomes an immense vehicle that will do its best to drive the world into a new religion, a new geography, a new mastery of the future.

Why Are We in Vietnam? is the only novel I ever finished under the mistaken belief I was writing another. Living in Province-town on the edge of those rare, towering, and windy dunes that give the tip of Cape Cod a fair resemblance to the desert of the Sahara, I had begun to think of a novel so odd and so horrible that I hesitated for years to begin it. I imagined a group of seven or eight bikers, hippies and studs plus a girl or two, living in the scrub thickets that sat in some of the valleys between the dunes. Only six feet high, those thickets were nonetheless forests, and if you could find a path through the thorns and cat briars, nobody could track you, not in a hurry. So I peopled the thickets with characters: My characters were as wild as anyone who ever came to Provincetown. It is not a tame place. Years ago, a first lady was once told it was "the Wild West of the East," and that is not a bad description. The tip of Cape Cod curls in on itself like a spiral— the long line of the dunes comes around like the curve of one's palm and fingers as they close into a fist. It is one of the very few places in America where one comes to the end of the road for a more profound reason than real estate ceasing to be profitable. In Provincetown, the land runs out, and you are surrounded by the sea.

So it is a strange place. The Pilgrims landed there before they went on to Plymouth—America began here. The Pilgrims lost interest in scrub pine, mournful winds, and sand. They moved on, left ghosts. Whaling captains settled in later, left ghosts. In winter, the town is filled with spirits. One can go mad in that rainy climate waiting for March to end. It is a place for murder-ers and suicides. If decades went by without a single recorded homicide, that record ended abruptly with a crime of true car-nage. Some years ago, a young Portuguese from a family of fish-ermen killed four girls, dismembered their bodies, and buried the pieces in twenty small and scattered graves.

That catastrophe was not a good deal worse than anything I had already contemplated for my gang, since I conceived of them making nocturnal trips from the dunes into town, where, out of the sheer boredom of an existence not nearly intense enough to satisfy their health, they would commit murders of massive brutality and then slip back to the dunes. Motiveless murders. I saw a string of such crimes.

I was, as I say, in fear of the book. I loved Provincetown and did not think that was a good way to write about it. The town is so naturally eerie in mid-winter and provides such sense of omens waiting to be magnetized into lines of force that the novel in my mind seemed more a magical object than a fiction, a black magic.

Nonetheless, I began the book in the spring of '66. It attracted me too much not to begin. Yet because I could not thrust Provincetown into such literary horrors without preparation, I thought I would start with a chapter about hunting bear in Alaska. A prelude. I would have two tough rich boys, each as separated from social convention as any two rich boys could be—Texans I would make them, out of reserve memories of Texans I had served with in the 112th Cavalry out of San Antonio. The boys would still be young, still mean rather than uncontrollably murderous—the hunting might serve as a bridge to get them ready for more. They would come back from the Alaskan hunting trip ready to travel; Provincetown would eventually receive them.

Now, anyone who reads the book which this preface serves will see that nobody ever gets to Provincetown. The chapter on hunting becomes half a dozen chapters; it ends up being all of the book. If I wrote those chapters wondering how long it would take to extricate myself with novelistic integrity from all the elaborations of the hunt I seemed more and more bound to get into, it was not until those boys were back in Dallas and I was getting ready to move them East that I realized two things:

(1) I had nothing further to say about them.

(2) Even if I did, I could no longer believe that Tex and D.J. could still be characters in the Provincetown novel. They had another quality by now.

So I lived with my manuscript for a few months and ended by recognizing that I hadn't been too bright. I had written a novel, not a prelude. The book was done. Later, a number of readers would think *Why Are We in Vietnam?* was far and away my best book. I thought I had never written one with so wild and happy a humor.

In the aftermath, I was less certain, however. For when Sharon Tate was murdered in the summer of '69 and the world heard of Charles Manson, I could wonder what state of guilt I might have been in if I had written that novel of desert murderers. How then could I ever have been certain Manson had not been sensitive to its message in the tribal air?

But then writing has its own occult force. At best, we never know where our writing comes from, or who gives it to us. Jack Kennedy's name is invoked in the first sentence of *An American Dream;* nine lines farther down that page a man named Kelly is mentioned. Later in the same chapter we learn that Kelly's middle name is Oswald—Barney Oswald Kelly. That chapter appeared in *Esquire* about a month after the assassination, but it had been written three months earlier, a coincidence to force one to contemplate the very design of coincidence.

So too had I written in *Barbary Shore* about a secret agent named McLeod, who had been, in his time, a particularly important Soviet agent. He lived in a cheap room on the top floor of a cheap rooming house just across the hall from the narrator. Writing that book, I always found it hard to believe that such a man would be found in such a place, and the simple difficulty of not quite believing what I wrote did not help to speed the writing of the book. A year after it was published, I rented a room in a dank old building with high ceilings, called Ovington Studios, on Fulton Street in Brooklyn, not half a mile from the rooming house in *Barbary Shore,* and on the floor below during those ten years I kept the studio was Colonel Rudolph Abel, the most important Soviet spy in America—or, at least, so he was described by the FBI when the arrest was finally made.

We will never know if primitive artists painted their caves to show a representation or whether the moving hand was looking to placate the forces above and the forces below. Sometimes I think the novelist fashions a totem just as much as an aesthetic and that his real aim, not even known necessarily to himself, is to create a diversion in the fields of dread, a sanctuary in some of the arenas of magic. The flaws of his work can even be a part of his magical strength, as if his real intent in writing is to alter the determinations of that invisible finger which has written and moved on. By such logic, many a book is a totem, not empty of amulets for the author against curses, static, and the malignity of electronic air.

The unconscious can lead one to startling conclusions. In *Ancient Evenings,* I named my protagonist Menenhetet and occasionally made it Meni for short. A couple of years later I came across the translated text of an inscription on an ancient Egyptian temple wall that described the battle of Kadesh, a key event in the novel. In this inscription was mentioned one Menni, Ramses the Second's equerry, which was exactly Menenhetet's role in that part of the book. Somehow, I did not think of the coincidence as eerie—comfirmative, rather, as if it proved that there was some very good reason I devoted so many years to the tome.

The story is that Robert Rauschenberg was once given the gift of a pastel from Willem de Kooning. Rauschenberg, with de Kooning's permission, erased the pastel and then signed it "Pastel by de Kooning Erased by Robert Rauschenberg," after which he sold it. The story bothered me. There was something profound there, but how to get ahold of it? Then it came to me: Rauschenberg was saying that the artist has the same right to print money as the financier. Money is nothing but authority imprinted upon emptiness.

I laid the story to rest and was content until the day I thought, Maybe the person who bought the pastel was neither a gambler nor an investor so aware of chic in painting that he knew he could make a profit from reselling it. Maybe if a truly talented painter erases the work of another truly talented painter, there's a resonance, an echo, in the lost work. If, let's say, Fidel Castro had executed Charles de Gaulle and buried him himself, that would not be ordinary burial ground. Students of the occult would pay great attention to the aura about the place. So I thought maybe that's what's transpiring here—some echo of de Kooning's original work might be *fortifying* the person who purchased it. Therefore, I am obsessed with the story again. One of two possibilities exists: Either this aesthetic act was an outrage, or it advances our comprehension of the occult.

Famous plant-man Backster, attaching the electrodes of his polygraph to a philodendron one night, wonders in the wake of this passing impulse how to test the plant for some emotional reaction. Abruptly, a current courses through the philodendron at the horror of this thought. When Backster cuts or burns the leaf, however, the polygraph registers little: The plant is numb. (Its telepathic sensitivity seems to be its life; its suffering, an abstention from life.) The experiment suggests plants may be a natural species of wireless. (What, indeed, did Picasso teach us if not that every form offers up its own scream?) Radio is then no more than a prosthetic leg of communication, whereas plants speak to plants and are aware of the death of animals on the other side of the hill. Some artists might even swear they have known this from the beginning, for they would see themselves as stimulants who inject perception into the blind vision of the century. (And, like a junkie, does the century move into apathy from the super-brilliance of its injections?)

The act of writing is a mystery, and the more you labor at it, the more you become aware after a lifetime of such activity that it is not answers which are being offered so much as a greater appreciation of the literary mysteries. The primal enigma of the profession—where do those words come from?—not only arouses fear at the thought of such powers disappearing but also inspires the happiness that one may be in contact with some embodiment of literature itself. Now, of course, we cannot talk directly of such matters; it is enough to amuse ourselves with our variety of approaches to the problem. In my college years, many of us used to have a certainty. It was that environment was all: One was the product of one's milieu, one's parents, one's food, one's conversations, one's dearest and/or most odious human relations. One was the sum of one's own history as it was cradled in the larger history of one's time. One was a product, and if one wrote novels, they were merely a product of the product. With this working philosophy, I wrote a book—it happened to be *The Naked and the Dead*—which was wholly comfortable to me. I would not have known then what an author meant by speaking of any of his works as uncomfortable or, worse, unnatural. *The Naked and the Dead* seemed a sure result of all I had learned up to the age of twenty-five, all I had experienced and all I had read. My characters had already been conceived and put in file boxes before they were ever on the page. I had hundreds of filled-out file cards before I ever began to write. The novel itself seemed merely the end of a long-active assembly line, and I felt able to account for each part of it.

The next book after *The Naked and the Dead*, however, was such a mystery to me that to this day I do not comprehend it. I can tell you what it is about, what I was trying to say, but do not ask me where *Barbary Shore* came from. I used to feel as if this second novel were being written by someone else. Where *The Naked and the Dead* had been put together with the solid, agreeable effort of a young carpenter constructing a decent house while full of the practices, techniques, and wisdom of those who built houses before him, *Barbary Shore* might as well have been dictated to me by a ghost in the middle of a forest. Each morning I would sit down to work with no notion at all of how to continue. My characters were strangers to me, and each day after a few hours of blind work (because I never seemed to get more than a sentence or two ahead of myself) I would push my plot and people three manuscript pages forward into their eventual denouement, but I never knew what I was doing or where it came from. It's fortunate that I had heard of Freud and the unconscious; if not, I would have had to postulate such a condition myself. An unconscious was the only explanation for what was going on. Now I was left aware of two presences cooperating in the production of a literary work, and the second had the capacity to take over the act of authorship from the first.

Sometimes, when I am feeling tolerant to the idea of karma, demiurges, spirits of the age, and the intervention of angels, saints, and demons, I also wonder if being a writer over a long career does not leave you open to more than one origin for your work. In a long career one may come forth with many books that are products of one's skill and vocational experience, of one's dedication, but I also wonder if once in a while the gods do not look about and have their own novels to propose and peer down among us and say, "Here's a good one for Bellow," or, "That would have been a saucy dish for Cheever, too bad he's gone," or, in my own case, "Look at poor old Mailer worrying about his job again. Let's make him the agent for this absolutely wicked little thing about Vietnam." Who knows? We may be sturdy literary engineers full of sound literary practice or, as equally, unwitting agents for forces beyond our comprehension. It matters less than the knowledge that our books can come from more than one wondrous place. After all, it is not so depressing to think that with all our hungers, we can also have the fortune to be handed in passing a few gifts we do not deserve. How agreeable to feel kin to the force that put paintings on the walls of caves, set stonecutters to exactitudes that would permit Gothic arches, gave the calculus to Newton's age and space travel to ours. No, it is not so ill to sense that we are also heir to emanations from some unaccountable and fabulous source. Nothing lifts our horizons like a piece of unexpected luck or the generosity of the gods.

The novel has its own particular resource, which is close to magical. If you write purely enough and your style's good enough, you can establish a communion between yourself and the reader that can be found in no other art, and this communion can continue not only for hours but for weeks, years. When the novel is dead, then the technological society will be totally upon us.

For six and a half centuries, we have been moving from the discovery of our humanity, good and evil, into the circulation of the name. By extension, the name is equal to money. Over the millennia, we have been extricating ourselves out of some primitive obeisance to dread so complete that painting once lay inert on the field of two dimensions (as if the medieval eye, like the primitive eye, did not feel ready to wander). Then art dared to rise into that Renaissance venture to liberate us from much of the weight of our anxiety. Painters entered the space-perspective of volume and depth. Now, with graffiti, we are back in the prison of two dimensions once more. Or is it the one dimension of the name—the art form screaming through space on a unilinear subway line?

At night, in the yards, the walls of the subway cars sit there possessed of soul—you are not just writing your name but trafficking with the iron spirit of the vehicle standing before you in the yard. What a set of inert iron beasts. There they stand in all the corrals of the yard! The graffiti-writers, stealthy as the near-to-silent sound of their movement, work up and down the line of cars, some darting in to squiggle a little toy of a name on twenty cars—their nerve has no larger surge—others embark on their first or their hundred-and-first masterpiece, daring the full enterprise of an hour of painting one masterpiece while they carry all the tension of waiting for the disturbance of their entrance to settle, waiting for the guards patrolling the lines of track to grow somnolent and descend into the early morning pall of the watchman. Sometimes the graffiti-writers would set out from their own turf at dark yet not begin to paint until two in the morning, hiding for hours in the surest corners of the yard or in and under the trains. What a quintessential marriage of cool and style to write your name in giant separate living letters, large as animals, lithe as snakes, mysterious as Arabic or Chinese curls of alphabet, and do it in the heart of a winter night, when the hands are frozen and only the heart is hot with fear. No wonder the best of the graffiti writers, those mountains of heavy-masterpiece production, STAY HIGH, PHASE 2, STAR III, get the respect, call it the glory, that they are as famous and luminous to their people as a rock star. It is their year. Nothing automatic about writing a masterpiece on a subway car. "I was scared," said Japan, "all the time I did it." And sitting in the station at 158th and St. Nicholas Avenue, watching the trains go by, talking between each wave of subway sound, he is tiny in size, his dark eyes as alert as any small and hungry animal who eats in a garden at night and does not know where the householder may be waiting with his varmint gun.

Now, as Japan speaks, his eyes never failing to take in the collection of names, hieroglyphs, symbols, stars, crowns, ribbons, masterpieces, and toys on every passing car, there is a sadness in his mood. The city has mounted a massive campaign. There was a period in the middle when it looked as if graffiti would take over the city, when a movement that began as an expression of tropical peoples living in a monotonous iron-gray and dull-brown-brick environment, surrounded by asphalt, concrete, and clangor, had erupted to save the sensuous flesh of their inheritance from the macadamization of the psyche, save the blank city wall by the exercise of their united brain, ready to paint the dead-ass wall with their equivalent of giant trees and petty plants of a tropical rain forest. Like such a jungle, every plant, large and small, spoke to one another, lived in the profusion *and* harmony of a forest. No one wrote over another name, no one was obscene—for that would have smashed the harmony. A communion took place over the city in this plant growth of names until every institutional wall, fixed or moving, every modern new school that looked like a brand-new factory, every old slum warehouse, every standing billboard, every huckstering poster, and the halls of every high-rise low-rent housing project that looked like a prison (and all did) were covered by a foliage of graffiti which grew seven or eight feet tall, even twelve feet high in those choice places worth the effort for one to stand on another, ah, if it had gone on, the entire city of blank architectural high-rise horrors would have been covered with paint.

Graffiti writers might have become mountaineers with pitons for the ascent of high-rise high-cost swinger-single apartments in the East Sixties and Seventies. The look of New York, and then the world, might have been transformed, and the interlapping of names and colors, those wavelets of ego forever reverberating upon one another, could have risen like a flood to cover the monstrosities of abstract empty techno-architectural twentieth-century walls where no design ever predominated over the most profitable (and ergo most monotonous) construction ratio implicit in a twenty-million-dollar bill.

The kids painted with less than this in view. Sufficient in the graffiti-proliferating years of the early Seventies to cover the front door of every subway car they could find. The ecstasy of the roller coaster would dive down into their chest if they were ever waiting in a station and a twelve-car train came stampeding in and their name, HONDO, WILDCAT, SABU, or LOLLIPOP, was on the *front*! Yes, the graffiti had not only the feel and all the super-powered whoosh and impact of all the bubble-letters in all the mad comic strips, but the *zoom*, the *aghr*, and the *ahhr* of screeching rails, the fast motion of subways roaring into stations, the comic strips come to life. So it was probably not a movement designed to cover the world so much as an extirpation of visual emptiness. Slum populations chilled on one side by the bleakness of modern design and brain-cooked on the other by comic strips and TV ads with zooming letters, even brain-cooked by the whip of the capital letters in the names of the products, and gut-picked by the sound of rock and soul screaming up into the voodoo of the firmament with the shriek of the performer's electronic strings coiling like neon letters in the blue satanic light, yes, all the excrescence of the highways and the fluorescent wonderlands of every Las Vegas sign frying through the Iowa and New Jersey night, all the stomach-tightening nitty-gritty of trying to learn to spell was in the writing, every assault on the psyche as the trains came slamming in. Maybe it was no more than a movement that looked to take some of the overflow left within and paint it out upon the world, no more than a species of collective therapy, of grace exhibited under pressure in which they never dreamed of going on to paint all of the blank and empty modern world, but the authority of the city reacted as if the city itself might be in greater peril from graffiti than from drugs, and a war had gone on, more and more implacable on the side of the authority with every legal and psychological weedkiller on full employ until the graffiti of New York was defoliated, cicatrized, Vietnamized. Now, as I sat in the station with John Naar and Japan and we watched the trains go by, aesthetic blight was on the cars. Few masterpieces remained. The windows were gray and smeared. The cars looked dull red or tarnished aluminum—their recent coat of paint remover having stripped all polish from the manufacturer's surface. New subway cars looked like old cars. Only the ghost-outline of former masterpieces remained. The kids were broken. The movement seemed over. Even cans of spray paint could no longer be stolen. Now the ones set out for store display were empty, the misdemeanors were being upped to felony, the fines were severe, the mood was vindictive. Two hideous accidents had occurred. One boy had been killed beneath a subway car, and another had been close to fatally burned by an inflammable spray can catching a spark, yes, a horror was on the movement and transit patrols moved through the yards and plugged the entrances. The white monoliths of the high-rise were safe. And the subways were dingier than they had ever been. The impulse of the jungle to cover the walled tombs of technology had been broken. Was there a clue to graffiti in the opposite passion to look upon monotony and call it health? As I walked the streets with John Naar, we passed a sign: DON'T POLLUTE—KEEP THE CITY CLEAN. "That sign," the photographer murmured, "is a form of pollution itself."

Years ago, back in the early Fifties, he conceived of a story he was finally not to write, for he lost his comprehension of it. A rich young artist in New York in the early Fifties, bursting to go beyond Abstract Expressionism, began to rent billboards on which he sketched huge, ill-defined (never say they were sloppy) works in paint chosen to run easily and flake quickly. The rains distorted the lines, made gullies of the forms, automobile exhausts laid down a patina, and comets of flying birds crusted the disappearing surface with their impasto. By the time fifty such billboards had been finished—a prodigious year for the painter —the vogue was on. His show was an event. They transported the billboards by trailer-truck and broke the front wall of the gallery to get the art objects inside. It was the biggest one-man exhibition in New York that year. At its conclusion, two art critics were arguing whether such species of work still belonged to art.

"You're mad," cried one. "It is not art, it is never art."

"No," said the other. "I think it's valid."

So would the story end. Its title, Validity. But before he had written a word he made the mistake of telling it to a young Abstract Expressionist whose work he liked. "Of course it's valid," said the painter, eyes shining with the project. "I'd do it myself if I could afford the billboards."

The story was never written. He had assumed he was proposing a satire, but it was evident he had no insight into how painters were ready to think. Some process had entered art and he could not discern it out.

Let us go back to the pastel by de Kooning which Rauschenberg erased. The details, when further inquiry is made, are less impromptu. Rauschenberg first informed de Kooning of what he would do, and de Kooning agreed. The work, when sold, bore the inscription "A drawing from Willem de Kooning erased by Robert Rauschenberg." Both artists are now proposing something more than that the artist has the same right as the financier to print money; they may even be saying that the meat and marrow of art, the painterly core, the life of the pigment, and the world of technique with which hands lay on that pigment are convertible to something other. The ambiguity of meaning in the twentieth century, the hollow in the heart of faith, has become such an obsessional hole that art may have to be converted into intellectual transactions. It is as if we are looking for stuff, any stuff with which to stuff the hole, and will convert every value into packing for this purpose. For there is no doubt that in erasing the pastel and selling it, art has been diminished but our knowledge of society is certainly enriched. An aesthetic artifact has been converted into a sociological artifact. It is not the painting that intrigues us now but the lividities of art fashion which made the transaction possible in the first place. Something rabid is loose in the century. Maybe we are not converting art into some comprehension of social process but rather are using art to choke the hole, as if society has become so hopeless, which is to say so twisted in knots of faithless ideological spaghetti, that the glee is in strangling the victims.

But take the example further. Let us imagine a show at the Guggenheim. It will be like many we have seen. Let us make it a plausible modern one-man show. Nothing will be exhibited but computer read-out sheets from a statistical operation. Hundreds of such sheets tacked to the wall. Somewhat irregularly. Attempts at neatness will be contradicted by a confusion in the style of placing them on the wall of the Guggenheim as it spirals up the ramp. Checkerboards alternate with ascending bands, then cul-de-sacs, paper stapled up every way.

We try to digest the aesthetic experience. Of what do the computer read-out sheets consist? What is the subject of their inquiry? we ask. And what is the motive of the artist? Is he telling us something about the order and disorder of the mind in relation to a technological world? Has he presented us with an ongoing composition of exceptional cunning? Is it possible he even has set the problem for the computer himself? Maybe the endless numbers on these computer sheets reflect some analogue to the tension of major themes in his brain. Do we then have here an arithmetical display whose relation to art is as complex as *Finnegans Wake* to literature?

Bullshit, responds the painter. The computer sheets were selected at random. Because the artist did not even wish to bear an unconscious responsibility for the selection, he chose an acquaintance with whom he shared no great psychic identity to pick up the computer sheets for him. Neither he nor the acquaintance ever inquired into the subject of the statistical problem, and he never took a look at what was brought back. Rather, he spoke to the janitor at the Guggenheim by telephone and told him to tack up the pages any way at all. The checkerboards and bands and cul-de-sacs of stapled paper were merely a reflection of the personnel: The janitor worked with two assistants. One was neat, the other drunk. And the painter never came to see the show. The show was the fact that people came, studied the walls, lived for an uncertain hour in the Guggenheim and went out again, their minds exercised by a question that not only had no answer, but may not even have been a question. The artist had done his best to have no intent. Not unless his intent was to demonstrate that most of the experience of viewing a painting is the context of the museum itself. We are next to one of John Cage's compositions in silence. Art has been saying with more and more intensity: The nature of the painting has become less interesting than the relation of painting to society—we can even erase Rauschenberg's erasure. Get the artist out of it altogether, and it is still art. The world is turning inside out.

What step is left to take? Only one. A show that offers no object at all. The last reference to painting or sculpture is the wall on which something can be hung, or the floor on which a piece can sit. That must now disappear. The art-piece enters the artist: The work can only be experienced within his psyche.

From *The New York Times*, September 2, 1973, by Peter Plagens:

a marksman-friend shot Chris Burden in the upper left arm with a .22 long-jacket before an audience of 12 intimates. He [Burden] figured on a graze wound with a Band-Aid slapped on afterward, but it "felt like a truck hit my arm at 80 miles per hour"; he went to the hospital, nauseous, and filed the requisite police report ("accident").

Plagens goes on to describe other "pieces." Burden chooses situations for their possibility of danger, pain, humiliation, or boredom. There is:

"Movie on the Way Down," in which Burden, hanging by his heels, nude, six feet off a gym floor with a movie camera in his hands, is summarily chopped loose.

The movie is presumably taken on the way down (is it filmed in slow motion?) and he ends with a cut lip. There are other pieces where he rockets flaming matches "at his nude supine wife" or sets ablaze two 16-foot wooden crosses on Laguna Canyon Road at 2 A.M.—"the intended audience for that piece," says Burden, "was the one guy driving down the road who saw it first." Ah, Los Angeles! For "Endurance/real time," he 1) stays in a locker for five days, 2) does 1,600 tours of a gallery on his bicycle, and 3) remains in bed for three weeks and a day. He also pretends to be a dead man lying under a tarpaulin on the street and is arrested by the police for creating a traffic hazard. He gets a hung jury at his trial and the case is dismissed but "one of the nine votes for conviction, a stewardess, told Burden if she ever saw him under a tarp again, she'd run over him herself." He even does a study in the shift of identity. For "I Became a Secret Hippie," Burden cuts his hair short and dresses in FBI clothes. "If you want to be a heavy artist nowadays," Plagens, reporting on Burden, concludes, "you have to do something unpleasant to your body, because everything *else* has been done. [Burden] may be a product of art-world art history—backed into some unten-able masochistic corner because all the other novelty territory has been claimed."

At the least, Burden is fulfilling the dictum of Jean Malaquais that once there are enough artists in the world, the work of art will become the artist himself. Burden is refining his personality. Through existential tests. Burden is exploring not his technique but his vibrations. The situations he chooses are, as Plagens describes, "edgy." They have nothing remotely resembling a boundary until they are done. In "Movie on the Way Down," Burden can hardly know if he will cut his lip or break his neck, feel a live instant on the descent or some dull anxiety. When he shoots lighted matches at his nude wife the areas defined are empty before the action begins. Given every variable from Women's Liberation to the sadomasochistic tales of Wilhelm Stekel, Burden can know in advance only that a psycho-dramatic enterprise will be commenced. But where it may end, and what everybody might feel—will the matches burn her skin?—will the marriage be fortified or scorched?—no, there is no confidence which question is going to offer an answer. Per-haps he is not refining his personality so much as attempting to clear a space in his psyche free of dread. But isn't that the fun-damental operation of the primitive at the dawn of civilization, the establishment of the ego? For what is the human ego but a clearing in the forest of the psyche free of dread? Money, held in one's hand, is free of time. Cash has no past; its future is assign-able. It is powerful and empty. So, too, is the ego. It bears the same relation to the psyche as cash bears to the security or com-fort of the body. The ego is virtually separate from the psyche even as money is still separate from every organic communicat-ing logic of nature.

We are back to the cave man and his cave painting. His hand draws the outline of the animal in defiance of those gods who watch him. Burden is smashing his nose on the floor or display-ing his wife in defiance of the last gods of conventional art. They are that audience remnant of a once-leviathan bourgeois cul-ture. They still trickle out to see Happenings, the desire of the middle class to preserve its last religion: the world of the artist, palette, museum and gallery wall. Middle-class passion is to ap-preciate the work of art.

But art may be the little ball rolling off the table. Perhaps art now signifies some unheard reverberation from the subterranean obsession of us all: Is civilization coming to an end? Is society burning? Is the day of the cave man returning? Has our search for ego which was once so routine—a useful (somewhat heartless) ego to be fashioned for a useful (if heartless) society—now gone past the measure of our experience so that we no longer try to construct a control center at the core of the mind, but plunge instead into absurdities which offer us that curious calm we find in the art of the absurd, even as the cave man, defying his gods, discovered he was not always dead on the next day?

But we are at the possible end of civilization, and tribal impulses start up across the world. The descending line of the isolated artist goes down from Michelangelo all the way to Chris Burden, who is finally more comfortable to us than the writers of graffiti. For Burden is the last insult from the hippie children of the middle class to the bourgeois art-patron who is their spiritual parent, but graffiti speaks of a new civilization where barbarism is stirring at the roots.

If at the beginning of Western painting, man was small and God was large; if, in the Renaissance, man was mysteriously large in his relation to God, now, in our times man has disappeared into God. He is mass-man without identity, and he is God. He is all the schizophrenia of the powerless and all-powerful in one psyche.

As we lose our senses in the static of the oncoming universal machine, so does our need to exercise the ego take on elephantiasistical proportions. Graffiti is the expression of a ghetto that is near to the plague, for civilization is now closed off from the ghetto. Too huge are the obstacles to any natural development of a civilized man. In the ghetto it is almost impossible to find some quiet identity. No, in the environment of the slum, the courage to display yourself is your only capital, and in the streets, crime is the only productive process that converts such capital to the modern powers of the world, ego and money. Art is not peace but war, and form is the record of that war.

Yet there is a mystery still. From which combat came these curious letters of graffiti, with their Chinese and Arabic calligraphies? Out of what connection to the past did these lights and touches of flame become so much like the Hebrew alphabet, where the form of the letter itself was worshipped as a manifest of the Lord? No, it is not enough to think of the childlike desire to see one's name ride by in letters large enough to scream your ego across the city, no, it is almost as if we must go back into some more primeval sense of existence. If our name is enormous to us, it is also not real—as if we have come from other places than the name, and lived in other lives.

Perhaps this is the unheard echo of graffiti, the vibration of that profound discomfort it arouses. Can the unheard music of its proclamation and/or its mess, the rapt intent seething of its foliage, be the herald of some oncoming apocalypse less and less far away, and so graffiti lingers on our subway door as a memento of all the lives ever lived, sounding now like the bugles of gathering armies across the unseen ridge. That sound will be muted and heard again and muted and heard and muted into all the decades of the century to come.

GIANTS

TOLSTOY*

Somewhere around the turn of the century, we have Chekhov visiting Tolstoy. He takes the train to the nearest station. Let's say it's wintertime. He rents two horses and a sled, and drives out through the snow to Yasnya Polyana. Tolstoy's pretty old by now, big, strong, severe, of course, and sits him right down and they talk. They drink tea and they talk. Tolstoy says: "Chekhov, you are a very good writer. You are excellent. Some of your short stories are so good I would have been pleased to have written them myself. But, Chekhov, I must tell you: You are a *terrible* playwright! You are awful! You are even worse than Shakespeare!"

Afterward, Chekhov drives back to the railroad station through the snow. In his journal he will write: "I whipped the horses. To the moon I shouted, 'I am even *worse* than Shakespeare!'"

It's a fine story, but if it's true, why did Tolstoy dislike Shake-

---

*In John Ford Noonan's very funny play *Talking Things Over with Chekhov,* a story is told. It lived for me with such intensity that I came to decide it was true. Whether or not it actually happened was beside the point. It was just too good a story not to believe it took place.

speare so? I expect the answer is that Tolstoy was always searching for subtle but precise moral judgment. That required a detailed sense of any sequence of events which had produced a
dramatic or tragic event. You had to know how to assess the
blame. For that, you needed to know exactly when and why
things happened.

But there, very much in the way, was Shakespeare, the greatest movie writer who ever existed—centuries before cinema had
a silver screen. For Shakespeare was not interested in making
careful connections with his characters. Shakespeare was looking to get the most dynamic actors together under any circum-
stance available, no matter how contrived (King Lear can be the
first example). He was looking for superb exchanges of dialogue
and fantastic moments, vertiginous possibilities for the English
language, whereas Tolstoy looked for sobriety of moral judgment. So he considered Shakespeare a monster who paid no attention to causality except when it was useful to him. Will's
people did incredible things, fell in love or murdered, the latter
with a minimum of preparation—Macbeth—and then had exceptional speeches that seared an audience's consciousness. To
Tolstoy, this was monstrous, and must have been equal to the
way some of us look these days upon advertising campaigns that
are stuffed with manipulation and little else.

But why Tolstoy would compare Chekhov to Shakespeare is
another question. I don't know that anyone is prepared to answer.

If there is a reason, I suspect it was for a different set of faults.
Tolstoy may have felt that Chekhov was a prelude to someone
yet to arrive, someone like Beckett. In his plays, Chekhov's people were simply not doing what they ought to be doing. What
had to irritate Tolstoy immensely was that Anton's play-actors sat
in their own spiritual excrement and made sweet speeches and
moaned a little and sighed and groaned and never got out of
their situation. To Tolstoy, this was a cardinal sin. One should
not live with the given when it is vapid and vaguely immoral.
That was one of Tolstoy's most basic notions. You may have to
endure a dreary given as a discipline, but you do not accept your
condition as eternal, as the meaning of life. He could not permit
that. Could not accept how Chekhov made so much of the essential inanition of the Russian middle class.

HUCKLEBERRY FINN—
ALIVE AT 100

———

I s there a sweeter tonic for the doldrums than old reviews of
great novels? In nineteenth-century Russia, *Anna Karenina*
was received with the following: "Vronsky's passion for his horse
runs parallel to his passion for Anna" . . . "Sentimental rubbish"
. . . "Show me one page," says *The Odessa Courier,* "that contains
an idea." *Moby-Dick* was incinerated: "Graphic descriptions of a
dreariness such as we do not remember to have met before in
marine literature" . . . "Sheer moonstruck lunacy" . . . "Sad stuff.
Mr. Melville's Quakers are wretched dolts and scrivellers and his
mad captain is a monstrous bore."

By this measure, *Huckleberry Finn* gets off lightly. *The Spring-
field Republican* judged it to be no worse than "a gross trifling
with every fine feeling. . . . Mr. Clemens has no reliable sense of
propriety," and the public library in Concord, Massachusetts,
was confident enough to ban it: "the veriest trash." *The Boston
Transcript* reported that "other members of the Library Committee characterize the work as rough, coarse, and inelegant, the
whole book being more suited to the slums than to intelligent,
respectable people."

All the same, the novel was not too unpleasantly regarded.
There were no large critical hurrahs, but the reviews were, on
the whole, friendly. A good tale, went the consensus. There was

no sense that a great novel had landed on the literary world of 1885. The critical climate could hardly anticipate T. S. Eliot and Ernest Hemingway's encomiums fifty years later. In the preface to the English edition, Eliot would speak of "a masterpiece . . . Twain's genius is completely realized," and Ernest went further. In *Green Hills of Africa,* after disposing of Emerson, Hawthorne, and Thoreau, and paying off Henry James and Stephen Crane with a friendly nod, he proceeded to declare, "All modern American literature comes from one book by Mark Twain called *Huckleberry Finn.* . . . It's the best book we've had. All American writing comes from that. There was nothing before. There has been nothing as good since."

Hemingway, with his nonpareil gift for nosing out the perfect *vin de pays* for an ineluctable afternoon, was more like other novelists in one dire respect: He was never at a loss to advance himself with his literary judgments. Assessing the writing of others, he used the working author's rule of thumb: If I give this book a good mark, does it help appreciation of my work? Obviously, *Huckleberry Finn* has passed the test.

A suspicion immediately arises. Mark Twain is doing the kind of writing only Hemingway can do better. Evidently, we must take a look. May I say it helps to have read *Huckleberry Finn* so long ago that it feels brand-new on picking it up again. Perhaps I was eleven when I saw it last, maybe thirteen, but now I only remember that I came to it after *Tom Sawyer* and was disappointed. I couldn't really follow *The Adventures of Huckleberry Finn.* The character of Tom Sawyer, whom I had liked so much in the first book, was altered, and did not seem nice anymore. Huckleberry Finn was altogether beyond me. Later, I recollect being surprised by the high regard nearly everyone who taught American Lit lavished upon the text, but that didn't bring me back to it. Obviously, I was waiting for an assignment from *The New York Times.*

Let me offer assurances. It may have been worth the wait. I suppose I am the ten millionth reader to say that *Huckleberry Finn* is an extraordinary work. Indeed, for all I know, it is a great novel. Flawed, quirky, uneven, not above taking cheap shots and cashing far too many checks (it is rarely above milking its humor)—all the same, what a book we have here! I had the most curious sense of excitement. After a while, I understood my peculiar frame of attention. The book was so up-to-date! I was not

reading a classic author so much as looking at a new work sent to
me in galleys by a publisher. It was as if it had arrived with one of
those rare letters that say, "We won't make this claim often, but
do think we have an extraordinary first novel to send out." So it
was like reading *From Here to Eternity* in galleys, back in 1950, or
Lie Down in Darkness, Catch-22, or *The World According to Garp*
(which reads like a fabulous first novel). You kept being alter-
nately delighted, surprised, annoyed, competitive, critical, and,
finally, excited. A new writer had moved onto the block. He
could be a potential friend or enemy, but he most certainly was
talented.

That was how it felt to read *Huckleberry Finn* a second time. I
kept resisting the context until I finally surrendered. One always does surrender sooner or later to a book with a strong
magnetic field. I felt as if I held the work of a young writer about
thirty or thirty-five, a prodigiously talented fellow from the Midwest, from Missouri probably, who had had the audacity to write
a historical novel about the Mississippi as it might have been a
century and a half ago, and this young writer had managed to
give us a circus of fictional virtuosities. In nearly every chapter
new and remarkable characters bounded out from the printed
page as if it were a tarmac on which they could perform their
leaps. The author's confidence seemed so complete that he
could deal with every kind of man or woman God ever gave to
the middle of America. Jail-house drunks like Huck Finn's
father take their bow, full of the raunchy violence that even gets
into the smell of clothing. Gentlemen and river rats, young, attractive girls full of grit and "sand," and strong old ladies with
aphorisms clicking like knitting needles, fools and confidence
men—what a cornucopia of rabble and gentry inhabit the author's river banks.

It would be superb stuff if only the writer did not keep giving
away the fact that he was a modern young American working in
1984. His anachronisms were not so much in the historical
facts—those seemed accurate enough—but the point of view was
too contemporary. The scenes might succeed—say it again, this
young writer was talented!—but he kept betraying his literary
influences. The author of *The Adventures of Huckleberry Finn* had
obviously been taught a lot by such major writers as Sinclair
Lewis, John Dos Passos, and John Steinbeck; he had certainly
lifted from Faulkner and the mad tone Faulkner could achieve

when writing about maniacal men feuding in deep swamps; he had also absorbed much of what Vonnegut and Heller could teach about the resilience of irony. If he had a surer feel for the picaresque than Saul Bellow in *Augie March,* still he felt derivative of that work. In places one could swear he had memorized *The Catcher in the Rye,* and he probably dipped into *Deliverance* and *Why Are We in Vietnam?* He might even have studied the mannerisms of movie stars. You could feel traces of John Wayne, Victor McLaglen, and Burt Reynolds in his pages. The author had doubtless digested many a Hollywood comedy on small-town life. His instinct for life in hamlets on the Mississippi before the Civil War was as sharp as it was farcical, and couldn't be more commercial.

No matter. With a talent as large as this, one could forgive the obvious eye for success. Many a large talent has to go through large borrowings in order to find his own style, and a lust for popular success, while dangerous to serious writing, is not necessarily fatal. Yes, one could accept the pilferings from other writers, given the scope of his work, the brilliance of the concept—to catch rural America by a trip on a raft down a great river! One could even marvel uneasily at the depth of the instinct for fiction in the author. With the boy Huckleberry Finn, this new novelist had managed to give us a character of no comfortable, measurable dimension. It is easy for characters in modern novels to seem more vivid than figures in the classics but, even so, Huckleberry Finn appeared to be more alive than Don Quixote and Julien Sorel, as naturally near to his own mind as we are to ours. But how often does a hero who is so absolutely natural on the page also succeed in acquiring convincing moral stature as his adventures develop?

It is to be repeated. In the attractive grip of this talent, one is ready to forgive the author of *Huckleberry Finn* for every influence he has so promiscuously absorbed. He has made such fertile use of his borrowings. One could even cheer his appearance on our jaded literary scene if not for the single transgression that goes too far. These are passages that do more than borrow an author's style—they copy it! Influence is mental, but theft is physical. Who can declare to a certainty that a large part of the prose in *Huckleberry Finn* is not lifted directly from Hemingway? We know that we are not reading Ernest only because the author, obviously fearful that his tone is getting too near, is careful to sprinkle his text with "a-clutterings" and "warn'ts" and "any-wheres" and "t'others." But we have read Hemingway—and so we see through it—we know we are reading pure Hemingway disguised:

> We cut young cottonwoods and willows, and hid the raft with them. Then we set out the lines. Next we slid into the river and had a swim . . . then we set down on the sandy bottom where the river was knee-deep and watched the daylight come. Not a sound anywheres . . . the first thing to see, looking away over the water, was a kind of dull line— that was the woods on t'other side; you couldn't make nothing else out; then a pale place in the sky; then more paleness spreading around; then the river softened up away off, and warn't black any more . . . by and by you could see a streak on the water which you know by the look of the streak that there's a snag there in a swift current which breaks on it and makes that streak look that way; and you see the mist curl up off the water and the east reddens up and the river.

Up to now I have conveyed, I expect, the pleasure of reading this book today. It is the finest compliment I can offer. We use an unspoken standard of relative judgment on picking up a classic. Secretly, we expect less reward from it than from a good contemporary novel. The average intelligent modern reader would probably, under torture, admit that *Heartburn* was more fun to read, minute for minute, than *Madame Bovary,* and maybe one even learned more. That is not to say that the first will be superior to the second a hundred years from now but that a classic novel is like a fine horse carrying an exorbitant impost. Classics suffer by their distance from our day-to-day gossip. The mark of how good *Huckleberry Finn* has to be is that one can compare it to a number of our best modern American novels and it stands up page for page, awkward here, sensational there—absolutely the equal of one of those rare incredible first novels that come along once or twice in a decade. So I have spoken of it as kin to a first novel because it is so young and so fresh and so all-out silly in some of the chances it takes and even wins. A wiser old novelist would never play that far out when the work was already well along and so neatly in hand, but Twain does.

For the sake of literary propriety, let me not, however, lose sight of the actual context. *The Adventures of Huckleberry Finn* is a novel of the nineteenth century and its grand claims to literary magnitude are also to be remarked upon. So I will say that the first measure of a great novel may be that it presents—like a human of palpable charisma—an all but visible aura. Few works of literature can be so luminous without the presence of some majestic symbol. In *Huckleberry Finn* we are presented (given the possible exception of Anna Livia Plurabelle) with the best river ever to flow through a novel, our own Mississippi, and in the voyage down those waters of Huck Finn and a runaway slave on their raft, we are held in the thrall of the river. Larger than a character, the river is a manifest presence, a demiurge to support the man and the boy, a deity to betray them, feed them, all but drown them, fling them apart, float them back together. The river winds like a fugue through the marrow of the true narrative, which is nothing less than the ongoing relation between Huck and the runaway slave, this Nigger Jim whose name embodies the very stuff of the slave system itself—his name is not Jim but Nigger Jim. The growth of love and knowledge between the runaway white and the runaway black is a relation equal to the relation of the men to the river, for it is also full of betrayal and nourishment, separation and return. So it manages to touch that last fine nerve of the heart where compassion and irony speak to one another and thereby give a good turn to our most protected emotions.

Reading *Huckleberry Finn,* one comes to realize all over again that the near burned-out, throttled, hate-filled dying affair between whites and blacks is still our great national love affair, and woe to us if it ends in detestation and mutual misery. Riding the current of this novel, we are back in the happy time when the love affair was new and all seemed possible. How rich is the recollection of that emotion! What else is greatness but the indestructible wealth it leaves in the mind's recollection after hope has soured and passions are spent? It is always the hope of democracy that our wealth will be there to spend again, and the ongoing treasure of *Huckleberry Finn* is that it frees us to think of democracy and its sublime, terrifying premise: Let the passions and cupidities and dreams and kinks and ideals and greed and hopes and foul corruptions of all men and women have their day and the world will still be better off, for there is more good than bad in the sum of us and our workings. Mark Twain, whole embodiment of that democratic human, understood the premise in every turn of his pen, and how he tested it, how he twisted and tantalized and tested it until we are weak all over again with our love for the idea.

ODDMENTS ON
HEMINGWAY

———

J. MICHAEL LENNON: I don't think anyone can deny the brilliance
of Hemingway in terms of style. But Hemingway could never
write a book like *The Naked and the Dead,* in which you're talking about fascism coming to America, technology, and the
kinds of themes you have dealt with over the past thirty years.

NORMAN MAILER: I didn't say Hemingway was brighter than I
was. I just said he writes better.

JML: But that's not the same as saying his talent is better.

NM: Well, I think it is. You can have marvelous character actors
like Charles Laughton, who can play just about any part.
Then you get someone like Marilyn Monroe, who, in the technical sense, has a small talent. But she can come out and hold
a mandolin and play a little ditty and wonderful things happen. Let's take an example we would argue about less. In the
technical sense, there were limitations, I suppose, to Charlie
Chaplin. Any number of actors can do a credible imitation
of Charlie Chaplin and, in addition, play fifty roles Chaplin
would never go near. Yet we could never argue that they were
greater than Chaplin. Even though they might achieve
ninety-five percent of him in an imitation, Chaplin plucked a
nerve in us that very few artists reach. What great artists do is
so profound, you don't debate with it.

Hemingway's style affected whole generations of us, the way a roomful of men are affected when a beautiful woman walks through—their night is turned for better or for worse. His style had the ability to hit young writers in the gut, and they weren't the same after that.

I guess I would say that he occupies the very center of American writing. No matter how serious or superficial a reader you are, you quickly sense that you are in the hands of someone who writes so well that your wits are keyed afterward to the flaws in the bad writing of others, and, worse, in yourself.

What characterizes every book about Hemingway I have read is the way his character remains out of focus. Even a writer with an edge as hard as Lillian Ross did not seem able to catch him properly in her famous *New Yorker* piece. Hemingway was there, but much too precise in his portrait, as if he had sat for one of those neo-realist paintings where the pride of the artist is to make the subject look as if he has been photographed, not painted.

For contrast, there is Carlos Baker's monumental biography, and it gives us an immense amount of day-to-day material somewhat modestly undigested. It is nonetheless an invaluable book that every ambitious biography to come will evaluate detail by detail, a necessary task, for Baker's book was written with a determinedly soft focus, as if the author felt his literary mission was not so much to present the man as to cover every year of Hemingway's existence in the recollections of his friends.

There is also A. E. Hotchner's book, which gives us a portrait, and most readable it is, but askew. Hotchner is using a wide-angle lens; the very nostrils of the great man are distorted. Sadly, we learn there is reason to believe the materials are transposed. A long and marvelously articulated speech which Hemingway makes once to Hotchner turns out in fact to have been taken from a letter. It is a minor literary peccadillo of the sort professional magazine writers commit often, since their skills mature in a school which demands you tell your story fast and make it track (and a quotation from a letter comes off slower than a man talking), but such methods breed distortion with their speed.

Now, we have here a book written by a son about his father,*

---

*Papa, by Gregory Hemingway.

written by a son who is not a professional writer, as he is quick to tell you (although he can write interestingly enough—it may even be a book which will be read at one sitting by more than half the readers who pick it up). That is because it is unlike most books written by sons about great fathers. There is nothing slavish here. The son lies to the father, and the father pays him back, meanly; the son loves the father and the father loves him back, but in his own style, and it is remote enough for the son to hate him a little as well. If it is a portrait written in love, it is with all the sweets and sours of love. What characterizes love when not wholly blissful is how damnably sweet and sour it gets. It kills any man or woman if they have the bad luck to be deeply in love with a veritable son of a bitch, and every bad thing we have ever heard about Hemingway can find its echo in this book. You do not have to wonder when you are done why any number of men and women could know Hemingway well and hate him. Yet everything fine, noble, attractive, and splendid in the man comes in with its echo as well. For once, you can read a book about Hemingway and not have to decide whether you like him or not. He is there. By God, he exists. He is a father, good and bad by turns, even sensational and godawful on different days of the year, and his contradictions are now his unity, his dirty fighting and his love of craft come out of the same blood. We can feel the man present before us, and his complexes have now become no more than his moods. His pride and his evasions have become one man, his innocence and sophistication, his honesty and outsize snobbery, his romantic madness and inconceivably practical sense of how to be outrageously romantic; it all comes through as in no other book about Hemingway, and for the simplest reason—the father was real to the son. Whereas those of us who approach Hemingway from without have been in the position of trying to find the reality behind the legend, and that is an especially contemporary form of analysis which tends to come out wrong. Hemingway, when all is said, was a Midwestern boy seized by success and ripped out of every root, and he spent the rest of his life trying to relocate some of his old sense of terra firma by following each movement of the wind (and there were many) through his talent and his dread. What a remarkable achievement that the sense of that talent and dread, while hardly ever referred to in these pages, is nonetheless in every paragraph of this unassuming and affective memoir.

THE TURD TEST

The cruelest criticism ever delivered of Henry James is that
he had a consciousness (and a style) so hermetic that his pen
would have been paralyzed if he had ever entered a town house,
removed his hat, and found a turd on his head (a matter we
would hope of small moment to Tolstoy or to Dostoyevsky or to
Stendhal). Hemingway would have been bothered more than he
liked. Miller would have loved it. How did his host react to the
shit? How did our host's wife? My God, the way she smacked her
nostrils, you can be sure her thighs were in a lather.

In fact, Hemingway would have hated such a scene. He was
trying to create a world where mood—which Hemingway saw as
the staff of life—could be cultivated by the scrupulosity with
which you kept mood aloft. Mood surviving through the excellence of your gravity, courage, and diction, that is to say, your
manners.

Hemingway's dreams must have looked down the long vista
of his future suicide. So he had a legitimate fear of chaos. He
never wrote about the river—he contented himself with the
quintessentially American aesthetic of writing about the camp
he set up each night by the side of the river: That was the night
we made camp at the foot of the cliffs just after the place where
the rapids were bad.

Miller became the other half of literature, an *espontaneo* without fear of his end, a literary athlete at ease in air, earth, or water. I am the river, he was always ready to say, I am the rapids and the placids, I'm the froth and the scum and the twigs—what a roar as I go over the falls. Who gives a fart? Let others camp where they may. I am the river and there is nothing I can't swallow.

Hemingway's world was doomed to collapse so soon as the forces of the century pushed life into a technological tunnel; with Hemingway, mood could not survive grinding gears, surrealist manners—here's shit in your hat—static, but Miller took off at the place where Hemingway stopped. In *Tropic of Cancer* he was saying—and it is the force of the book—I am obliged to live where mood is in the meat grinder, so I know more about it. I know all of the spectrum that runs from good mood to bad mood, and can tell you—a stinking mood is better than no mood. Life has been designed to run in the stink.

Miller bounces in it. We read *Tropic of Cancer,* that book of horrors, and feel happy. It is because there is honor in the horror, and metaphor in the hideous. How, we cannot even begin to say. Maybe mood is vastly more various, self-regenerative, hearty, and sly than Hemingway ever guessed. Maybe mood is not a lavender lady but a barmaid. Without stoicism or good taste, or even a nose for the nicety of good guts under terrible pressure, Miller is still living closer to death than Hemingway, certainly he is closer if the sewer is nearer to our end than the wound.

History proved to be on Miller's side. Twentieth-century life was leaving the world of individual effort, liquor, and tragic wounds, for the big-city garbage can of bruises, migraines, static, mood chemicals, amnesia, absurd relations, and cancer. Down in the sewers of existence where the cancer was being cooked, Miller was cavorting. Look, he was forever saying, you do not have to die of this crud. You can breathe it, eat it, suck it, fuck it, and still bounce up for the next day. There is something inestimable in us if we can stand the smell. Considering where the world was going—right into the worldwide sewer of the concentration camps—Miller may have had a message that gave more life than Hemingway.

HENRY MILLER

His work embraced, which is to say swallowed in four or five weeks, and then re-read over another month or two, can sit in one's mind with all the palpability of a huge elm lying in the backyard. The nobility of the trunk is on the ground for you to examine, not to speak of the rich nightmare of the roots and crawlers. To read Miller in that short a period reopens the old question, which is always too large: What is a man? Just as our uprooted elm would take on constellations of meaning as it lay in the yard until finally it could be reminiscent of a battleship, or a host of caverns in Hieronymus Bosch, so might you be forced to ask: What the devil is a tree? Just so does Miller return us to the first question of humanism. What, finally, is a Man? Nothing is settled after all. We have been given the illusion that we know Miller, know every one of his vices, peccadilloes, hustles, horrors, cadges, gifts, flaws, and transcendent generosities, are, yes, familiar with that man who is by his own description "confused, negligent, reckless, lusty, obscene, boisterous, thoughtful, scrupulous, lying, diabolically truthful . . . filled with wisdom and nonsense." Nonetheless, when we are done reading, we wonder if we know anything. It is not that he bears no relation to the Henry Miller who is the protagonist of his books. (That Henry Miller is, indeed, the ultimate definition of the word *protagonist*.) No, the real Henry Miller, which is to say, the corporeal protean Miller whom a few writers knew intimately and wrote about well, Anaïs Nin being the first, is not very different from his work, but more like a transparency placed over a drawing, and then skewed a degree. He is just a little different from his work. But in that difference is all the mystery of his own personality, and the paradoxes of a great artist. And the failure. For it is impossible to talk of a great artist without speaking of failure. The greater they are, the more they do not fulfill their own idea of themselves. Miller was never able to come to focus on the one subject which cried out to him: D. H. Lawrence's old subject— what is to be said of love between a man and a woman? Miller saw that Lawrence had come to grips with the poetry of sex but none of the sewer gas. Miller would strike matches to the sewer gas and set off literary explosions, but he never blew himself over to the other side of the divide. While nobody can be more poetic than Miller about fornication itself—two hundred beer-hall accordions might as well be pumping away as he describes the more heavenly engagements he has played—the writing becomes an evocation of some disembodied but divine cunt and what it is doing to him—his appreciation equal to the enjoyment of a great symphony, yet he still cannot write about fucking with love. (Of course, it is fair to ask, who can?) Miller nonetheless pounds away on the subject like a giant phallus trying to enter a tiny vagina—in the pounding is one simple question: How the hell do you get in?

Miller has not lacked for adulation. A small but accountable part of the literary world has regarded him as the greatest living American writer for the last four decades, and indeed, as other American writers died, and Hemingway was there no longer, nor Faulkner and Fitzgerald, not Wolfe, not Steinbeck, nor Dos Passos, and Sinclair Lewis long gone, Dreiser dead and Farrell in partial obscurity, who else could one speak of as the great American author? Moreover, Miller provided his considerable qualifications. One had to go back to Melville to find a rhetoric that could prove as noble under full sail. Miller at his best wrote a prose more overpowering than Faulkner's—the good reader is revolved in a farrago of light with words heavy as velvet, brilliant as gems; eruptions of thought cover the page. You could be in the vortex of one of Turner's oceanic holocausts, where the sun shines in the very center of the storm. No, there is nothing like Henry Miller when he gets rolling. Men with literary styles as full as Hawthorne's appear by comparison stripped of their rich language; one has to take English back to Marlowe and Shakespeare before encountering a wealth of imagery equal in intensity.

Yet it can hardly be said that the American Establishment walks around today thinking of Henry Miller as our literary genius or one of the symbols of human wealth in America. Born in 1891, he will be eighty-five by December 26 of 1976, an artist of incomparably larger dimensions than Robert Frost, yet who can conceive of a President inviting him to read from his work on Inauguration Day—no, the irony is that a number of good and intelligent politicians might even have a slight hesitation over whether it is Arthur Miller or Henry Miller being talked about.

"Oh yes, *Henry* Miller," they might say at last, "the guy who writes the dirty books."

In the literary world, however, Miller's reputation also survives in a vacuum. It is not that he lacks influence. It is not even excessive to say that Henry Miller had influenced the style of half the good American poets and writers alive today: Would books as different as *Naked Lunch, Portnoy's Complaint, Fear of Flying,* and *Why Are We in Vietnam?* have been as well received (or as free in language) without the irrigation Henry Miller gave to American prose? Even a writer so removed in purpose from Miller as Saul Bellow shows a debt in *Augie March*. Miller has had his effect. Thirty years ago, young writers learned to write by reading him along with Hemingway and Faulkner, Wolfe and Fitzgerald. With the exception of Hemingway, he has had perhaps the largest stylistic influence of them all. Yet there is still that critical space. Miller has only been written about in terms of adulation or dismissal. One does not pick up literary reviews with articles entitled "Ernest Hemingway and Henry Miller— Their Paris Years," or "The Social Worlds of F. Scott Fitzgerald and Henry Miller," no comments on "The Apocalyptic Vision of Henry Miller and Thomas Wolfe as Reflected in Their Rhetoric." Nor is there bound to be a work titled "Henry Miller and the Beat Generation" or "Henry Miller and the Revolution of the Sixties." Young men do not feel they are dying inside because they cannot live the way Henry Miller once lived. Yet no American writer came closer to the crazy bliss of being alone in a strange city with no money in your pocket, not much food in your stomach, and a hard-on beginning to stir, a "personal" hard-on (as one of Miller's characters nicely describes it).

The paradox therefore persists. It is a wonder. To read *Tropic of Cancer* today is to take in his dimension. He is a greater writer than one thought. It is one of the few great novels of our American century, a revolution in style and consciousness equal to *The Sun Also Rises*. You cannot pass through the first twenty pages without knowing that a literary wonder is taking place—nobody has ever written in just this way before, nobody may ever write by this style so well again. A time and a place have come to focus in a writer's voice. It is like encountering an archaeological relic. Given enough such novels, the history of our century could never be lost: There would be enough points of reference.

It is close therefore to incomprehensible that a man whose literary career has been with us over forty years, an author who wrote one novel that may yet be considered equal to the best of Hemingway, and probably produced more than Thomas Wolfe day by day, and was better word for word, and purple passage for purple passage, a writer finally like a phenomenon, has somehow, with every large acceptance, and every respect, been nonetheless ignored and near to discarded.

We must assume there was something indigestible about Miller that went beyond his ideas. His condemnations are virtually comfortable to us today, yet he is not an author whose complexities are in harmony with our own. Hemingway and Fitzgerald may each have been outrageous pieces of psychic work, yet their personalities haunt us. Faulkner inspires our reverence and Wolfe our tenderest thoughts for literary genius. They are good to the memories we keep of our reading of them—they live with the security of old films. But Miller does not. He is a force, a value, a literary sage, and yet in the most peculiar sense he does not become more compatible with time—he is no better beloved today than twenty, thirty, or forty years ago—it is as if he is almost not an American author; yet nobody could be more American. So he evades our sense of classification. He does not become a personality; rather he maintains himself as an enigma.

The authors who live best in legend offer personalities we can comprehend like movie stars. Hemingway and Fitzgerald impinge on our psyche with the clarity of Bogart and Cagney. We comprehend them at once. Faulkner bears the same privileged relation to a literary Southerner as Olivier to the London theatregoer. A grand and cultivated presence is enriching the marrow of your life. Nobody wishes to hear a bad story about Olivier or Faulkner.

Henry Miller, however, exists in the same relation to legend that anti-matter shows to matter. His life is antipathetic to the idea of legend itself. Where he is complex, he is too complex—we do not feel the resonance of slowly dissolving mystery but the madness of too many knots; where he is simple, he is not attractive—his air is harsh. If he had remained the protagonist by which he first presented himself in *Tropic of Cancer*—the man with iron in his phallus, acid in his mind, and some kind of incomparable relentless freedom in his heart, that paradox of tough misery and keen happiness, that connoisseur of the spectrum of odors between good sewers and bad sewers, a noble rat gnawing on existence and impossible to kill, then he could indeed have been a legend, a species of Parisian Bogart or American Belmondo. Everybody would have wanted to meet this post-gangster barbarian-genius. He would have been the American and heterosexual equivalent of Jean Genet. But that was not his desire. Paradoxically, he was too separate from his work.

In fact, he could never have been too near to the character he made of himself in *Tropic of Cancer*. One part never fits. It is obvious he must have been more charming than he pretends—how else account for all the free dinners he was invited to, the people he lived on, the whores who loved him? There had to be something angelic about him. Anaïs Nin when describing the apartment in Clichy that Miller kept with Alfred Perles made the point that Miller was the one tidying the joint. "Henry keeps house like a Dutch housekeeper. He is very neat and clean. No dirty dishes about. It is all monastic, really, with no trimmings, no decoration."* Where in all of *Tropic of Cancer* is this neat and charming man?

His novel must be more a fiction, then, than a fact. Which, of course, is not to take away a particle of its worth. Perhaps it becomes even more valuable. After all, we do not write to recapture an experience; we write to come as close to it as we can. Sometimes we are not very close, and yet, paradoxically, are nearer than if we had a photograph. Not nearer necessarily to the verisimilitude of what happened but to the mysterious reality of what can happen on a page. Oil paints do not create clouds but the image of clouds; a page of manuscript can only evoke that special kind of reality which lives on the skin of the writing paper, a rainbow on a soap bubble. Miller is forever accused of caricature by people who knew his characters, and any good reader knows enough about personality to sense how much he must be leaving out of his people. Yet what a cumulative reality they give us. His characters make up a Paris more real than its paving stones until a reluctant wonder bursts upon us—no French writer, no matter how great, not Rabelais, nor Proust, not de Maupassant, Hugo, Huysmans, Zola, or even Balzac, not even Céline has made Paris more vivid to us. Whenever before has a foreigner described a country better than its native writ-

---

The Diary of Anaïs Nin (Vol. 1) (New York: The Swallow Press and Harcourt, Brace & World, Inc., 1966), p. 62.

ers? For in *Tropic of Cancer* Miller succeeded in performing one high literary act: He created a tone in prose which caught the tone of a period and a place. If that main character in *Tropic of Cancer* named Henry Miller never existed in life, it hardly matters—he is the voice and spirit which existed at the time. The spirits of literature may be the nearest we come to historical truth.

For that matter, the great confessions of literature are apart from their authors. Augustine recollecting his sins is not the sinner but the pieties. Stendhal is not Julien Sorel, nor Kierkegaard the seducer. *On the Road* is close to Jack Kerouac, yet he gives us a happier Kerouac there than the one who died too soon. Proust was not his own narrator, even as homosexuality is not heterosexuality but another land, and if we take *The Sun Also Rises* as the purest example of a book whose protagonist created the precise air of a time and a place, even there we come to the realization that Hemingway at the time he wrote it could not have been equal to Jake Barnes—he had created a consciousness wiser, drier, purer, more classic, more sophisticated, and more graceful than his own. He was still gauche in relation to his creation.

The difference between Hemingway and Miller is that Hemingway set out thereafter to grow into Jake Barnes and locked himself, for better and worse, for enormous fame and eventual destruction, into that character who embodied the spirit of an age. Miller, following, had only to keep writing *Tropic of Cancer* over and over, refining his own personality to become less and less separate from his book, and he could have entered the American life of legend. But Henry, eight years older than Hemingway, yet arriving at publication eight years later, and so sixteen years older in 1934 than Hemingway was in 1926, chose to go in the opposite direction. He proceeded to move away from the first Henry Miller he had created. He did not wish to be a character but a soul—he would be various. He was.

D. H. LAWRENCE

———

Not until his last book did one of Lawrence's romances end with the heroine pregnant, tranquil, and fulfilled. Lawrence's love affairs were more likely to come in like winds off *Wuthering Heights*—yet never had a male novelist written more intimately about women—heart, contradiction, and soul; never had a novelist loved them more, been so comfortable in the tides of their sentiment, and so ready to see them murdered. His work held, on the consequence, huge fascination for women. Since by the end he was also the sacramental poet of the sacramental act, for he believed nothing human had such significance as the tender majesties of a man and woman fucking with love, he was also the most appalling subversive to the single permissive sexual standard. The orgy, homosexuality, and the inevitable promiscuity attached to a sexual search repelled him, and might yet repel many of the young as they become bored with the similarity of the sexes.

Indeed, which case-hardened guerrilla of Women's Liberation might not shed a private tear at the following passage:

> *And if you're in Scotland and I'm in the Midlands, and I can't put my arms round you, and wrap my legs round you, yet I've got something of you. My soul softly flaps in the little pentecost flame with*

you, like the peace of fucking. We fucked a flame into being. Even the flowers are fucked into being between the sun and the earth. But it's a delicate thing, and takes patience and the long pause.

So I love chastity now, because it is the peace that comes of fucking. I love being chaste now. I love it as snowdrops love the snow. I love this chastity, which is the pause of peace of our fucking, between us now like a snowdrop of forked white fire. And when the real spring comes, when the drawing together comes, then we can fuck the little flame brilliant and yellow. . . .

Yes, which stout partisan of the Liberation would read such words and not go soft for the memory of some bitter bridge of love she had burned behind. Lawrence was dangerous. So delicate and indestructible an enemy to the cause of Liberation that to expunge him one would have to look for Kate Millett herself. If she is more careful with Lawrence than with Henry Miller, acting less like some literary Molotov, if her disrespect for quotation is in this place more guarded, if she even functions as a critic and so gives us a clue to the meaning of Lawrence's life and work, she has become twice adroit at hiding the real evidence. So she rises from abuse to night-school legal briefs—it is crucial to her case that Lawrence actually be the "counterrevolutionary sexual politician" she terms him, but since women love his work, and remember it, she is obliged to bring in the evidence more or less fairly, and only distort it by small moves, brief elisions in the quotation, the suppression of passing contradictions, in short bring in all the evidence on her side of the case and only harangue the jury a little. Since she has a great deal of evidence, only a careful defense can overthrow her case. For Lawrence can be hung as a counterrevolutionary sexual politician out of his own words and speeches. There is a plethora of evidence—in his worst books. And in all his books there are unmistakable tendencies toward the absolute domination of women by men, mystical worship of the male will, detestation of democracy. There is a stretch in the middle of his work, out in such unread tracts as *Aaron's Rod* and *Kangaroo*, when the uneasy feeling arrives that perhaps it was just as well Lawrence died when he did, for he could have been the literary adviser to Oswald Mosley about the time Hitler came in; one can even ingest a comprehension of the appeal of fascism to Pound and Wyndham Lewis, since the death of nature lived already in the air of the contract between corporate democracy and technology, and who was then to know that the marriage of fascism and technology would be even worse, would accelerate that death. Still, such fear for the end of Lawrence is superficial. He was perhaps a great writer, certainly full of faults, and abominably pedestrian in his language when the ducts of experience burned dry, he was unendurably didactic then, he was a pill, and at his worst a humorless nag; he is pathetic in all those places he suggests that men should follow the will of a stronger man, a purer man, a man conceivably not unlike himself, for one senses in his petulance and in the spoiled airs of his impatient disdain at what he could not intellectually dominate that he was a momma's boy, spoiled rotten, and could not have commanded two infantrymen to follow him, yet he was still a great writer, for he contained a cauldron of boiling opposites—he was on the one hand a Hitler in a teapot, on the other he was the blessed breast of tender love, he knew what it was to love a woman from her hair to her toes, he lived with all the sensibility of a female burning with tender love—and these incompatibles, enough to break a less extraordinary man, were squared in their difficulty by the fact that he had intellectual ambition sufficient to desire the overthrow of European civilization, his themes were nothing if not immense—in *The Plumed Serpent* he would even look to the founding of a new religion based on the virtues of the phallus and the submission of women to the wisdom of that principle. But he was also the son of a miner; he came from hard practical small-minded people, stock descended conceivably from the Druids, but how many centuries had hammered the reductive wisdom of pounds and pennies into the genes? So a part of Lawrence was like a little tobacconist from the English Midlands who would sniff the smoke of his wildest ideas—notions, we may be certain, which ran completely off the end of anybody's word system—and hack out an irritable cough at the intimate intricate knobby knotty contradictions of his ideas when they were embodied in people. For if we can feel how consumed he was by the dictatorial pressure to ram his sentiments into each idiot throat, he never forgets that he is writing novels, and so his ideas cannot simply triumph, they have to be tried and heated and forged, and finally be beaten into shapelessness against the anvil of his own British skepticism which would not buy his ideas, not outright, for even his own characters seem to wear out in them. Kate Leslie, the heroine of *The Plumed Serpent*, a proud, sophisticated Irish lady, falls in love with one of the Mexican leaders of a new party, a new faith, a new ritual, gives herself to the new religion, believes in her submission—but not entirely! At the end she is still attached to the ambivalence of the European mind. Lilly, the hero of *Aaron's Rod,* finally preaches "deep fathomless submission to the heroic soul in a greater man" and the greater man is Lilly, but he is a slim, small, somewhat ridiculous figure, a bigger man for example strikes him in front of his wife and he is reduced to regaining his breath without showing he is hurt; he is a small hard-shelled nut of contradictions, much like Lawrence himself, but the grandeur of the ideas sound ridiculous in the little cracked shell. Of course, Lawrence was not only trying to sell dictatorial theorems, he was also trying to rid himself of them. We can see by the literary line of his life that he moves from the adoration of his mother in *Sons and Lovers* and from close to literal adoration of the womb in *The Rainbow* to worship of the phallus and the male will in his later books. In fact, Millett can be quoted to good effect, for her criticism is here close to objective, which is to say not totally at odds with the defense:

> Aaron's Rod, Kangaroo, *and* The Plumed Serpent *are rather neglected novels, and perhaps justly so. They are unquestionably strident, and unpleasant for a number of reasons, principally a rasping protofascist tone, an increasing fondness of force, a personal arrogance, and innumerable racial, class, and religious bigotries. In these novels one sees how terribly Lawrence strained after triumph in the "man's world" of formal politics, war, priestcraft, art and finance. Thinking of* Lady Chatterley *or the early novels, readers often equate Lawrence with the personal life which generally concerns the novelist, the relations of men and women—for whether he played a woman's man or a man's man, Lawrence was generally doing so before an audience of women, who found it difficult to associate him with the public life of male authority. After* Women in Love, *having solved, or failed to solve, the problem of mastering the female, Lawrence became more ambitious. Yet he never failed to take his sexual politics with him, and with an astonishing consistency of motive, made it the foundation of all his other social and political beliefs.*

It is fair analysis as far as it goes, but it fails to underline the heroism of his achievement, which is that he was able finally to leave off his quest for power in the male world and go back to what he started with, go back after every bitterness and frustration to his first knowledge that the physical love of men and women, insofar as it was untainted by civilization, was the salvation of us all, there was no other. And in fact he had never ceased believing that, he had merely lost hope it could be achieved.

Millett's critical misdemeanor is to conceal the pilgrimage, hide the life, cover over that emotional odyssey which took him from adoration of the woman to outright lust for her murder, then took him back to worship her beauty, even her procreative beauty. Millett avoids the sympathy this might arouse in her female readers (which lover is more to be cherished than the one who returned at the end?), yes, avoids such huge potential sympathy by two simple critical stratagems; she writes about his last book first, which enables her to end her very long chapter on Lawrence with an analysis of his story "The Woman Who Rode Away." Since it may be the most savage of his stories and concludes with the ritual sacrifice of a white woman by natives, Millett can close on Lawrence with the comment, "Probably it is the perversion of sexuality into slaughter, indeed, the story's very travesty and denial of sexuality, which accounts for its monstrous, even demented air." Not every female reader will remind herself that Lawrence, having purged his blood of murder, would now go on to write *Lady Chatterley*. But then Millett is not interested in the dialectic by which writers deliver their themes to themselves; she is more interested in hiding the process, and so her second way of concealing how much Lawrence has still to tell us about men and women is simply to distort the complexity of his brain into snarling maxims, take him at his worst and make him even worse, take him at his best and bring pinking shears to his context. Like a true species of literary Mafia, Millett works always for points and the shading of points. If she can't steal a full point, she'll cop a half.

Examples abound, but it is necessary to quote Lawrence in some fullness; a defense of his works rests naturally on presenting him in uninterrupted lines, which indeed will be no hardship to read. Besides, the clearest exposure of the malignant literary habits of the prosecutor is to quote her first and thereby give everyone an opportunity to see how little she shows, how much she ignores, in her desire to steal the verdict.

"You lie there," he orders. She accedes with a "queer obedience"—Lawrence never uses the word female in the novel without prefacing it with the adjectives "weird" or "queer": this is presumably

*done to persuade the reader that woman is a dim prehistoric crea-
ture operating out of primeval impulse. Mellors concedes one kiss
on the navel and then gets to business:*

And he had to come into her at once, to enter the peace on
earth of that soft quiescent body. It was the moment of pure
peace for him, the entry into the body of a woman. She lay
still, in a kind of sleep, always in a kind of sleep. The activity, the orgasm was all his, all his; she could strive for herself
no more.

This is the passage from which she has drawn her quotation:

*"You lie there," he said softly, and he shut the door, so that it was
dark, quite dark.*

*With a queer obedience, she lay down on the blanket. Then she
felt the soft, groping, helplessly desirous hand touching her body,
feeling for her face. The hand stroked her face softly, softly, with infinite soothing and assurance, and at last there was the soft touch of
a kiss on her cheek.*

*She lay quite still, in a sort of sleep, in a sort of dream. Then she
quivered as she felt his hand groping softly, yet with queer thwarted
clumsiness among her clothing. Yet the hand knew, too, how to
unclothe her where it wanted. He drew down the thin silk sheath,
slowly, carefully, right down and over her feet. Then with a quiver
of exquisite pleasure he touched the warm soft body, and touched
her navel for a moment in a kiss. And he had to come into her at
once, to enter the peace on earth of her soft, quiescent body. It was
the moment of pure peace for him, the entry into the body of a
woman.*

*She lay still, in a kind of sleep, always in a kind of sleep. The ac-
tivity, the orgasm was his, all his; she could strive for herself no
more. Even the tightness of his arms round her, even the intense
movement of his body, and the springing seed in her, was a kind of
sleep, from which she did not begin to rouse till he had finished and
lay softly panting against her breast.*

It is a modest example, but then it is a modest act and Con-
stance Chatterley is exhausted with the emotional costs of her
previous world. Since she and her new lover will make other
kinds of love later, the prosecutor will have cause enough to be

further enraged, but the example can show how the tone of Lawrence's prose is poisoned by the acids of inappropriate comment. "Mellors concedes one kiss on the navel and then gets to business." Indeed! Take off your business suit, Comrade Millett.

But it is hardly the time for a recess. We will want to look at another exhibit. The quoted lines up for indictment are from *Women in Love:*

> *Having begun by informing Ursula he will not love her, as he is interested in going beyond love to "something much more impersonal and harder," he goes on to state his terms: "I've seen plenty of women, I'm sick of seeing them. I want a woman I don't see . . . I don't want your good looks, and I don't want your womanly feelings, and I don't want your thoughts nor opinions nor your ideas." The "new" relationship, while posing as an affirmation of the primal unconscious sexual being, to adopt Lawrence's jargon, is in effect a denial of personality in the woman.*

Or is it a denial of personality in Lawrence? Witness how our literary commissar will void the strength of Lawrence's style by cutting off our acquaintance with the marrow of his sensibility, the air of his senses. For Lawrence is always alert to the quiet ringing of the ether, the quick retreat of a mood, the awe of the thought about to be said, then left unsaid, then said after all. But his remarks cannot be chopped out of their setting. A bruised apple at the foot of a tree is another reality from a bruised apple in the frigidaire.

> *There was silence for some moments.*
> *"No," he said. "It isn't that. Only—if we are going to make a relationship, even of friendship, there must be something final and irrevocable about it."*
> *There was a clang of mistrust and almost anger in his voice. She did not answer. Her heart was too much contracted. She could not have spoken.*
> *Seeing she was not going to reply, he continued, almost bitterly, giving himself away:*
> *"I can't say it is love I have to offer—and it isn't love I want. It is something much more impersonal and harder—and rarer."*
> *There was a silence, out of which she said:*
> *"You mean you don't love me?"*

She suffered furiously, saying that.
"Yes, if you like to put it like that. Though perhaps that isn't true.
I don't know. At any rate, I don't feel the emotion of love for you—
no, and I don't want to. Because it gives out in the last issues. . . ."

How different is all this from "going beyond love to 'something much more impersonal and harder,'" how much in fact we have the feeling they are in love.

"If there is no love, what is there?" she cried, almost jeering.
"Something," he said, looking at her, battling with his soul, with all his might.
"What?"
He was silent for a long time, unable to be in communication with her while she was in this state of opposition.
"There is," he said, in a voice of pure abstraction, "a final me which is stark and impersonal and beyond responsibility. So there is a final you, and it is there I would want to meet you—not in the emotional, loving plane—but there beyond, where there is no speech and no terms of agreement. There we are two stark, unknown beings, two utterly strange creatures, I would want to approach you, and you me. And there could be no obligation, because there is no standard for action there, because no understanding has been reaped from that plane. It is quite inhuman—so there can be no calling to book, in any form whatsoever—because one is outside the pale of all that is accepted, and nothing known applies. One can only follow the impulse, taking that which lies in front, and responsible for nothing, asking for nothing, giving nothing, only each taking according to the primal desire."
Ursula listened to this speech, her mind dumb and almost senseless, what he said was so unexpected and so untoward.
"It is just purely selfish," she said.
"If it is pure, yes. But it isn't selfish at all. Because I don't know what I want of you. I deliver myself *over to the unknown, in coming to you, I am without reserves or defenses, stripped entirely, into the unknown. Only there needs the pledge between us, that we will both cast off everything, cast off ourselves even, and cease to be, so that that which is perfectly ourselves can take place in us."*

As we shall soon see, Lawrence will go further than this, he will come to believe that a woman must submit completely, bet on it. Yet in that book where such submission takes place, in *The Plumed Serpent,* where Kate Leslie has her most profound sex with a man who insists on remaining a stranger and an Indian, the moral emerges that he wants her by the end, wants Kate Leslie just so deeply as she desires him. Lawrence's point, which he refines over and over, is that the deepest messages of sex cannot be heard by taking a stance on the side of the bank, announcing one is in love, and then proceeding to fish in the waters of love with a creel full of ego. No, he is saying again and again, people can win at love only when they are ready to lose everything they bring to it of ego, position, or identity—love is more stern than war—and men and women can survive only if they reach the depths of their own sex down within themselves. They have to deliver themselves "over to the unknown." No more existential statement of love exists, for it is a way of saying we do not know how the love will turn out. What message more odious to the technologist? So Millett will accuse him endlessly of patriarchal male-dominated sex. But the domination of men over women was only a way station on the line of Lawrence's ideas—what he started to say early and ended saying late was that sex could heal, sex was the only nostrum which could heal, all other medicines were part of the lung-scarring smoke of factories and healed nothing, were poison, but sex could heal only when one was without "reserves or defenses." And so men and women received what they deserved of one another. Since Women's Lib has presented itself with the clear difficulty of giving modern woman a full hard efficient ego, Lawrence's ideas could not be more directly in the way. Still, it is painful to think that, quickly as men are losing any sense of fair play, women—if Millett can model for her sex—are utterly without it. Maybe Millett is not so much Molotov as Vishinsky. What a foul exhibit must now be displayed!

Passive as she is, Connie fares better than the heroine of The Plumed Serpent, *from whom Lawrentian man, Don Cipriano, deliberately withdraws as she nears orgasm, in a calculated and sadistic denial of her pleasure:*

By a swift dark instinct, Cipriano drew away from this in her. When, in their love, it came back on her, the seething electric female ecstasy, which knows such spasms of delirium, he recoiled from her. . . . By a dark and powerful instinct he drew away from her as soon as this desire rose again in her, for the white ecstasy of frictional satisfaction, the throes of Aphrodite of the foam. She could see that to him, it was repulsive. He just removed himself, dark and unchangeable, away from her.

The passage restored will be of interest to any jury looking for further evidence on the virtues or deterrents of the clitoral come:

> *She realised, almost with wonder, the death in her of the Aphrodite of the foam: the seething, frictional, ecstatic Aphrodite. By a swift dark instinct, Cipriano drew away from this in her. When, in their love, it came back on her, the seething electric female ecstasy, which knows such spasms of delirium, he recoiled from her. It was what she used to call her "satisfaction." She had loved Joachim for this, that again, and again, and again he could give her this orgiastic "satisfaction," in spasms that made her cry aloud.*
>
> *But Cipriano would not. By a dark and powerful instinct he drew away from her as soon as this desire rose again in her, for the white ecstasy of frictional satisfaction, the throes of Aphrodite of the foam. She could see that to him, it was repulsive. He just removed himself, dark and unchangeable, away from her.*
>
> *And she, as she lay, would realise the worthlessness of this foam-effervescence, its strange externality to her. It seemed to come upon her from without, not from within. And succeeding the first moment of disappointment, when this sort of "satisfaction" was denied her, came the knowledge that she did not really want it, that it was really nauseous to her.*
>
> *And he, in his dark, hot silence, would bring her back to the new, soft, heavy, hot flow, when she was like a fountain gushing noiseless and with urgent softness from the volcanic deeps. Then she was open to him soft and hot, yet gushing with a noiseless soft power. And there was no such thing as conscious "satisfaction." What happened was dark and untellable. So different from the friction which flares out in circles of phosphorescent ecstasy, to the last wild spasm which utters the involuntary cry, like a death-cry, the final love-cry. This she had known, and known to the end, with Joachim. And now this too was removed from her. What she had with Cipriano was curiously beyond her knowing: so deep and hot and flowing,*

as it were subterranean. She had to yield before it. She could not grip it into one final spasm of white ecstasy which was like sheer knowing.

And as it was in the love-act, so it was with him. She could not know him. *When she tried to know him, something went slack in her, and she had to leave off. She had to let be. She had to leave him, dark and hot and potent, along with the things that* are, *but are not known. The presence. And the stranger. This he was always to her.*

Yes, sex was the presence of grace and the introduction of the stranger into oneself. That was the only medicine for the lividities of the will. So Lawrence would preach, but he was a man in torture. If Millett had wished to get around Lawrence in the easiest way for the advance of the Liberation, she would have done better to have built a monument to him and a bridge over his work rather than making the mean calculation she could bury him by meretricious quotation. For Lawrence is an inspiration, but few can do more than respect him on the fly (the way a Soviet official might duck into an Orthodox church to smell the incense). The world has been technologized and technologized twice again in the years since his death; the citizens are technologized as well. Who will go looking for the "new, soft, heavy, hot flow," or the "urgent softness from the volcanic deeps" when the air of cities smells of lava and the mood of the streets is like the bowels turned inside out? What he was asking for had been too hard for him; it is more than hard for us—his life was, yes, a torture, and we draw back in fear, for we would not know how to try to burn by such a light.

Yet he was a man more beautiful perhaps than we can guess, and it is worth the attempt to try to perceive the logic of his life, for he illumines the passion to be masculine as no other writer, he reminds us of the beauty of desiring to be a man, for he was not much of a man himself, a son despised by his father, beloved by his mother, a boy and young man and prematurely aging writer with the soul of a beautiful woman. It is not only that no other man writes so well about women, but indeed is there a woman who can? Useless for Millett to answer that here is a case of one man commending another man for his ability to understand women—what a vain and pompous assumption, she will hasten to jeer, but such words will be the ground meat of a dull cow. The confidence is that some of Lawrence's passages have a ring—perhaps it is an echo of that great bell which may toll whenever the literary miracle occurs and a writer sets down words to resonate with that sense of peace and proportion it is tempting to call truth. Yet whoever believes that such a leap is not possible across the gap, that a man cannot write of a woman's soul, or a white man of a black man, does not believe in literature itself. So, yes, Lawrence understood women as they had never been understood before, understood them with all the tortured fever of a man who had the soul of a beautiful, imperious, and passionate woman, yet was locked into the body of a middling male physique, not physically strong, of reasonable good looks, a pleasant to somewhat seedy-looking man, no stud. What a nightmare to balance that soul! to take the man in himself, locked from youth into every need for profound female companionship, a man almost wholly oriented toward the company of women, and attempt to go out into the world of men, indeed even dominate the world of men so that he might find balance. For his mind was possessed of that intolerable masculine pressure to command which develops in sons outrageously beloved by their mothers—to be the equal of a woman at twelve or six or any early age which reaches equilibrium between the will of the son and the will of the mother, strong love to strong love, is all but to guarantee the making of a future tyrant, for the sense of where to find one's inner health has been generated by the early years of that equilibrium—its substitute will not be easy to create in maturity. What can then be large enough to serve as proper balance to a man who was equal to a strong woman in emotional confidence at the age of eight? Hitlers develop out of such balance derived from imbalance, and great generals and great novelists (for what is a novelist but a general who sends his troops across fields of paper?).

So we must conceive then of Lawrence arrogant with mother love and therefore possessed of a mind which did not believe any man on earth had a mind more important than his own. What a responsibility then to bring his message to the world, unique message which might yet save the world! We must conceive of that ego equal already to the will of a strong woman while he was still a child—what long steps had it taken since within the skull! He needed an extraordinary woman for a mate, and he had the luck to find his Frieda. She was an aristocrat and he was a miner's son, she was large and beautiful, she was passionate, and he stole her away from her husband and children—they could set out together to win the world and educate it into ways to live, do that, do all of that out of the exuberance of finding one another.

But she was a strong woman, she was individual, she loved him but she did not worship him. She was independent. If he had been a stronger man, he could perhaps have enjoyed such personal force, but he had become a man by an act of will, he was bone and blood of the classic family stuff out of which homosexuals are made; he had lifted himself out of his natural destiny, which was probably to have the sexual life of a woman, had diverted the virility of his brain down into some indispensable minimum of phallic force—no wonder he worshiped the phallus; he, above all men, knew what an achievement was its rise from the root, its assertion to stand proud on a delicate base. His mother had adored him. Since his first sense of himself as a male had been in the tender air of her total concern—now, and always, his strength would depend upon just such outsize admiration. Dominance over women was not tyranny to him but equality, for dominance was the indispensable elevator which would raise his phallus to that height from which it might seek transcendence. And sexual transcendence, some ecstasy where he could lose his ego for a moment, and his sense of self and his will, was life to him—he could not live without sexual transcendence. If he had had an outrageously unequal development—all fury to be a man and all the senses of a woman—there was a direct price to pay: He was not healthy. His lungs were poor, and he lived with the knowledge that he would likely have an early death. Each time he failed to reach a woman, each time he failed particularly to reach his own woman, he was dying a little. It is hopeless to read his books and try to understand the quirky changeable fury-ridden relationships of his men and women without comprehending that Lawrence saw every serious love affair as fundamental do-or-die: He knew he literally died a little more each time he missed transcendence in the act. It was why he saw lust as hopeless. Lust was meaningless fucking and that was the privilege of the healthy. He was ill, and his wife was literally killing him each time she failed to worship his most proud and delicate cock. Which may be why he invariably wrote on the edge of cliché—we speak in simples as experience approaches the enormous, and Lawrence lived with the monumental gloom that his death was already in him, and sex—some transcendental variety of sex—was his only hope, and his wife was too robust to recognize such tragic facts.

By the time of writing *Women in Love,* his view of women would not be far from the sinister. One of the two heroines would succeed in driving her man to his death. His rage against the will of women turns immense, and his bile explodes on the human race, or is it the majority of the races?—these are the years when he will have a character in *Aaron's Rod,* Lilly, his mouthpiece, say:

> *I can't do with folk who teem by the billion, like the Chinese and Japs and Orientals altogether. Only vermin teem by the billion. Higher types breed slower. I would have loved the Aztecs and the Red Indians. I* know *they hold the element in life which I am looking for—they had living pride. Not like the flea-bitten Asiatics. Even niggers are better than Asiatics, though they are wallowers. The American races—and the South Sea Islanders—the Marquesans, the Maori blood. That was true blood. It wasn't frightened. All the rest are craven. . . .*

It is the spleen of a man whose organs are rotting in parts and so, owner of a world-ego, he will see the world rotting in parts.

These are the years when he flirts with homosexuality, but is secretly, we may assume, obsessed with it. For he is still in need of that restorative sex he can no longer find, and since his psyche was originally shaped to be homosexual, homosexuality could yet be his peace. Except it could not, not likely, for his mind could hardly give up the lust to dominate. Homosexuality becomes a double irony—he must now seek to dominate men physically more powerful than himself. The paradoxes of this position result in the book *Aaron's Rod,* which is about a male love affair (which never quite takes place) between a big man and a little man. The little man does the housework, plays nursemaid to the big man when he is ill, and ends by dominating him, enough to offer the last speech in the book.

> *All men say, they want a leader. Then let them in their souls* submit *to some greater soul than theirs. . . . You, Aaron, you too have the need to submit. You, too, have the need livingly to yield to a more heroic soul, to give yourself. You know you have [but] perhaps you'd rather die than yield. And so, die you must. It is your affair.*

He has separated the theme from himself and reversed the roles, but he will die rather than yield, even though earlier in the book he was ready to demonstrate that platonic homosexuality saves. It is the clear suggestion that Aaron recovers only because Lilly anoints his naked body, lays on hands after doctors and medicines had failed.

Quickly he uncovered the blond lower body of his patient, and began to rub the abdomen with oil, using a slow, rhythmic, circulating motion, a sort of massage. For a long time he rubbed finely and steadily, then went over the whole of the lower body, mindless, as if in a sort of incantation. He rubbed every speck of the man's lower body—the abdomen, the buttocks, the thighs and knees, down to his feet, rubbed it all warm and glowing with camphorated oil, every bit of it, chafing the toes swiftly, till he was almost exhausted. Then Aaron was covered up again, and Lilly sat down in fatigue to look at his patient.

He saw a change. The spark had come back into the sick eyes, and the faint trace of a smile, faintly luminous, into the face. Aaron was regaining himself. But Lilly said nothing. He watched his patient fall into a proper sleep.

Another of his heroes, Birkin, weeps in strangled tones before the coffin of Gerald. It is an earlier period in Lawrence's years of homosexual temptation; the pain is sharper, the passion is stronger. "He should have loved me," he said. "I offered him." And his wife is repelled, "recoiled aghast from him as he sat . . . making a strange, horrible sound of tears." They are the sickly sounds of a man who feels ready to die in some part of himself because the other man would never yield.

But homosexuality would have been the abdication of Lawrence as a philosopher-king. Conceive how he must have struggled against it! In all those middle years he moves slowly from the man who is sickened because the other did not yield, to the man who will die because he, himself, will not yield. But he is bitter, and with a rage ready to set fire to half the world.

Then it is too late. He is into his last years. He is into the five last years of his dying. He has been a victim of love, and will die for lack of the full depth of a woman's love for him—what a near to infinite love he had needed. So he has never gotten to that place where he could deliver himself to the unknown, be "without reserves or defenses . . . cast off everything . . . and cease to be, so that that which is perfectly ourselves can take place in us," no, he was never able to go that far. By the time he began *Lady Chatterley,* he must have known the fight was done; he had never been able to break out of the trap of his lungs, nor out of the cage of his fashioning. He had burned too many holes in too many organs trying to reach into more manhood than the course of his nerves could carry, he was done; but he was a lover, he wrote *Lady Chatterley,* he forgave, he wrote his way a little further toward death, and sang of the wonders of creation and the glory of men and women in the rut and lovely of a loving fuck.

> *"When a woman gets absolutely possessed by her own will, her own will set against everything, then it's fearful, and she should be shot at last."*
> *"And shouldn't men be shot at last, if they get possessed by their own will?"*
> *"Ay!—the same!"*

The remark is muttered, the gamekeeper rushes on immediately to talk of other matters, but it has been made, Lawrence has closed the circle, the man and the woman are joined, separate and joined.

A LAGNIAPPE
FOR THE READER

———

Name any great novel that didn't weary you first time through. A great novel has a consciousness that is new to us. We have to become imbued with this new consciousness before we can enjoy the work. I've been bored in part by *Moby-Dick*, *The Red and the Black*, *Anna Karenina*, *The Scarlet Letter*, *Remembrance of Things Past*, *Ulysses*, *The Magic Mountain*. Hell, even *The Sun Also Rises*. Of course, I was a Freshman then.

James Jones and I used to feel in the early Fifties that we were the two best writers around. Unspoken was the feeling that there was room for only one of us. I remember that Jones inscribed my copy of *From Here to Eternity* "For Norman, my dearest enemy, my most feared friend."

Capote wrote the best sentences of anyone of our generation. He had a lovely ear. He did not have a good mind. I don't know if a large idea ever bothered him. While he wrote poetically, he did not think like a poet. But he did have a sense of time and place. *Breakfast at Tiffany's*, for example, is a slight book. Looking at it with a hard eye, it's a charlotte russe. On the other hand, if you are looking to capture a particular period in the Fifties in

New York, no other book may have done it so well. In that sense, Capote is a bit like Fitzgerald. If I were to mount them on one wall, however, I'd certainly put Truman under Scott.

All the same, Truman Capote was wonderful when all was said. I think of that tiny man who lived through his early years with the public laughing at him. To go from being a pampered little darling with a few friends who catered to him egregiously on to mustering the balls, the enormous balls, to decide he was going to be a major figure in American life—that was his achievement. To hell with writing. He was going to give up writing in order to be a major social figure, and in doing this, I think he sacrificed the last ten or twenty years of his talent.

Kurt Vonnegut and I are friendly with one another but wary. There was a period when we used to go out together fairly often because our wives liked each other, and Kurt and I would sit there like bookends. We would be terribly careful with one another; we both knew the huge cost of a literary feud, so we certainly didn't want to argue. On the other hand, neither of us would be caught dead saying to the other, "Gee, I liked your last book," and then be met with silence because the party of the second part could not reciprocate. So we would talk about anything else—we would talk about Las Vegas or the Galápagos Islands. We only had one literary conversation and that was over an evening in New York. Kurt looked up and sighed, "Well, I finished my novel today and it like to killed me." When Kurt is feeling heartfelt, he tends to speak in an old Indiana accent. His wife said, "Oh, Kurt, you always say that whenever you finish a book," and he replied, "Well, whenever I finish a book I do say it, and it is always true, and it gets more true, and this last one like to killed me more than any."

Reading Toni Morrison, I say to myself: I know so little of black women who don't have a voice, and after all, I should know more. Toni certainly has a deep sense of such women, no question. But how good is she on black men? I feel less certain of those portraits. Finally, I decide that what she does with black women is an education and I respect her for that. I've only read one or two of her novels, by the way, so I may be reacting on too narrow a base.

Picasso had his bleak, dark, ugly view of women. On the other hand, he had the same hard view of other men and of himself. If you can pass through Picasso and still have a little love left for humanity, then you have arrived at some kind of peace. Picasso is like a doctor who's cleaning out a very ugly wound, the filth embedded in humanity.

It's the guys who pen wonderfully sweet books, however, who are the real monsters. You know—they kick the wife, cuff the kids, and have the dog shrinking in horror. Then their books come out: "X once again delights the reader with his sense of joy."

Back in school, we had a joke we used to repeat. It went:
   "Whom are you talking about?"
   "Herbert Hoover."
   "Never heard of him."
   "Never heard of whom?"
   "Herbert Hoover."
   "Who's he?"
   "He's the man you mentioned."
   "Never heard of Herbert Hoover."
   So it went. So goes *Catch-22*. It's the rock and roll of novels. One finds its ancestor in Basic Training. We were ordered to have clean sheets for Saturday inspection. But one week we were given no clean sheets from the Post laundry, so we slept on our mattress covers, which got dirty. After inspection, the platoon was restricted to quarters. "You didn't have clean sheets," our sergeant said.
   "How could we have clean sheets if the clean sheets didn't come?"
   "How do I know?" said the sergeant. "The regulations say you gotta have clean sheets."
   "But we can't have clean sheets if there are no clean sheets."
   "That," said the sergeant, "is tough shit."
   Which is what *Catch-22* could have been called. The Army is a village of colliding bureaucracies whose colliding orders cook up impossibilities. Heller takes this one good joke and exploits it into two thousand variations of the same good joke, but in the act he somehow creates a rational vision of the modern world. Of course, the crisis of reason is that it can no longer compre-

hend the modern world. Heller demonstrates that a rational man devoted to reason must arrive at the conclusion that either the world is mad and he is the only sane man in it or (and this is the weakness of *Catch-22*—it never explores this possibility) the sane man is not really sane, because his rational propositions are without existential reason.

On page 178, there is a discussion about God.

> ". . . how much reverence can you have for a Supreme Being who finds it necessary to include such phenomena as phlegm and tooth decay in His divine system of creation. . . . Why in the world did He ever create pain?"
>
> "Pain?" Lieutenant Scheisskopf's wife pounced upon the word victoriously. "Pain is a useful symptom. Pain is a warning to us of bodily dangers."
>
> . . . "Why couldn't he have used a doorbell instead to notify us, or one of His celestial choirs?"

Right there is planted the farthest advance of the flag of reason in Heller's cosmology. There is, however, an answer, which might go that God gave us pain for the same reason the discovery of tranquilizers was undertaken by the Devil: If we have an immortal soul, some of us come close to it only through pain. A season of sickness can be preferable to a flight from disease, for it discourages the onrush of a death which begins in the center of oneself.

Some of the best prose in America is graffiti found on men's-room walls. It is prose written in bone, etched by acid, it is the prose of harsh truth, the virulence of the criminal who never found his stone walls and so settles down on the walls of the john, it is the language of hatred unencumbered by guilt, hesitation, scruple, or complexity. Burroughs must be the greatest writer of graffiti who ever lived. His style has the snap of a whip, and it never relents. Every paragraph is quotable. Here's a jewel among a thousand jewels:

DR. BENWAY . . . looks around and picks up one of those rubber vacuum cups at the end of a stick they use to unstop toilets . . . "Make an incision, Doctor Limpf. . . . I'm going to massage the heart." . . . Dr. Benway washes the suction cup by swishing it around in the toilet-bowl. . . .

DR. LIMPF: "The incision is ready, doctor."

Dr. Benway forces the cup into the incision and works it up and down. Blood spurts all over the doctors, the nurse and the wall. . . .

NURSE: "I think she's gone, doctor."

DR. BENWAY: "Well, it's all in the day's work."

Punch and Judy. Mr. Interlocutor and Mr. Bones. One, two, three, bam! two, four, eight, bam! The drug addict lives with a charged wire so murderous he must hang his nervous system on a void. Burroughs's achievement, his great achievement, is that he has brought back snowflakes from this murderous void. Burroughs is the surgeon of the novel.

Yet he is something more. It is his last ability which entitles him to a purchase on genius. Through the fantasies runs a vision of a future world, a half-demented welfare state, an abattoir of science fiction with surgeons, bureaucrats, perverts, diplomats, a world not describable short of getting into the book. The ideas have pushed into the frontier of an all-electronic universe. One holds on to a computer in some man-eating machine of the future that has learned to use language. The words come out in squeaks, spiced with static, sex coiled up with technology like a scream on the radar. Bombarded by his language, the sensation is like being in a room where three radios, two television sets, stereo hi-fi, a pornographic movie, and two automatic dishwashers are working at once while a mad scientist conducts the dials to squeeze out the maximum disturbance. If this is a true picture of the world to come, and it may be, then Burroughs is a great writer. Yet there is sadness in reading him, for one gets intimations of a mind which might have come within distance of Joyce, except that a catastrophe has been visited on it, a blow by a sledgehammer, a junkie's needle which left the crystalline brilliance crashed into bits.

Bellow's main character, Henderson, is a legendary giant American, an eccentric millionaire, six-four in height, with a huge battered face, an enormous chest, a prodigious pot belly, a wild crank's gusto for life, and a childlike impulse to say what he thinks. He is a magical hybrid of Jim Thorpe and Dwight Macdonald. And he is tormented by an inner voice, which gives him no rest and poisons his marriages and pushes him to go forth. So he chooses to go to Africa (after first contemplating a visit to the Eskimos) and finds a native guide to take him deep into the interior.

The style gallops like Henderson, full of excess, full of light, loaded with irritating effusions, but it is a style that moves along. *The Adventures of Augie March* was written in a way which could only be called *all writing*. That was one of the troubles with the book. Everything was smothered by the style. But Henderson talks in a free-swinging, easy bang-away monologue that puts your eye in the center of the action. I don't know if Bellow ever visited Africa, I would guess he didn't, but his imaginative faculty—which has always been his loot—pulls off a few prodigies. I don't know if any other American writer has done Africa so well. As for instance:

> I was in tremendous shape those first long days, hot as they were. At night, after Romilayu had prayed, and we lay on the ground, the face of the air breathed back on us, breath for breath. And then there were the calm stars, turning around and singing, and the birds of the night with heavy bodies, fanning by. I couldn't have asked for anything better. When I laid my ear to the ground, I thought I could hear hoofs. It was like lying on the skin of a drum.

After a series of tragicomic adventures, Henderson reaches a royal almost Oriental tribe with a culture built upon magic and death. He is brought to the King, Dahfu, who lives in a wooden palace attended by a harem of beautiful Amazons. (One could be visiting the royalest pad in Harlem.) Dahfu is a philosopher-king, large in size, noble, possessed of grace, complex, dignified, elegant, educated, living suspended between life and death. The King, delighted with his new friend, takes him into the secrets of his mind and his palace, and one begins to read the book with a vast absorption because Bellow is now inching more close to the Beast of mystery than any American novelist before him. Dahfu is an exceptional creation, a profoundly sophisticated man with a deep acceptance of magic, an intellectual who believes that civilization can be saved only by a voyage back into the primitive, an expedition which he is of course uniquely suited to lead.

As the action explores its way down into an underworld of plot and magical omens, one ceases to know any longer whether Dahfu is potentially an emperor who can save the world or a noble man lost in a Faustian endeavor. The book is on the threshold of a stupendous climax—for the first time in years I had the feeling I was going to learn something large from a novel—and then like a slow leak the air goes out of the book in the last fifty pages. Dahfu is killed in a meaningless action, Henderson goes home to his wife, and the mystery that Bellow has begun to penetrate closes over his book, still intact.

He is a curious writer. He has the warmest imagination, I think, of any writer in my generation, and this gift leads him to marvelous places—it is possible that Bellow succeeds in telling us more about the depths of the black man's psyche than either Baldwin or Ellison. He has a widely cultivated mind, which nourishes his gift. He has a facility for happy surprises, and in Henderson, unlike Augie March, he has developed a nose for where the treasure is buried. Yet I still wonder if he is not too timid to become a great writer. A novelist like Jones could never have conceived *Henderson the Rain King* (no more could I), but I know that Jones or myself would have been ready to urinate blood before we would have been ready to cash our profit and give up as Bellow did on the possibilities of a demonically vast ending. The clue to this capitulation may be detected in Bellow's one major weakness, which is that he creates individuals and not relations between them, at least not yet. Augie March travels alone, the hero of *Seize the Day* is alone, Henderson forms passionate friendships but they tend to get fixed, and the most annoying aspect of the novel is the constant repetition of the same sentiments, as if Bellow is knocking on a door of meaning that will not open for him. It is possible that the faculty of imagination is opposed to the gift of grasping relationships—in the act of coming to know somebody else well, the point of the imagination may be dulled by the roughness of the other's concrete desires and the attrition of living not only in one's own boredom but someone else's. Bellow has a lonely gift, but it is a gift. I would guess he is more likely to write classics than major novels, which is a way of saying that he will give intense pleasure to particular readers over the years but is not too likely to seize the temper of our time and turn it.

I haven't looked at Jonathan Franzen's work yet, but by some reports, *The Corrections* is the first important novel that's come along in quite a while. Obviously, it has to be read if one wants any sense at all of what's going on in American letters. And I noticed when looking at the blurbs on the back that something like twenty writers and reviewers all gave their salute, and most of them were of Franzen's generation. Updike wasn't there; not Bellow, not Roth; I wasn't there—the oldest was Don DeLillo, who gave the smallest praise. The others were new, respected names like David Foster Wallace, Michael Cunningham, and a host of others, all contemporary. Apparently, *The Corrections* is the book of a generation that wants to wipe the slate clean and offer a new literary movement.

I think the younger writers are sick of Roth, Bellow, Updike, and myself the way we were sick of Hemingway and Faulkner. When I was a young writer we never talked about anyone but them, and that feeling grew into resentment. Since they had no interest in us, we began to think, Yeah, they're great—now get off the stage! We want the lights on us!

Since writing the above, I've read *The Corrections*. It is very good as a novel, very good indeed, and yet most unpleasant now that it sits in memory, as if one has been wearing the same clothes for too many days. Franzen writes superbly well sentence for sentence, and yet one is not happy with the achievement. It is too full of language, even as the nouveaux riches are too full of money. He is exceptionally intelligent, but like a polymath, he lives much of the time in Wonkville Hollow, for Franzen is an intellectual dredging machine. Everything of novelistic use to him that came up on the Internet seems to have bypassed the higher reaches of his imagination—it is as if he offers us more human experience than he has literally mastered, and this is obvious when we come upon his set pieces on gourmet restaurants or giant cruise ships or modern Lithuania in disarray. Such sections read like first-rate magazine pieces, but no better—they stick to the surface. When he deals with what he does know directly and intimately, which is the family at the core of his book—an old father, a late-middle-aged mother, two grown sons, and a daughter—he is an exceptionally gifted observer. What waste, however! Nothing much is at stake for us with his people. They have almost no changing relation to each other (considering that they have something like six hundred pages to work up a few new mutual stances.) Three, maybe four of the five can legitimately be characterized as one-note characters—only the daughter, who becomes a passionate lesbian, has much to tell us. It is not only that—dare I use the old book reviewer's clichés?—they offer us very little rooting interest and are, for the most part, *dank*. Worse!—nothing but petty, repetitious conflicts arise from them. They wriggle forever in the higher reaches of human mediocrity and incarcerated habit. The greatest joy to lift from the spine of the book is the author's vanity at how talented he is. He may well have the highest IQ of any American novelist writing today, but unhappily, he rewards us with more work than exhilaration, since rare is any page in *The Corrections* that could not be five to ten lines shorter.

All this said, exceptional potential still remains. I think it is the sense of his potential that excites so many. Now, the success of *The Corrections* will change his life and charge it. Franzen will begin to have experiences at a more intense level; the people he encounters will have more sense of mission, will be more exciting in their good and in their evil, more open at their best, more crafty in their use of closure. So if he is up to it, he will grow with his new experiences (which, as we ought to have some idea by now, is no routine matter), but if he succeeds, yes, he has the potential to become a major writer on a very high level indeed. At present, his negative characteristics predominate. Bellow and Company can still rest on their old laurels, I think I am almost ready to say, "Alas!"

THE ARGUMENT
REINVIGORATED

Good writing is not an act to excite tolerance because it is good, but anguish because it is not better. Who can swear there has not been something catastrophic to America in the failure of her novelists? Maybe we are the last liberators in the land, and if we continue to thrive on much less than our best, then the being of all of us may be deadened before we are done.

That is a statement which sups on the essence of extravagance, and yet it is the distance of the bridge to be built. It may be necessary that a communication of human experience, of the deepest and most unrecoverable human experience, must yet take place if we are to survive. Such at least is the not-so-covert opinion beneath the address to the Modern Language Association that ends this book.

Assume I am a lecturer in the fields of Fellowship surrounding American Literature and am trying to draw some grand design on a twenty-minute talk devoted to "The Dynamic of American Letters." Knowing attention is iron for the blood of a Fellow, I will not be so foolish as to perish without a look at the topical. No, I will use "The Dynamic of American Letters" as preparation for a lightning discussion of *Herzog* and Terry Southern, with a coda on the art of the absurd. Let me then have my first sentence as a lecturer: "There has been a war at the center of American letters for a long time." That is not so poor. The look of absolute comprehension on the face of the audience encourages the lecturer to go on.

The war began as a class war; an upper middle class looked for a development of its taste, a definition of its manners, a refinement of itself to prepare a shift to the aristocratic—that was its private demand upon culture. This upper-class development of literature was invaded, however, at the beginning of the twentieth century, by a counterliterature, whose roots were found in poverty, industrial society, and the emergence of a new class. It was a literature which grappled with a peculiarly American phenomenon—a tendency of American society to alter more rapidly than the ability of its artists to record that change. Now, of course, one might go back two thousand years into China to find a society which did not alter more rapidly than its culture, but the American phenomenon had to do with the very rate of acceleration. The order of magnitude in this rate had shifted. It was as if everything changed ten times as fast in America, and this made for extraordinary difficulty in creating a literature. The sound, sensible, morally stout delineation of society which one found in Tolstoy and Balzac and Zola, in Thackeray and in Trollope, had become impossible. The American novelist of manners had to content himself with manners—he could not put a convincing servant into his work, and certainly not a working man, because they were moving themselves in one generation out from the pantry into the morning dress of the lady in the parlor and up from the foundry to the master of the factory. The novelist of manners could not go near these matters—they promised to take over all of his book. So the job was left to Howells, Stephen Crane, to Dreiser, and in lesser degree to such writers as Norris, Jack London, Upton Sinclair—let us say it was left to Dreiser. A fundamental irony of American letters had now presented itself. For in opposition to Dreiser was the imperfectly developed countertradition of the genteel. The class that wielded the power which ran America and the class which most admired that class banded instinctively together to approve a genteel literature, which had little to do with power or the secrets of power. They encouraged a literature about courtship and marriage and love and play and devotion and piety and style, a literature which had to do finally with the *excellence* of belonging to their own genteel tradition. Thus it was a literature that borrowed the forms of its conduct from European models. The people who were most American by birth, and who had the most to do with managing America, gave themselves a literature which had the least to say about the real phenomena of American life, most particularly the accelerated rate, the awful rate, of growth and anomaly through all of society. That sort of literature and that kind of attempt to explain America was left to the sons of immigrants, who, if they were vigorous enough, and fortunate enough to be educated, now had the opportunity to see that America was a phenomenon never before described, indeed never before visible in the record of history. There was something going on in American life that was either grand or horrible or both, but it was going on—at a dizzy rate—and the future glory or doom of the world was not necessarily divorced from it. Dreiser labored like a titan to capture the phenomenon; he became a titan; Thomas Wolfe, his only peer as giant (as the novelist-as-giant), labored also like a titan, but for half as long and died in terror of the gargantuan proportions of the task. Yet each failed in one part of the job. They were able to describe society—Wolfe like the greatest fifteen-year-old alive, an invaluable achievement, and Dreiser like some heroic tragic entrepreneur who has reasoned out through his own fatigue and travail very much how everything works in the iron mills of life but is damned because he cannot pass on the knowledge to his children. Dreiser and Wolfe were up from the people, and Dreiser particularly came closer to understanding the social machine than any American writer who ever lived, but he paid an unendurable price—he was forced to alienate himself from manner in order to learn the vast amount he learned. Manner insists one learn at a modest rate, that one absorb each step with grace before going on to the next. Dreiser was in a huge hurry, he had to learn everything—that was the way he must have felt his mission, so there is nothing of manner in his work; which is to say, nothing of tactics.

If the upper class quite naturally likes a literature which is good for them, a literature at the surface perhaps trivial but underneath amusing, elucidative, *fortifying*, it is because this kind of literature elaborates and clarifies the details of their life and thus adjusts their sense of power, their upper-class sense of power, which is invariably lubricated by a sense of detail. So too does that other class of readers in American literature, that huge, loose, all but unassociated congregation of readers— immigrant, proletarian, entrepreneur—wish in turn for a litera- ture which is equally good for them. That is where Dreiser had to fail. He was only half-good for such readers. He taught them strategy as Americans had never gotten it before in a novel. If they were adventurers, he was almost as useful to them as Sten- dhal was exceptionally useful to a century of French intellectuals who had come to Paris from the provinces. But not quite. Dreiser, finally, is not quite as useful, and the difference is cru- cial. Because a young adventurer reads a great novel in the un- voiced hope it is a grindstone which sharpens his ax sufficiently to smash down doors now locked to him. Dreiser merely located the doors and gave warnings about the secret padlocks and the traps. But he had no grindstone, no manner, no eye for the deadly important manners of the rich—he was obliged to call a rich girl "charming"; he could not make her charming when she spoke, as Fitzgerald could, and so he did not really prepare the army of his readers for what was ahead. His task was doubly dif- ficult—it was required of him to give every upstart fresh strategy and tactics. No less than the secret sociology of society is what is needed by the upstart and that strategy Dreiser gave him. But tactics—the manners of the drawing room, the deaths and lifes of the drawing room, the cocktail party, the glorious tactics of the individual kill—that was all beyond him. Dreiser went blind climbing the mountains of society, so he could not help anyone see what was directly before him—only what had happened and what might come next.

That was the initial shape of the war, Naturalism versus the Genteel Tradition it has been called, and one might pose Henry James against Dreiser, but James is sufficiently great a writer to violate the generalizations one must make about the novel of manners, which must always—precisely because it deals with manners—eschew the overambitious, plus extremes of plot— which James of course did not. So let us say the war was between Dreiser and Edith Wharton, Dreiser all strategy, no tactics and Wharton all tactics. Marvelous tactics they were—a jewel of a writer and stingy as a parson—she needed no strategy. The upper-class writer had all strategy provided him by the logic of his class. Maybe that is why the war never came to decision, or even to conclusion. No upper-class writer went down into the pits to bring back the manner alive of the change going on *down there,* certainly not Edith Wharton, not James Branch Cabell, of course not, nor Hergesheimer nor even Cather or Glasgow, not Elinor Wylie, no, nor Carl Van Vechten, and no diamond in the rough was ever reshaped by the cutters of Newport. The gap in American letters continued. Upper-class writers like John Dos Passos made brave efforts to go down and get the stuff and never quite got it, mainly in Dos Passos's case because they lacked strategy for the depths—manners may be sufficient to delineate the rich, but one needs a vision of society to comprehend the poor, and Dos Passos had only revulsion at injustice, which is ultimately a manner. Some upper-class writers like Fitzgerald turned delicately upon the suppositions of their class, lost all borrowed strategy and were rudderless, were forced therefore to become superb in tactics, but for this reason perhaps a kind of hysteria lived at the center of their work; lower-class writers like Farrell and Steinbeck described whole seas of the uncharted ocean, but their characters did not push from one milieu into another, and so the results were more taxonomic than apocalyptic.

Since then the war has shifted. No writer succeeded in doing the single great work which would clarify a nation's vision of itself as Tolstoy had done perhaps with *War and Peace* or *Anna Karenina* and Stendhal with *The Red and the Black;* no one novel came along which was grand and daring and comprehensive and detailed, able to give sustenance to the adventurer and merriment to the rich, leave compassion in the icechambers of the upper class and energy as alms for the poor. (Not unless it was *Tropic of Cancer.*) Dreiser came as close as any, and never got close at all, for he could not capture the moment, and no country in history has lived perhaps so much for the moment as America. After his heroic failure, American literature was isolated—it was necessary to give courses in American literature to Americans, either because they would not otherwise read it or because, reading it, they could not understand it. It was not quite vital to them. It did not save their lives, make them more ambitious, more moral, more tormented, more audacious, more ready for love, more ready for war, for charity and for invention. No, it tended to puzzle them. The realistic literature had never caught up with the rate of change in American life, indeed it had fallen further and further behind, and the novel gave up any desire to be a creation equal to the phenomenon of the country itself; it settled for being a metaphor. Which is to say that each separate author made a separate peace. He would no longer try to capture America; he would merely try to give life to some microcosm in American life, some metaphor—in the sense that a drop of water is a metaphor of the seas, or a hair of the beast is for some a metaphor of the beast—and in that metaphor he might —if he was very lucky—have it all, rich and poor, strategy and tactics, insight and manner, detail, authority, the works. He would have it all for a particular few. It was just that he was no longer writing about the beast but, as in the case of Hemingway (if we are to take the best of this), about the paw of the beast or in Faulkner about the dreams of the beast. What a paw and what dreams! Perhaps they are the two greatest writers America ever had, but they had given up on trying to do it all. Their vision was partial, determinedly so; they saw that as the first condition for trying to be great—that one must not try to save. Not souls, and not the nation. The desire for majesty was the bitch that licked at the literary loins of Hemingway and Faulkner: The country could be damned. Let it take care of itself.

And of course the country did. Just that. It grew by itself. Like a weed and a monster and a beauty and a pig. And the task of explaining America was taken over by Luce magazines. Those few aristocratic novelistic sensibilities which had never seen the task of defining the country as one for them—it was finally most unamusing as a task—grew smaller and smaller and more and more superb. Edith Wharton reappeared as Truman Capote, even more of a jewel, even stingier. Of writers up from the bottom there were numbers: Dreiser's nephews were as far apart as Saul Bellow and James Jones. But the difference between the two kinds of writers had shifted. It had begun to shift somewhere after the Second World War, and the shift had gone a distance. One could not speak at all now of aristocratic writers and novelists whose work was itself the protagonist to carry the writer and his readers through the locks of society; no, the work had long since retreated, the great ambition was gone, and then it was worse, even the metaphor was gone, the paw of the beast and the dreams of the beast, no, literature was down to the earnest novel and the perfect novel, to moral seriousness and Camp. Herzog and Candy had become the protagonists.

Frank Cowperwood once amassed an empire. Herzog, his

bastard great-nephew, diddled in the ruins of an intellectual warehouse. Where once the realistic novel cut a swath across the face of society, now its reality was concentrated into moral seriousness. Where the original heroes of naturalism had been active, bold, self-centered, close to tragic, and up to their nostrils in their exertions to advance their own life and force the webs of society, so the hero of moral earnestness, the hero Herzog and the hero Levin in Malamud's *A New Life,* are men who represent the contrary—passive, timid, other-directed, pathetic, up to the nostrils in anguish: The world is stronger than they are; suicide calls.

Malamud's hero is more active than Herzog, he is also more likeable, but these positive qualities keep the case from being so pure. There is a mystery about the reception of *Herzog.* For beneath its richness of texture and its wealth of detail, the fact remains: Never has a novel been so successful when its hero was so dim. Not one of the critics who adored the book would ever have permitted Herzog to remain an hour in his house. For Herzog was defeated, Herzog was an unoriginal man, Herzog was a fool—not an attractive God-anointed fool like Gimpel the Fool, his direct progenitor, but a sodden fool, over-educated and inept, unable to fight, able to love only when love presented itself as a gift. Herzog was intellectual but not bright, his ideas not original, his style as it appeared in his letters unendurable—it had exactly the leaden-footed sense of phrase that men laden with anxiety and near to going mad put into their communications. Herzog was hopeless. We learned nothing about society from him, not even anything about his life. And he is the only figure in the book. His wives, his mistress, his family, his children, his friends, even the man who cuckolds him are seen on the periphery of a dimming vision. Like all men near to being mad, his attention is within, but the inner attention is without genius. Herzog is dull, he is unendurably dull—he is like all those bright pedagogical types who have a cavity at the center of their brain.

Yet the novel succeeds. There is its mystery. One reads it with compassion. With rare compassion. Bored by Herzog, still there is a secret burning of the heart. One's heart turns over and produces a sorrow. Hardly any books are left to do that.

Of course, Herzog is alive on sufferance. He is a beggar, an extraordinary beggar who fixes you with his eye, his breath, his clothing, his dank near-corrupt presence; he haunts. Something goes on in Herzog's eye. It says: I am debased, I am failed, I am near to rotten, and yet something just as good and loving resides in me as the tenderest part of your childhood. If the prophet Elijah sent me, it is not to make you feel guilt but to weep. Suddenly, Herzog inspires sorrow—touch of alchemy to the book— Herzog is at the center of the modern dilemma. If we do not feel compassion for him, a forceful compassion that sends blood to warm the limbs and the heart, then we are going to be forced to shoot him. Because if Herzog does not arouse your compassion, there is no other choice—he is too intolerable a luxury to keep alive in his mediocrity unless he arouses your love. The literary world chose to love him. We were not ready to shoot Herzog. It all seemed too final if we did. Because then there would be nothing left but Camp, and Camp is the art of the cannibal; Camp is the art which evolved out of the bankruptcy of the novel of manners. It is the partial thesis of these twenty minutes that the pure novel of manners had watered down from *The House of Mirth* to the maudlin middle reaches of *The Rector of Justin;* had in fact gone all the way down the pike from *The Ambassadors* to *By Love Possessed.* So one does not speak of the novel of manners any longer—one is obliged to look at the documentary, *In Cold Blood,* or one is obliged to look at satire. The aristocratic impulse turned upon itself produced one classic—Terry Southern's *The Magic Christian.* Never had distaste for the habits of a mass mob reached such precision, never did wit falter in its natural assumption that the idiocies of the mass were attached breath and kiss to the hypocrisies, the weltering grandeurs, and the low stupidities of the rich, the American rich. The aristocratic impulse to define society by evocations of manner now survived only in the grace of any cannibal sufficiently aristocratic to sup upon his own family. *The Magic Christian* was a classic of Camp.

Note then: The two impulses in American letters had failed— the realistic impulse never delivered the novel that would ignite a nation's consciousness of itself, and the aristocratic impulse clawed at the remaining fabric of a wealthy society it despised and no longer wished to sustain. Like a Tinguely machine that destroys itself, Camp amused by the very act of its destruction.

Literature then had failed. The work was done by the movies, by television. The consciousness of the masses and the culture of the land trudged through endless mud.

The American consciousness, in the absence of a great tradition in the novel, ended by being developed by the bootlicking pieties of small-town newspaper editors and small-town educators, by the worst of organized religion, a formless force filled with the terrors of all the Christians left to fill the spaces left by the initial bravery of the frontiersman, and these latterday Christians were simply not as brave. That was one component of the mud. The other was the sons of the immigrants. Many of them hated America, hated it for what it offered and did not provide, what it revealed of opportunity and what it excluded from real opportunity. The sons of these immigrants and the sons' sons took over the cities and began to run them, high up in the air and right down into the ground; they plucked and they plundered and there was not an American city which did not grow more hideous in the last fifty years. Then they spread out—they put suburbs like blight on the land—and piped mass communications into every home. They were cannibals selling Christianity to Christians, and because they despised the message and mocked at it in their own heart, they succeeded in selling something else, a virus perhaps; an electronic nihilism went through the mass media of America and entered the Christians and they were like to being cannibals, they were a tense and livid people, swallowing their own hate with the tranquilizers and the sex in the commercials, whereas all the early cannibals at the knobs of the mass media made the mistake of passing on their bleak disease and were left now too gentle, too liberal, too programmatic, filled with plans for social welfare, and they looked and talked in Show Biz styles that possessed no style and were generally as unhealthy as Christians who lived in cellars and caves.

Yes, the cannibal sons of the immigrants had become Christians, and the formless form they had evolved for their mass media, the hypocritical empty and tasteless taste of the television arts they beamed across the land encountered the formless form and the all but tasteless taste of the small-town cannibal mind at its worst, and the collision produced schizophrenia in the land. Half of America went near-insane with head colds and medicaments and asthmas and allergies, hospitals and famous surgeons with knives to cut into the plague, welfares and plans and committees and cooperations and boredom, boredom plague deep upon the land; and the other part of America went ape, and the motorcycles began to roar like lions across the land and all the beasts of all the buried history of America turned in their circuit and prepared to slink toward the market place. One thought of America and one thought of aspirin, kitchen-commercials, and blood. One thought of Vietnam.

It has been said more than once that Tolstoy and Dostoyevsky divided the central terrain of the modern novel between them. Tolstoy's concern—even in the final pessimism of *The Kreutzer Sonata*—was with men-in-the-world, and indeed the panorama of his books carries to us an image of a huge landscape peopled with figures who changed that landscape, whereas the bulk of Dostoyevsky's work could take place in ten closed rooms: It is not society but a series of individuals we remember, each illuminated by the terror of exploring the mystery of themselves. This distinction is not a final scheme for classifying the novel. If one can point to *Moby-Dick* as a perfect example of a novel in the second category—a book whose action depends upon the voyage of Ahab into his obsession—and to *An American Tragedy* as a virile example of the first kind of novel, one must still come up short before the work of someone like Henry James, who straddles the categories, for he explores into society as if the world were a creature in a closed room and he could discover its heart. Yet the distinction is probably the most useful single guide we have to the novel and can even be given a modern application to Proust as a novelist of the developed, introspective, but still objective world, and Joyce as a royal, demented, most honorable traveler through the psyche. The serious novel begins from a fixed philosophical point—the desire to discover reality—and it goes to search for that reality in society or else must embark on a trip up the upper Amazon of the inner eye.

It is this necessity to travel into one direction or the other up to the end which makes the writing of novels perilous to one's talent and finally to one's health, as the horns of a bull can be doom for the suit of lights. If one explores the world, one's talent must be blunted by punishment, one's artistic integrity by corruption: Nobody can live in the world without shaking the hand of people he despises; so an ultimate purity must be surrendered. Yet it is as dangerous to travel unguided into the mysteries of the Self, for insanity prepares an ambush. No man or woman explores into his or her own nature without submitting to a curse from the root of biology, since existence would cease if it were natural to turn upon oneself.

This difficulty has always existed for the novelist, but today it may demand more antithesis and more agony than before. The writer who would explore the world must encounter a society that is now conscious of itself and so resistant (most secretly) to an objective eye. Detours exist everywhere. There was a time when a writer had to see just a little bit of a few different faces in the world and could know that the world was still essentially so simple that he might use his imagination to fill in the unknown colors. Balzac could do that, and so could Zola. But the arts of the world suffered a curious inversion as man was turned by the twentieth century into mass man rather than democratic man. The heartland which was potential in everyone turned upon itself; people used their personal arts to conceal from themselves the nature of their work. They chose to become experts rather than artists. The working world was no longer a panorama of factories and banks so much as it was reminiscent of hospitals and plastic recreation centers. Society tended to collect in small stagnant pools. Now, any young man trying to explore that world is held up by pleasures that are not sufficiently intense to teach him and is dulled by injustices too elusive to fire his rage. The Tolstoyan novel begins to be impossible. Who can create a vast canvas when the imagination must submit itself to a plethora of detail in each joint of society? Who can travel to many places when the complexity of each pool sucks up one's attention like a carnivorous flower?

Yet a turn in the other direction, into the world of the Self, is not less difficult. An intellectual structure which is debilitating to the instinct of the novelist inhabits the crossroads of the inner mind—*psychoanalysis*. An artist must not explore into himself with language given by another. A vocabulary of experts is a vocabulary greased out and sweated in committee and so is inimical to a private eye. One loses what is new by confusing it with what may be common to others. The essential ideas of psychoanalysis are reductive and put a dead weight on the confidence of the venture. If guilt, for example, is neurotic, a clumsy part of the functioning in a graceful machine, then one does not feel like a hero studying his manacles or a tragic victim regarding his just sentence but instead is a skilled mechanic trying to fix his tool. Brutally, simply, mass man cannot initiate an inner voyage unless it is conducted by an expert graduated by an institution.

Yet the difficulty goes beyond the country of psychoanalysis. There are hills beyond that hill. The highest faces an abyss. Man in the Middle Ages or the Renaissance, man even in the nineteenth century, explored deep into himself that he might come closer to a vision of a God or some dictate from eternity, but that exploration is suspect in itself today, and in the crucial climactic transcendental moments of one's life, there is revealed still another dilemma. God, is it God one finds, or madness? The suggestion of still another frontier for the American novel is here. A war has been fought by some of us over the years to open the sexual badlands to our writing, and that war has been won. Can one now begin to think of an attack on the stockade—those dead forts where the spirit of twentieth-century man, frozen in flop and panic before the montage of his annihilation, has collected, like castrated cattle behind the fence? Can the feet of those infantrymen of the arts, the novelists, take us beyond the churches, to where the real secrets are stored? We are the last of the entrepreneurs, and one of us homeless guns had better make it or the future will smell like the dead air of the men who captured our time during that huge collective cowardice which was the aftermath of the Second War. Nothing less than a fresh vision of the ongoing and conceivably climactic war between God and the Devil can slake our moral thirst now that we have passed through the incomprehensibilities of the last century. Before us stand the dire omens of the new hundred to come.

If this is prodigiously gloomy, I can only add that I am not able to believe in my own pessimism too thoroughly or why would I have bothered to put together this book? It obviously assumes that novelists will continue to appear, will write better and better, and may yet—given the ripening consciousness of the world— be as able as any statesman, doctor, or politician to give life to our beleaguered earth, our would-be great society dwelling still in the bonds of misperception that Marx once thought could be liberated entirely by a new vision of economics.

No, it is the theological misperception that enchains us, the notion that the Creator is All Good and All Powerful, when indeed it is enough that He (or—is it possible?—She) has been the apocalyptic and still searching Artist who is now in need of us. For we, we humans, are the most advanced presence to emerge from that ongoing exploratory Creation these many millions of years old, this Creation with all its evolutionary triumphs and defeats, its errors, its tragedies, its disasters, its catastrophes, and its ongoing creative hope of a more creative world. How much we are needed! How much God is in need of all we may yet discover if we do not destroy it all. Let us never assume there is not more and more, and more and more, and then more to write about—yes, we are the philosophers who are there to make sense of those concentrated if frozen fantasies we pretend to call facts. Someday, may it be, we will say, those old fantasies we *used* to call facts until we learned how to unpack them. What characterizes the beauty and the terror of the Creation is that it is not fixed, not absolute, not imperishable, but is existence itself and so may rise to more, or decompose and/or explode into less. How much fear this arouses in us, and, on rare splendid days, what exaltation.

ACKNOWLEDGMENTS

There are scores of people I wish to thank. First would be my good friend Michael Lennon, who not only urged this book upon me but then demonstrated that there were hundreds of relevant remarks made over forty years of my interviews that he had collected for my archive. Presented with the cache, I began to perceive that the form of a legitimate work was present, barely visible, but with the unmistakable heft of a book.

Lennon made a first classification of the topics. I went on to pursue another scheme, which owes a fair amount of its shape to his first assemblage. From such gleanings and sortings was this book initially put together. Needless to add, much new material was then added by me: Dwelling upon these matters naturally incited a good number of new thoughts, anecdotes, and small essays.

In addition, the need arose for more interviews to fill a few thematic gaps. In London, Peter Florence brought together several young men and women to put queries to me (referred to in the Source Notes as the London Master Class); James Fleming, of Suffolk University, assembled a larger group (the Suffolk University Master Class), and Larry Shainberg and I had a most useful conversation on Samuel Beckett.

Let me thank by name the five members of the London Master Class: Martin Aaron, Peter Florence, Mark Mills, Merope Mills, Clare Sears; also, the many who offered their stimulus to the Suffolk group: Josette Akresh, Blair Bigelow, Jane Brox, Peter Caputo, Thomas Connolly, Carol Dine, James Fleming, Nick Kain, George Kalogeris, Kristy Langone, Barry Leeds, J. Michael Lennon, Michael Madden, Betty Mandl, Fred Marchant, Anthony Merzlak, Quentin Miller, John Mulrooney, Larry Shainberg, Christopher Sherman, Alexandra Todd, and, to my great pleasure at his presence, Christopher Ricks.

In addition, I want to offer my appreciation to the men and women whose interviews across the last four decades contribute directly to matters here. These extracts, stripped for the most part of their questions, would leave them anonymous but for Lennon's source notes. One needs, then, the compensatory pleasure of citing them here, with my thanks and, on occasion, my gratitude.

They are: Sean Abbott, Laura Adams, John W. Aldridge, Harvey Aronson, Paul Attanasio, William Baises, Robert Begiebing, Melvyn Bragg, the late Vincent Canby, Anthony R. Cannela, the late Paul Carroll, the late Frank Crowther, Robin Davies, Edward de Grazia, Digby Diehl, the late Buzz Farbar, Debbie Forman, David Frost, Matthew Grace, Jorie Green, Lawrence Grobel, Robert Harvey, Patricia Holt, Peter E. Howard, Richard Howard, Carolyn T. Hughes, Samuel M. Hughes, Stan Isaacs, Michiko Kakutani, Eugene Kennedy, Julia Braun Kessler, Ramona Koval, Paul Krassner, Brian Lamb, Marshall Ledger, Michael Lee, Barry H. Leeds, J. Michael Lennon, Robert F. Lucid, Michael Mailer, Carole Mallory, Steven Marcus, Carol McCabe, Joseph McElroy, Jay McInerney, Alastair McKay, Cathleen Medwick, Robert Merrill, Hilary Mills, Lewis Nichols, Henry Nuwer, Brian Peterson, George Plimpton, Tammy Polonsky, Dermot Purgavie, Steve Roday, Charles Ruas, Eric James Schroeder, Michael Schumacher, Barbara Probst Solomon, Scott Spencer, Richard G. Stern, Curt Suplee, Toby Thompson, Dan Treisman, Michael Ventura, Bill Vitka, W. J. Weatherby, William Wilborn, David Young.

I also wish to acknowledge a debt to my assistant, Judith McNally, for her astute and classy insights into the occasional merits and demerits of *The Spooky Art*, to Veronica Windholz for her—as always—impeccable copy-editing, and to Ann Godoff for her incisive overview of how to publish this work. In addition, I want to thank my sister, Barbara Wasserman, and my son John Buffalo Mailer for their early and sensitive readings of the manuscript.

Last, and never least—to my wife, Norris, that most talented lady, who offers (among her other gifts) one indispensable ingredient: the creation of a daily atmosphere in which one can count on getting the work out without shifts of weather and/or marital mishaps. That is no mean virtue to find in a mate when the lady is, in her own right, one hell of a bang-up novelist.

SOURCE NOTES

BY J. MICHAEL LENNON, EDITOR

From an initial pool of approximately eight hundred items, Mailer selected about 190, drawing on nearly a hundred different sources. He then added approximately fifty more items, which either were written expressly for this book or were taken from the transcripts of unpublished interviews or forums on writing. In all but a few instances, he has incorporated the questions of his interviewers in his replies. Sometimes he has expanded his comments; just as often he has cut them, as comparison with the originals will demonstrate. But in all cases he has respected the spirit of the exchanges: His interlocutors of the past will easily recognize Mailer's answers.

To satisfy those who wish to know the provenance of an item, the following source notes give both the original place of publication and, whenever possible, the most readily available reprint. To aid readers who would like to obtain the full original source, inclusive page numbers are given in each instance. Those seeking more context or nuance on these matters are advised to consult a recently published reference work, *Norman Mailer: Works and Days*, by J. Michael and Donna Pedro Lennon, published by Sligo Press, 67 South Pioneer Avenue, Shavertown, Pennsylvania, 18708. Website: normanmailerworks anddays.com.

PART I

LIT BIZ

5   **I am tempted:** First publication.
5   **In 1963:** First publication.
5   **Steven Marcus: Do you need:** "Norman Mailer: The Art of Fiction XXXII," interview with Steven Marcus, *Paris Review* no. 31 (winter–spring 1964): 28–58; rpt: *Conversations with Norman Mailer*, ed. J. Michael Lennon (Jackson: University Press of Mississippi, 1988).
9   **I don't know:** Preface, *Fiction Writer's Handbook*, by Hallie and Whit Burnett (New York: Harper and Row, 1975) xvii–xxi.

11 **That is the best:** Personal interview, Larry Shainberg, 10 and 17 March 2002, Provincetown, Massachusetts.

12 **In any event:** Suffolk University Master Class, Boston, 3 March 2002, organized by James Fleming. Participants: Josette Akresh, Blair Bigelow, Jane Brox, Peter Caputo, Thomas Connolly, Carol Dine, James Fleming, Nick Kain, George Kalogeris, Kristy Langone, Barry Leeds, J. Michael Lennon, Michael Madden, Bette Mandl, Fred Marchant, Anthony Merzlak, Quentin Miller, John Mulrooney, Christopher Ricks, Larry Shainberg, Christopher Sherman, Alexandra Todd.

13 **How I aspired:** "Norman's Conquests," interview with Julia Braun Kessler, *Daily News Magazine* [Van Nuys, Calif.] 29 May 1983: 25–27.

13 **Samuel Goldwyn:** Introduction, *A Transit to Narcissus* (New York: Howard Fertig, 1978) vii–x.

19 **Soon after finishing:** "A Conversation with Norman Mailer," interview with Michael Lee, *Cape Cod Voice* 2–15 August 2001: 12–13, 53–54.

19 **Steven Marcus: Can you say:** Marcus interview.

21 **I think I suffered:** "In and Out of Books," interview with Lewis Nichols, *The New York Times Book Review* 14 March 1965: 8.

21 **Fifty years after:** Introduction, *The Naked and the Dead,* fiftieth anniversary edition (New York: Henry Holt, 1998) xi–xiii.

23 **Steven Marcus: What methods:** Marcus interview.

25 *Barbary Shore:* London Master Class, Savoy Hotel, 5 February 2002, organized by Peter Florence. Participants: Martin Aaron, Peter Florence, Mark Mills, Merope Mills, Clare Sears.

26 **Steven Marcus: What about *The Deer Park:*** Marcus interview.

28 **In his review:** "The Mind of an Outlaw," *Esquire* November 1959: 87–94; rpt: as "Fourth Advertisement for Myself: The Last Draft of *The Deer Park,*" *Advertisements for Myself* (New York: Putnam, 1959).

49 **Now that this:** First publication.

49 **Writing a best-seller:** "A Man Half Full," rev. of *A Man in Full,* by Tom Wolfe, *The New York Review of Books* 17 December 1998: 18, 20–23; rpt: *The Time of Our Time* (1998; New York: Modern Library, 1999).

49 **The ideal:** London Master Class.

50 **Today, large literary canvases:** "Una Conversación con Norman Mailer," interview with Barbara Probst Solomon, *El País* [Madrid] 4 October 1981: 10–15; rpt: in Solomon's collection, *Horse-Trading and Ecstasy* (San Francisco: North Point Press, 1989).

50 **It's counterproductive:** "The Critic's Choice: Norman Mailer Talks About Journalism and Millennialism," interview with Jorie Green and Tammy Polonsky, *Daily Pennsylvanian* 4 April 1995: 3.

50 **A best-seller strategy:** "A Man Half Full."

51 **Editing tends to make:** "Mailer: It's Easier to Talk of Sex Than Death," interview with Eugene Kennedy, *Chicago Tribune Bookworld* 10 April 1983: 1, 7.

51 **My literary generation:** "A Literary Lion Roars," interview with Carolyn T. Hughes, *Poets and Writers* 29 (March–April 2001): 40–45.

51 **Right now the smart money:** Untitled interview with William Baises, Robert Harvey, Robert Merrill, Henry Nuwer, and William Wilborn,

Brushfire [University of Nevada at Reno] 23 (November–December 1973): 7–20.

52 **Bookstore managers:** "Mailer Back in Arena, Pushing 'Oswald,'" interview with Carol McCabe, *Providence Journal* 28 May 1995: E1, E9.

53 **I treat bad reviews:** "Unbloodied by the Critical Pounding, Norman Mailer Defends the Egyptian Novel that Took a Decade to Write," interview with George Plimpton, *People* 30 May 1983: 53–54, 59–60, rpt: *Conversations with Norman Mailer*.

54 **Michael Schumacher: Should a writer:** "Modern Evenings: An Interview with Norman Mailer," *Writer's Digest* October 1983: 30–34.

54 **It usually doesn't matter:** Lee interview.

55 **Large literary success:** London Master Class.

55 **Ah, publicity:** First publication.

55 **I think for any novelist:** "Mailer Talking," interview with Michiko Kakutani, *The New York Times Book Review* 6 June 1982: 3, 38–41; rpt: *Conversations with Norman Mailer*.

56 **For literary people:** Kakutani interview.

56 **Every time a story:** Kakutani interview.

56 **If you are ever:** Suffolk Master Class.

57 **On this practical note:** Interview with Edward de Grazia, *Girls Lean Back Everywhere: The Law of Obscenity and the Assault on Genius,* by Edward de Grazia (New York: Random House, 1992) 520–21.

57 **I remember, years ago:** "The Big Bite," *Esquire* June 1963: 23–24, 28, 32; "Some Children of the Goddess: Further Evaluations of the Talent in the Room," *Esquire* July 1963: 63–69, 105. These two essays are combined as "Some Children of the Goddess" in *Cannibals and Christians* (New York: Dial, 1966).

59 **One more note:** First publication.

60 **One of the cruelest remarks:** First publication.

61 **Being a novelist:** "Prisoner of Success," interview with Paul Attanasio, *Boston Phoenix* 24 February 1981: 1–2, 11; rpt: *Pieces and Pontifications* (Boston: Little Brown, 1982).

62 **It's not advisable:** Attanasio interview.

62 **I remember saying:** "Mailer Opus," interview with Sean Abbott, *At Random Magazine* May 1998 <http://www.randomhouse.com/atrandom/normanmailer/index/html>.

63 **Sometimes you write:** Suffolk Master Class.

CRAFT

67 **Before we can talk:** First publication.

67 **The piece that follows:** First publication.

67 **I am going to speak:** "The Hazards and Sources of Writing," *Michigan Quarterly Review* 24 (summer 1985): 391–402; rpt: *Speaking of Writing: Selected Hopwood Lectures,* ed. Nicholas Delbanco (Ann Arbor: University of Michigan Press, 1990).

73 **To the risks:** London Master Class.

74 **Style, of course:** Preface, *Advertisements for Myself* (1959; New York: Berkley, 1976) v–vii; rpt: *Pieces and Pontifications.*

76 **In *The Deer Park:*** "The Pursuit of Experience," interview with W. J. Weatherby, *Manchester Guardian Weekly* 28 September 1961: 14.

76 **Finding one's own manner:** London Master Class.

77 **Style is character:** Marcus interview.

77 **Style is also a reflection:** London Master Class.

77 **It is comforting:** Plimpton, *People*.

78 **You know, a good skier:** "Norman Crosses Swords with Women's Lib," interview with Digby Diehl, *Los Angeles Times Calendar* 14 February 1971: 1, 56.

78 **There are two kinds:** "Toward a Concept of Norman Mailer," interview with Samuel M. Hughes, *Pennsylvania Gazette* [Alumni Magazine of University of Pennsylvania] May 1995: 20–27.

78 **Metaphors? You ask:** "Literary Ambitions," interview with J. Michael Lennon, *Pieces and Pontifications* 163–71.

79 **On the other hand:** Shainberg interview.

79 **A short fictional piece:** "A Man Half Full."

79 **Larry Shainberg: You used:** Shainberg interview.

79 **While Dwight Macdonald:** Preface, *Discriminations: Essays and Afterthoughts,* by Dwight Macdonald (New York: Grossman, 1985) vii–ix.

80 **As a corollary:** "Some Children of the Goddess."

84 **Third person and first person:** "Norman Mailer Interview," with Romona Koval, *Books and Writing* 1 September 2000 <http://www.abc.net.au/arts_0192000html>.

84 **In the first person:** London Master Class.

85 **First person point of view:** "A Conversation with Norman Mailer," with J. Michael Lennon, *New England Review* 20 (summer 1999): 138–48.

86 **It was not until:** Abbott interview.

86 **Nonetheless, I have considerable:** London Master Class.

89 **The CIA:** "Mailer's American Dream," interview with Patricia Holt, *San Francisco Chronicle* 17 October 1991: 1, 4.

90 **The decisions you make:** Lennon, *New England Review.*

90 **Working on *The Executioner's Song:*** "Mailer's America," interview with J. Michael Lennon, *Chicago Tribune* 29 September 1991: Sec. 13, 18–19, 27.

90 **I no longer work:** "Creators on Creating: Norman Mailer," interview with Hilary Mills, *Saturday Review* January 1981: 46–49, 52–53; rpt: *Pieces and Pontifications.*

91 **For that matter:** Plimpton, *People.*

91 **Many young novelists:** Suffolk Master Class.

92 **Some of my characters:** "Norman Mailer: Fact and Fiction," interview with Harvey Aronson, *PD: Sunday Magazine of the St. Louis Post-Dispatch* 16 December 1984: 4–6, 22–23.

92 **Graham Greene:** Aronson interview.

93 **Up to now:** Marcus interview.

93 **The question remains:** Marcus interview.

93 **I've spoken of characters:** Marcus interview.

94 **Hearn's death:** "Norman Mailer at Columbia," interview with Joseph McElroy and Columbia students, *Columbia: A Magazine of Poetry and Prose* no. 6 (spring–summer): 103–15; rpt: *Pieces and Pontifications.*

95 **When it comes:** Lennon, "Literary Ambitions."

95 **I'd say try not:** "Norman Mailer: 'The Hubris of the American Vision,'" interview with Eric James Schroeder, *Vietnam, We've All Been There: Interviews with American Writers*, ed. Eric James Schroeder (Westport, Conn.: Praeger, 1992) 91–105.

95 **Hemingway suffered:** Shainberg interview.

95 **I've been asked:** Marcus interview.

96 **If a novelist:** Attanasio interview.

96 **The characters you create:** "Norman Mailer: I'm Like a Minor Champ," interview with Stan Isaacs, *LI: Newsday's Magazine* 21 September 1975: 10–13, 22–26.

97 **I am not sure:** Marcus interview.

97 **In large part:** "An Author's Identity," interview with J. Michael Lennon, *Pieces and Pontifications* 151–57.

97 **One example:** London Master Class.

98 **I think Capote's book:** "An Interview with Norman Mailer," with John W. Aldridge, *Partisan Review* 47 (July 1980): 174–82; rpt: *Conversations with Norman Mailer.*

98 **If you find:** McElroy interview.

99 **Let me take:** McElroy interview.

99 **The influence of Henry Adams:** Solomon interview.

99 **Literary influence:** "Mailer and Vidal: The Big Schmooze," interview with Carole Mallory, *Esquire* May 1991: 105–12.

100 **It's disturbing to read:** Mallory interview.

101 **I'm now eighty:** Abbott interview.

101 **I remember in the summer:** McElroy interview.

102 **A large part of writing:** London Master Class.

102 **Writing is wonderful:** "The Surreal Professor," interview with Marshall Ledger, *Pennsylvania Gazette* May 1983: 14–22.

102 **There's nothing glorious:** Kakutani interview.

103 **I used to have:** "Norman Mailer," interview with Brian Lamb, *Booknotes: America's Finest Authors on Reading, Writing, and the Power of Ideas,* ed. Brian Lamb (New York: Random House, 1997) 162–65.

103 **When I read something:** London Master Class.

103 **I never know what:** "Style Is Character: An Interview with Norman Mailer," with Cathleen Medwick, *Vogue* May 1983: 279, 343.

104 **I think it's important:** Marcus interview.

105 **Indeed, many good writers:** Schumacher interview.

106 **Of course, it's virtually:** Marcus interview.

106 **If you can:** McElroy interview.

106 **Once you are committed:** "Norman Mailer: Stupidity Brings Out the Violence in Me," interview with Lawrence Grobel, *Endangered Species: Writers Talk About Their Craft, Their Lives,* ed. Lawrence Grobel (Cambridge, Mass.: Da Capo Press, 2001) 289–316.

106 **I've often felt:** "Thoughts of a Tough Guy," interview with Richard Howard, *Mail on Sunday Magazine* [London] 14 October 1984: 78.

107 **A few words:** McElroy interview.

107 **Research is another matter:** McElroy interview.

108 **By now, I'm a bit cynical:** Marcus interview.

PSYCHOLOGY

113 **If I place:** First publication.

113 **Having, at the age of twenty-five:** London Master Class.

113 **Some artists:** Lennon, "An Author's Identity."

114 **My case was different:** Mills, "Creators on Creating: Norman Mailer."

114 **People who suffer:** "Norman and Norris Mailer Seem Letter-Perfect for Roles of Literary Legends Who Lived Large," interview with Debbie Forman, *Cape Cod Times* 15 September 2001: B1–B2.

115 **I was successful and alienated:** Mills, "Creators on Creating: Norman Mailer."

115 **Let me see:** "Still Stormin'," interview with Alastair McKay, *The Scotsman: S2 Weekend* 22 July 2000: 2–5.

115 **Moreover, there's an irony:** "Mailer, Between Lives," interview with Curt Suplee, *Washington Post Style* 20 April 1983: B1, B11.

116 **On the other hand:** First publication.

116 **James Jones:** Lennon, *New England Review*.

116 **But I kept wanting:** Interview with Bill Vitka, "The Source," CBS Radio, October 1984.

117 **I've always been fascinated:** "The Old Man and the Novel," interview with Scott Spencer, *The New York Times Magazine* 22 September 1991: 28–31, 40, 42, 47.

118 **Since good novelists:** "Norman Mailer Face-to-Face," interview with Dan Treisman and Robin Davis, *Isis: Oxford University Magazine* November– December 1984: 8–9.

118 **If you start:** "Norman Mailer Face-to-Face," interview with Anthony R. Cannela, *Hartford Courant* 6 December 1998: B1, B3.

118 **I've virtually said:** London Master Class.

119 **The energy I put:** Mills interview.

119 **City life produces:** "Mailer: Tough Guy at Ease in P'town," interview with Peter E. Howard, *Cape Cod Times* 12 August 1984: 1, 12–13.

119 **In the world:** "Existential Aesthetics: An Interview with Norman Mailer," with Laura Adams, *Partisan Review* 42 (summer 1975) 197–214; rpt: *Conversations with Norman Mailer* and, in part, *The Time of Our Time*.

119 **You also have to learn:** Lee interview.

120 **I think Hemingway:** "Mailer on Mailer: An Interview," with Matthew Grace and Steve Roday, *New Orleans Review* 3.3 (1973): 229–34.

120 **Hemingway's death:** Solomon interview.

120 **All the same:** "Some Children of the Goddess."

121 **Few good writers:** "Norman Mailer," interview with Charles Ruas, *Conversations with American Writers* (New York: Random House, 1985) 18–36.

121 **One of the hardest:** "Mailer's Alpha and Omega," interview with Toby Thompson, *Vanity Fair* October 1991: 150–62.

121 **The literary world:** Mills interview.

122 **A writer, no matter:** "Some Children of the Goddess."

124 **When it comes:** Suffolk Master Class.

125 **It may be that part:** "Twelfth Round: An Interview with Norman Mailer," with Robert Begiebing, *Harvard Magazine* 85 (March–April 1983): 40–50; rpt: *Conversations with Norman Mailer*.

125 **Only another writer:** "A Conversation with Norman Mailer," with Barry H. Leeds, *Connecticut Review* 10 (spring 1988): 1–15; rpt: *Conversations with Norman Mailer.*

126 **Writing can also be:** Kakutani interview.

127 **There is always fear:** Begiebing interview.

127 **I'm always a little:** Lennon, "An Author's Identity."

128 **Usually, on an average:** Grace and Roday interview.

128 **When I'm writing:** Diehl interview.

128 **Today, most of my ideas:** Kakutani interview.

129 **I can sit:** Shainberg interview.

129 **On the other hand:** Suffolk Master Class.

131 **If you believe:** Suffolk Master Class.

131 **Another word on gender:** Suffolk Master Class.

132 **The narcissist suffers:** "Narcissism," *Pieces and Pontifications* 106–14; rpt: from *Genius and Lust: A Journey Through the Major Writings of Henry Miller* (New York: Grove, 1976).

135 **A corollary of narcissism:** First publication.

135 **Paul Krassner: Do you think:** "An Impolite Interview with Norman Mailer," with Paul Krassner, *The Realist* no. 40 (December 1962): 1, 13–23, 10; rpt: *Advertisements for Myself.*

138 **In the course:** Shainberg interview.

140 **Part of the art:** Suffolk Master Class.

141 **I've found that I can't:** Mills interview.

141 **Sometimes, the only way:** Solomon interview.

142 **I've always had the feeling:** Begiebing interview.

142 **Over the years:** Suffolk Master Class.

144 **The rule in capsule:** Ledger interview.

PHILOSOPHY

147 **Since the primitive had senses:** "Norman Mailer on Science and Art," interview with David Young, *Antaeus* nos. 13/14 (spring–summer 1974): 334–45; rpt: *Pieces and Pontifications.*

148 **Primitive man had to see:** Abbott interview.

148 **The artist seeks:** Young interview.

149 **While the physicist:** Young interview.

149 **An equation sign:** Young interview.

149 **I've long had the notion:** "Norman Mailer Talks to Melvyn Bragg About the Bizarre Business of Writing a Hypothetical Life of Marilyn Monroe," interview with Melvyn Bragg, *Listener* 20 December 1973: 847–50; rpt: *Conversations with Norman Mailer.*

150 **J. Michael Lennon: Many of your characters:** Lennon, "Literary Ambitions."

151 **Back to Kierkegaard:** Adams interview.

151 **The moment you moralize:** Medwick, "Style Is Character."

152 **I've used this example:** Lennon, "An Author's Identity."

152 **I may not be a good:** Lennon, "An Author's Identity."

154 **Readers often have:** Suffolk Master Class.

155 **I've always been drawn:** Suffolk Master Class.

155 **Borges has a magical:** Lennon, "An Author's Identity."

155 **Paranoia? It is either:** "Frank Crowther: Norman Mailer, Part II," interview with Frank Crowther, *Changes* no. 86 (January 1974): 25–26.

155 **There is a famous:** "Writers and Boxers," interview with J. Michael Lennon, *Pieces and Pontifications* 158–62.

156 **The twentieth-century artist:** Ruas interview.

156 **In line with Picasso:** Ruas interview.

156 **We tell ourselves:** "Mailer Admits Someone's Better," interview with Brian Peterson, *Grand Forks* [North Dakota] *Herald* 22 March 1985: A1, A8.

158 **The great economists:** First publication.

158 **Obviously, Freud:** Lennon, "Literary Ambitions."

160 **Back in 1959:** Begiebing interview.

160 **You cannot have:** Vitka interview.

161 **I don't like to say:** Schroeder interview.

161 **I feel that the final purpose:** "Hip Hell and the Navigator: An Interview with Norman Mailer," with Richard G. Stern and Robert F. Lucid, *Western Review* 23 (winter 1959): 101–9; rpt: *Advertisements for Myself* and *The Time of Our Time.*

161 **The logic of reincarnation:** "Mailer on Marriage and Women," interview with Buzz Farbar, *Viva* October 1973: 74–76, 144–52; rpt: *Pieces and Pontifications* and, in part, *The Time of Our Time.*

161 **Speaking at the MacDowell:** Preface, *Some Honorable Men: Political Conventions, 1960–1972* (Boston: Little, Brown, 1976) vii–xii.

162 **I'm right and I'm wrong:** Begiebing interview.

162 **Yes, it is no ordinary:** Adams interview.

162 **When we read Proust:** "A Murderer's Tale: Norman Mailer Talking to Melvyn Bragg," with Melvyn Bragg, *Listener* 15 November 1979: 660–62; rpt: *Conversations with Norman Mailer.*

162 **I go back again:** Shainberg interview.

163 **Writers aren't taken seriously:** "I Ask the Questions (Such As: What's an Old Warhorse like You Doing Drinking Iced Tea?)" interview with Dermot Purgavie, *Mail on Sunday* [London] 24 September 1995: 3.

163 **If I could give:** Crowther interview.

164 **The reader will be aware:** Marcus interview.

165 **I've never felt close:** Shainberg interview.

167 **In parallel, the essence:** Shainberg interview.

169 **I can see some reasonably:** De Grazia interview.

169 **You can tell a lot:** Crowther interview.

170 **One can say that if Picasso:** "Mailer on Mailer," interview with Michael Mailer, *Time Out* [*New York*] 11–18 October 1995: 20–21, 23.

170 **A great many artists:** Michael Mailer interview.

170 **I've always felt:** Mallory interview.

171 **Which opens a useful:** First publication.

171 **But now that:** First publication.

171 **Abraham Lincoln:** First publication.

171 **"Merit envies success:** First publication.

171 **One good reason:** First publication.

171 **Example: "The whole problem:** First publication.

172 **"Rudeness is the weak man's:** First publication.

PART II

GENRE

177 **Genre, as used here:** First publication.

177 **Certain human relations:** Farbar interview.

178 **Centuries from now:** Preface, *Some Honorable Men.*

178 **I began my forays:** Preface, *Some Honorable Men.*

179 **The excerpt that follows:** First publication.

179 **Remember the old joke:** "Ten Thousand Words a Minute," *Esquire* February 1963: 109–20; rpt: *The Presidential Papers* (New York: Putnam, 1963) 213–67, and, in part, *The Time of Our Time.*

185 **The problem of going out:** McElroy interview.

186 **During sports events:** Solomon interview.

186 **Almost always a reporter:** Baises, Harvey, Merrill, Nuwer, and Wilborn interview.

187 **One of the elements:** Solomon interview.

187 **On the other hand:** Attanasio interview.

188 **In a novel:** Isaacs interview.

189 **It is painful:** "A Harlot High and Low: Reconnoitering Through the Secret Government," *New York* 16 August 1976: 22–32, 35–38, 43–46; rpt: *Pieces and Pontifications* and *The Time of Our Time.*

190 **A novelist ought:** Suffolk Master Class.

191 **Larry Schiller:** Shainberg interview.

192 **Already there have been:** "Of a Small and Modest Malignancy, Wicked and Bristling with Dots," *Esquire* November 1977: 125–48; rpt: *Pieces and Pontifications.*

198 **The making of my first:** "When Irish Eyes Are Smiling, It's Norman Mailer," interview with Vincent Canby, *The New York Times* 27 October 1968: Sec. 2, 15; rpt: *Conversations with Norman Mailer.*

198 **Movies are more likely:** "Dance of a Tough Guy," interview with Michael Ventura, *L.A. Weekly* 18–24 September 1987: 14–19; rpt: *Conversations with Norman Mailer.*

199 **Time is your money:** Ventura interview.

200 **All this is easy:** First publication.

200 **Perhaps a thousand:** "A Course in Film-Making," *New American Review* no. 12 (August 1971): 200–241; rpt: *Existential Errands* (Boston: Little, Brown, 1972).

210 **The first time:** "Norman Mailer on Love, Sex, God, and the Devil," interview with Cathleen Medwick, *Vogue* December 1980: 268–69, 322; rpt: *Pieces and Pontifications.*

211 **To pay one's $5:** "A Transit to Narcissus," rev. of *Last Tango in Paris,* dir. Bernardo Bertolucci, *The New York Review of Books* 17 May 1973: 3–10; rpt: *Existential Errands.*

229 **I may as well confess:** First publication.

230 **Many a fiction writer:** First publication.

230 **Sometimes, it is as if:** Foreword, *Unholy Alliance: A History of Nazi Involvement with the Occult,* by Peter Levenda (1995; New York: Continuum, 2002) 1–4.

233 ***Why Are We in Vietnam?*** **is the only:** Preface, *Why Are We in Vietnam?* (1967; New York: Berkley, 1977) vii–x; rpt: *Pieces and Pontifications.*

235 **The unconscious can lead:** Kennedy interview.

236 **The story is:** "The Hazards and Sources of Writing."

236 **Famous plant-man:** *The Faith of Graffiti*, documented by Mervyn Kurlansky and Jon Naar, Prepared by Lawrence Schiller, Text by Norman Mailer (New York: Praeger, 1974); rpt: *The Time of Our Time*.

237 **The act of writing:** "The Hazards and Sources of Writing."

239 **The novel has:** "Playboy Interview: Norman Mailer," with Paul Carroll, *Playboy* January 1968: 69–84; rpt: *Pieces and Pontifications*.

239 **For six and a half:** *The Faith of Graffiti*.

242 **Years ago:** *The Faith of Graffiti*.

GIANTS

251 **Somewhere around the turn:** Shainberg interview. The Chekhov-Tolstoy anecdote is derived from John Ford Noonan's play *Talking Things Over with Chekhov* (New York: Samuel French, 1991).

253 **Is there a sweeter:** "Huckleberry Finn, Alive at 100," *The New York Times Book Review* 9 December 1984: 1, 36–37; rpt: *The Time of Our Time*.

260 **J. Michael Lennon: I don't think:** Lennon, "Literary Ambitions."

261 **Hemingway's style:** Kakutani interview.

261 **I guess I would say:** Attanasio interview.

261 **What characterizes every book:** Preface, *Papa: A Personal Memoir*, by Gregory Hemingway, M.D. (Boston: Houghton Mifflin, 1976) xi–xiii.

263 **The cruelest criticism:** "Miller and Hemingway," *Pieces and Pontifications* 86–93; rpt: from *Genius and Lust*.

265 **His work embraced:** "Miller and Hemingway."

271 **Not until this last:** [D. H. Lawrence], *The Prisoner of Sex* (Boston: Little, Brown, 1971) 133–60; rpt: *The Time of Our Time*.

287 **Name any great novel:** Grobel interview.

287 **James Jones and I:** "Author to Author: Norman Mailer Talks to Jay McInerney," interview with Jay McInerney, *Providence Phoenix* 10 November 1995: Sec. 1, 10–11, 15.

287 **Capote wrote:** Interview with George Plimpton, *Truman Capote: In Which Various Friends, Enemies, Acquaintances, and Detractors Recall His Turbulent Career*, by George Plimpton (New York: Random House, 1997) 238–40.

288 **All the same:** Mallory interview.

288 **Kurt Vonnegut:** "The Hazards and Sources of Writing."

288 **Reading Toni Morrison:** London Master Class.

289 **Picasso had:** McInerney interview.

289 **It's the guys:** "Talking with David Frost," PBS, 24 January 1992.

289 **Back in school:** "Some Children of the Goddess."

293 **I haven't looked:** London Master Class.

294 **Since writing the above:** First publication.

296 **Good writing is not:** "Modes and Mutations: Quick Comments on the Modern American Novel," *Commentary* March 1966: 37–40; rpt: as "The Argument Reinvigorated" in *Cannibals and Christians*.

307 **If this prodigiously:** First publication.

INDEX

ABOUT THE AUTHOR

NORMAN MAILER was born in 1923 and published his first book, *The Naked and the Dead,* in 1948. *The Armies of the Night* won the National Book Award and the Pulitzer Prize in 1969; Mailer received another Pulitzer in 1980 for *The Executioner's Song.* He lives in Provincetown, Massachusetts, and Brooklyn, New York.

ABOUT THE TYPE

This book was set in Baskerville, a typeface which was designed by John Baskerville, an amateur printer and typefounder, and cut for him by John Handy in 1750. The type became popular again when the Lanston Monotype Corporation of London revived the classic Roman face in 1923. The Mergenthaler Linotype Company in England and the United States cut a version of Baskerville in 1931, making it one of the most widely used typefaces today.